A Socio-Criminological Analysis of the HIV Epidemic

by
Bruno Meini

Series in Sociology
VERNON PRESS

In the Americas:
Vernon Press
1000 N West Street,
Suite 1200, Wilmington,
Delaware 19801
United States

In the rest of the world:
Vernon Press
C/Sancti Espiritu 17,
Malaga, 29006
Spain

Series in Sociology

Library of Congress Control Number: 2020938732

ISBN: 978-1-64889-170-0

Also available: 978-1-64889-054-3 [Hardback]; 978-1-64889-079-6 [PDF, E-Book]

Table of contents

List of figures

Introduction

Health, and especially human immunodeficiency virus (HIV), has become a global issue which requires solutions that all countries can agree upon. The majority of global infections in 2018 were among key populations and their sexual partners. Key populations constitute a small percentage of the general population, but they are most at risk of acquiring or transmitting HIV, regardless of the legal and policy environment. Available data suggest that the risk of HIV acquisition among gay men and other men who have sex with men was 22 times higher in 2018 than it was among all adult men. Similarly, the risk of acquiring HIV for people who inject drugs was 22 times higher than for people who do not inject drugs, 21 times higher for sex workers than adults aged 15–49 years, and 12 times higher for transgender people than adults aged 15–49 years (UNAIDS 2019, 9).

Based on the above, it follows that the expansion of the drug and sex markets has played an essential role in the spread of HIV to almost every corner of the world, thus prompting international organisations to take initiatives on a global scale (WHO 2019; WHO 2015). The international community has operated directly through the action of specialised bodies, such as the World Health Organization (WHO) (Kim 2015). It has also succeeded in having the health theme added to the agendas of international summits and major international conventions, as well as to some documents of the United Nations Secretary-General. In this context, the theme of quality in healthcare systems is gradually assuming universal proportions. In most countries, quality has become pivotal in the realisation of adequate social and health service policies. International organisations have had an important role in the promotion of qualitative health-service development projects in low-income countries (Beigbeder 2004, 1–7).

The global dimension of HIV can be inferred by the spread of the virus throughout the world. At the end of 2018, there were 37.9 million [32.7 million–44.0 million] people living with HIV. Of these, about 61 per cent are in Sub-Saharan Africa, the region hardest hit by the epidemic (UNAIDS 2019, 16–17). The number of HIV-positive people is rising as more people are living longer because of antiretroviral therapy, alongside the number of new HIV infections which, although declining, is still very high (Ghys et al. 2018). Globally, new HIV infections among young women aged 15–24 years were reduced by 25 per cent between 2010 and 2018. These encouraging data, however, are not able to gloss over what remains unacceptable, namely the fact that every week 6,000 adolescent girls and young women become infected with HIV (UNAIDS 2019, 2).

HIV remains one of the most feared viruses in society and often fuels the so-called AIDS phobia which is the irrational fear of getting infected with HIV or the fear you have already been infected despite evidence to the contrary. From this phobia, collective reactions of hysteria and panic can sometimes arise because HIV is the virus that causes the deadly disease AIDS (Hood 2013). However, these reactions do not justify unfair attitudes towards those social groups which are already socially-excluded because of their risk-taking behaviours, especially in developing countries (Chingwaru and Vidmar 2018). This tagging process can lead to being suspicious about any individual who comes into contact with key populations at higher risk of HIV exposure and is influenced by a sentiment of repulsion for the modes by which a healthy individual can be infected by an HIV-positive person (Mawar et al. 2005). Moral disapprovals not only affect those who display a precarious state of health, but end up also including those behaviours which most increase the risk of transmitting or being infected by the virus, namely high-risk sexual behaviours such as having unprotected vaginal, anal, or oral sex (Kalichman et al. 2007), having multiple and casual sex partners without using a condom during sexual intercourse (Steffenson et al. 2011), having unprotected sex with a partner who injects drugs (Chikovani et al. 2013), and having unprotected sexual intercourse with sex workers (Mulieri et al. 2014).

In everyday life, from media-watching to pub talk, HIV is rarely out of public consciousness. The volume of coverage diverges quite a bit from country to country. In the 1980s, the media's initial excessive interest in the disease soon seemed to wane. Later, at the beginning of the 1990s, news accounts tended to put on a more sensationalised and extreme tone than in the past. This new trend contributed considerably to making it appear increasingly and unequivocally evident that the most exposed to the infection were those populations which, well before the advent of HIV, were already discriminated, socially-excluded and stigmatised within each society such gay men and other men who have sex with men, sex workers, transgender people and people who inject drugs (Aggleton et al. 2005).

HIV-related stigma and discrimination negatively affect people living with HIV who are considered dangerous because of their disease status (Phillips and Saewyc 2010, 369–370). Consequently, the reduction of HIV-related stigma and discrimination may dramatically improve the lives of people who are more vulnerable to HIV infection by implementing an effective social-inclusion programme that facilitates a process of optimisation of the investments in HIV prevention, care and treatment (Carr et al. 2010).

HIV is a significant social issue which has also mobilised the scientific interest of numerous researchers. Medical research is experimenting a multiplicity of strategies in the hope of either totally eradicating HIV from the body (a sterilising cure) or limiting it to such a low level that the immune system can retain control without antiretroviral drugs (a functional cure). Most researchers seek to discover a successful vaccine against HIV while others experiment with a range of drugs in order to find an effective treatment (Highleyman 2011). Medical scientific research has undoubtedly made enormous steps forward, while in the social research field, the route is still at the initial stages and many await a satisfactory response. However, with the overcoming of a cultural climate typical of emergency situations, the social sciences, and particularly sociology, have begun to produce several significant works on HIV (Watkins-Hayes 2014).

This volume offers a comprehensive analysis of the multifaceted socio-criminological dimensions of the HIV epidemic and positively contributes to the ongoing sociological debate on infectious diseases. The author intends to create an independent and original epistemology of HIV to explicate the social forces that impact and determine the course and experience of the epidemic and also seeks to reframe the popular discourse on HIV to reflect sociological conceptualisations (Lemelle Jr., Harrington, and LeBlanc 1999). This step leads to identifying the concept of social interaction as an appropriate tool for highlighting the complex social nature of the virus (Derlega and Barbee 1998).

The book is composed of six chapters. The first summarises all of the main aspects of the HIV epidemic and offers a detailed source of information readily available. The second chapter focuses on the sociological analysis of HIV with particular reference to Parsons' concept of the 'sick role'. The deviance issue related to health emerges not only in this context but also when taking the children orphaned by AIDS into consideration. The third chapter examines the effects of HIV-related stigma and discrimination on children made orphans by AIDS, and other children made vulnerable by HIV and on how to promote a strategy that draws these minors into social protection schemes and programmes. The fourth chapter addresses the links between violence against women and children and the risk of HIV infection by taking into consideration the South African reality as an illuminating example. The fifth chapter illustrates the potential association between the harmful aspects of widow inheritance, virginity testing, female genital mutilation, and HIV transmission in adolescent and adult females. This chapter significantly contributes to the multifaceted field of the victimology of human rights. The sixth chapter investigates the linked issues of HIV, crime, security and governance. It recognises that 'health' is part of the fabric of what constitutes a country's security, not only due to the impact that a disease can pose to a state's stability, but also to the state's ability to maintain internal stability and external security.

Chapter 1

HIV: The basic aspects

Health and illness

The dual concept of health and illness can be interpreted on the basis of three distinct aspects: those that are either healthy or ill (subjective); the doctor (professional); and the technical tools (objective) which can identify, measure and represent the illness in various ways. When ill health relates to an organic malfunction, it is referred to as 'disease', while the situation that a sick person experiences and how they perceive it is referred to as illness. An illness conditions the degree of adhesion to a therapy and, in some cases, the choice of a therapist. However, the meaning that each individual gives to their state of ill health is not entirely subjective, although it is always socially conditioned. A sociologist has more to say about the concept of illness than of disease, as the interpretation which a sick person gives to their state of ill health is mediated by a social perspective. Indeed, it is the social scientist that describes and explains how society and its segments give rise to the illness jointly with the individual. In addition, the field of study is vast. It is only necessary, for instance, to think about the illnesses related to unhealthy lifestyles or alcoholism (Cipolla 2002a, 12–13). A person's lifestyle alone can thus be the cause of grave disadvantages and accounts for the development of less serious pathologies (for example, cardiovascular conditions) or their absence over the past decades (Cipolla 2002b, 22). Lastly, sickness refers to the actual social scope of an illness; in other words, the capacity of an individual to accomplish those tasks in which the activity of a community is brought into fruition. When an individual cannot carry out these tasks, due to the onset of a disease or illness, other individuals define them as an ill person (Larsen, Lewis, and Lubkin 2006, 23–44).

The origin of AIDS

From the second half of the nineteenth century, the first bio-medical models presented disease as an accidental event caused by organic and environmental factors such as a virus, bacteria or pollution; factors which succeed in overcoming the barrier of the human body's defence mechanisms. Later, in the early twentieth century, a bio-psychosocial perspective developed. According to this perspective, health risks are the consequence of the interaction between the individual (bio and psycho) and the surrounding environment (social). More recently, this was replaced by an interpretation of health risk according to which the risk stems from the individual's insufficient control of their changing inner impulses (Ogden 1995, 412–413). Building on this assumption, the author can now turn his attention to AIDS. In 1981, the description of five cases of pneumocystis pneumonia[1] among homosexual men in Los Angeles in the *Morbidity and Mortality Weekly Report*, a publication of the Centers for Disease Control and Prevention (CDC) in Atlanta (the United States epidemiological authority)[2], was the first published report about an illness that would become known as acquired immunodeficiency syndrome (AIDS) (Curran and Jaffe 2011, 64). First identified in 1981[3], but officially classified in 1982, AIDS is a disease caused by a virus called human immunodeficiency virus (HIV), which belongs to a subgroup of retroviruses known as lentivirus, whose main characteristic is to subtly penetrate the control centre of the human immune system and progressively deprive it of its capacity to counter infectious agents (Douek, Roederer, and Koup 2009).

After describing AIDS in homosexuals, US epidemiological authorities established a national monitoring system, and, for statistical reasons, decided to give a definition for AIDS cases which could comply with specific parameters. According to this definition, an individual has acquired immunodeficiency syndrome when the following conditions exist: a) they have been plausibly diagnosed with an illness (for example, Kaposi's sarcoma and Pneumocystis carinii pneumonia) that suggests a lack of cellular immunity; b) the disease occurs in the absence of other well-known causes of cellular immunity deficiency (for example, the use of immunosuppressive drugs). In 1982, during an epidemiological investigation, the scientists at the CDC reached an interesting conclusion by employing the aforementioned definition of AIDS: all

---

[1] The disease PCP is a form of pneumonia, caused by the fungus Pneumocystis jirovecii. It is relatively rare in people with normal immune systems, but common among people with weakened immune systems, such as premature or severely malnourished children, the elderly, and especially persons living with HIV (in whom it is most commonly observed) (Aliouat-Denis et al. 2008, 708–726).

[2] Eventually, a single common factor was conceived for diverse clinical pictures. The syndrome was characterised by the onset of infections and/or tumours defined as opportunistic (because they take advantage of a serious deficiency of the organism's immune system, which allows them to develop) and conditioned by the presence of an immune deficiency. Acquired Immunodeficiency Syndrome, or AIDS, thus came into being (Elder, Baker, and Ribes 2004, 281–288).

[3] After lengthy controversies of a scientific and politico-legal nature on the paternity of the identification of the virus between the French group led by Luc Montagnier and the US group led by Robert Gallo, an agreement was reached which also provided that a single name be used to refer to the virus; hence it was established that it should be HIV, standing for Human Immunodeficiency Virus (Vahlne 2009).

the cases (save one) concerned men, 92 % of whom were homosexual and bisexual. These results led to the erroneous assumption that AIDS was an exclusively homosexual disease linked with a particular kind of sexual intercourse, a high degree of change in sexual partners and the use of stimulating substances (CDC 1982a). Consequently, the stigma attached to AIDS as a disease was based on a pre-existing stigma (Herek and Glunt 1988, 887), so much so that initially the disease was labelled with the acronym GRID (Gay-Related Immunodeficiency) (Altman 1982); in other words, sexual orientation became the defining criterion of the disease. However, the development of other opportunistic infections similar to those described in homo-bisexual patients with HIV-related diseases were soon also detected in many heterosexual people who inject drugs, in some heterosexual haemophiliac patients and in several Haitian immigrants in the United States. Successively, AIDS was detected in the female partners of HIV-positive individuals and in children born from mothers belonging to the previously-listed groups. Moreover, the conviction that the disease could be transmitted via a viral agent and by sexual and parenteral modes similar to those of the Hepatitis B virus became stronger. In 1982, this conviction was substantiated by the identification of the virus in transfusion recipients (CDC 1982b).

The Haitian controversy

Beginning in the 1960s, Haitians had been immigrating to the US both legally and illegally, by air and by sea, often driven by the same reasons that had pushed and pulled other waves of immigrants; to wish to flee from violence and poverty and to work to support their families. These immigrants were not welcome in the United States; consequently, many of them were held in detention centres of the United States Immigration and Naturalization Service. This agency maintained that the Haitians could not be admitted as refugees, while many Haitians and several American human rights defenders argued the opposite and denounced the illegality of the detention. The AIDS epidemic occurred precisely at the climax of this debate. In November 1981, only a few months after the medical literature announced what would later be called AIDS, several Haitian immigrants with infections typical of the syndrome were examined in various hospitals in Florida. Moreover, many other cases were immediately discovered among the Haitian community in New York (Pitchenik et al. 1983). In 1982, the US epidemiological authorities announced that 34 Haitians residing in the United States had been suffering from opportunistic infections (CDC 1982c). Unlike other North American patients who met the HIV-related disease diagnostic criteria, the Haitians denied being involved in risky behaviours such as unprotected sex among men, use of non-sterile drug injecting equipment, or transfusion of infected blood. Almost all the cases of the syndrome known at that time implied one or more of these behaviours; thus, according to many studies, the HIV cases among the Haitian immigrant community posed an absolute mystery. Hence, health workers in the United States were compelled to determine the origin of these non-classifiable cases. In order to accurately establish the risk of exposure to HIV among the Haitian immigrant community, an adequate knowledge of the population size was necessary. However, since no relevant data were available, instead of admitting that the risk could not be quantified, the unrealistically-low number of 200,000 recently-immigrated Haitians was initially used. The logical step that followed was that the CDC added all the Haitians belonging to the four main key populations at higher risk of exposure to HIV to that number. The members of these populations were defined as the club of the four Hs; homosexuals, Haitians, haemophiliacs and heroin users (Farmer 1992, 211–212).

The press did not hesitate to publish the CDC's conclusions and unflattering images of Haitian and Haitian-American HIV-positive patients. Moreover, Haiti was accused of being the place of origin of the infection on account of the transfusions, only one of which was actually carried out in Haiti on an unspecified date (Siegal and Siegal 1983, 85). These circumstances nurtured a climate of racism which became quite evident when the United States Coast Guard did not allow Haitian ships to berth (Nachman and Dreyfuss 1986, 33). The protests of the Haitian community were motivated by scientific data which proved that the percentage of people infected with HIV in Haiti was lower than in many other Caribbean islands and in many cities in the United States. However, these data did not lead the domestic authorities to intervene rapidly in favour of the Haitian population.

Consequently, the pressure from the public became so strong that the CDC was forced to eliminate Haitians from the key populations at higher risk of HIV exposure in April 1985 (Farmer 1992, 217), albeit without admitting the previously erroneous designation (Sabatier 1988, 46). However, the US Food and Drug Administration's ban prohibiting Haitians, who had arrived in the United States after 1977, to donate blood was still in force (Salbu 1996, 952). On 5 February 1990, the Food and Drug Administration's Center for Biologics Evaluation and Research issued a directive which extended the ban on blood or blood product donation to all Haitians regardless of when they had immigrated to the USA (Fairchild and Tynan 1994, 2013). This decision triggered protests throughout the USA, which culminated in a huge gathering held on 20 April 1990 in New York. Caught off guard, the Food and Drug Administration (FDA) immediately appointed a commission, which suggested that the blood-donating ban based on nationality or geographic origin be lifted; however, the FDA did not take their advice (Sharif 1990, 13). Demonstrators gathered to protest in all the major cities in the US, including Washington, where they marched right up to the FDA's headquarters. In December 1990, the FDA decided to formally remove the ban prohibiting Haitians from donating blood (Somerville 1990).

Features of the HIV epidemic

From the beginning, AIDS has proved to be far more dangerous than other viral diseases such as measles and hepatitis, diseases whose minor or severe symptoms appear within a week and which the body is able to overcome thanks to its antibodies. This does not happen with HIV infection, which hardly manifests any symptoms during its development. The individual may feel in good health for a long time, though they are not, and thus unknowingly be a threat to others. Currently, especially in Western countries, the treatment used for HIV infection is in the form of Highly Active Antiretroviral Therapy (HAART), consisting of opportune combinations of antiretroviral drugs (Schneider et al. 2005). The majority of HIV-positive patients develop AIDS within the first decade of diagnosis. Most patients who receive HAART will survive more than ten years from initiation of AIDS, whereas the majority of the patients who do not receive HAART die within two years of the onset of AIDS (Poorolajal et al. 2016). Therefore, a patient cannot be cured of human immunodeficiency virus at the moment, as a vaccine capable of immunising infected individuals does not yet exist. Medical research continues to work on a cure for HIV. In the meantime, combination antiretroviral therapy preserves the health of a patient with HIV. It does this by reducing the levels of the virus in the blood to an undetectable level. This so-called viral suppression helps prevent progression from HIV to AIDS. Consequently, it is of fundamental importance for the patient to follow their therapy plan accurately (Johnson 2019).

Many scholars and investigators have analysed the epidemic for the purpose of highlighting the failures of institutions to isolate HIV and organise efficient public health strategies. Paula Treichler (1987) coined the concept 'epidemic of signification', a broad map and analysis of the many meanings of HIV, to provide an official definition which could establish the policies, rules and practices that were able to govern the future of human beings with respect to the epidemic. She foresaw that this project was essential for democratically determining the authentic meaning of HIV (Kane 1994, 326). Charles Perrow and Mauro F. Guillén (1990) explained the HIV epidemic in the city of New York as being the product of the systematic incapacity of complex organisations to deal with emergency crises. Gerald Oppenheimer (1992) focused on the professional aspect of the epidemic. He specifically described the ways in which the professional paradigm of the epidemic incorporated social and cultural ideas capable of isolating a certain number of variables that could perform the transmission processes of HIV. He also stressed that the epidemiological issue retransmitted these ideas via well-grounded scientific claims. These theoretical grounds were useful to Oppenheimer for explaining how the CDC prematurely identified AIDS as a disease of homosexual men and how this erroneous interpretation affected early public prevention policies (Musheno 1994, 237).

Lastly, it is important to understand that AIDS should be classified among long-wave events in which negative and vast-scale effects gradually surface with time. This kind of phenomenon is different from diseases with short incubation periods and high mortality rates. For example, cholera is a short-wave event or an event whose course is predictable as soon as the individual contracts the disease. According to the MacKinder Centre for the Study of Long Wave Events at the London School of Economics, long-wave events[4] share specific characteristics:

o   Their onset is not apparent.
o   Once their presence, dynamics and effects are known, it takes a long time to slow them down or stop them (in several cases the event is inexorable).
o   Their management is different from that of short-wave events.
o   Institutions hesitate to employ the resources required to take appropriate action due to the fact that politicians restrict themselves to approving measures that remain in force for five years at the most, while these events generally extend over several decades.
o   The management of their consequences generates new questions which human experience is not always able to answer.
o   Their treatment calls for extraordinary administrative and political skills.
o   Once they have been identified, an emergency approach is used for dealing with them, which eventually worsens the situation.

AIDS is a long-wave event on account of the distinctive and specific characteristics of the disease's pathogen, HIV (Barnett 2006, 302–303).

The routes of transmission of HIV

Studies carried out after the identification of HIV as the causative agent of AIDS enabled the definition of its biological characteristics and the ascertainment of its routes of transmission, which are the main ways in which someone can become infected with HIV. HIV is transmitted in human bodily fluids by three routes: sexual intercourse through vaginal, rectal or penal tissues (sexual

---

[4] These also comprise global climatic change, the problem of obesity in some societies, and many other phenomena.

transmission); direct contact with contaminated and non-sterile drug injecting equipment or other piercing medical and non-medical equipment, and transfusion of contaminated blood and exposure to untreated plasma products (parenteral transmission); and from HIV-positive mother to child during pregnancy, labour and delivery and through breastfeeding (mother-to-child transmission) (Shaw and Hunter 2012).

HIV is transmitted primarily via unprotected sexual intercourse (including anal and oral sex). Sexual transmission theoretically depends on the following risk factors: the probability that the partner is HIV infected, the number of partners a person has sex with in their lifetime, the type of sexual contact involved, the amount of virus present in the blood or secretions of the infected partner, and the presence in one or both partners of other sexually transmitted infections and/or genital lesions (Ferris, Mizwa, and Schutze 2010, 120–122). Ulcerative genital lesions, such as those seen in chancroid, syphilis, or herpes simplex virus infection, appear to increase susceptibility to infection (Gillespie et al. 2013, 468–469). Unprotected oral sex is considered to carry the lowest risk of transmission; the risk is so low that researchers have had difficulty quantifying it. The probability of HIV transmission during one act of unprotected vaginal intercourse is often stated to be approximately 0.1%, or 1 in 1,000 (Powers et al. 2008; Boily et al. 2009). Unprotected anal intercourse is considered riskier, with an estimated per-act risk of 1 in 100 to 1 in 50, which is 10 to 20 times higher than for unprotected vaginal intercourse. Anal intercourse may substantially increase HIV transmission risk as the anal mucosa is more vulnerable to the penetration of the virus (Halperin et al. 2002; Baggaley, White, and Boily 2010). However, among discordant heterosexual couples, male-to-female transmission of HIV is relatively more efficient than female-to-male transmission (Nicolosi et al. 1994; Padian et al. 1997). The most likely explanation for this difference in ease of HIV spread from seropositive men to their uninfected sexual partners relates to the larger volume of semen compared with cervicovaginal secretions and to the higher concentration of HIV on average in seminal fluid (Cohn and Clark 2014, 1592).

Parenteral transmission is defined as that which occurs outside of the alimentary tract, such as in subcutaneous, intravenous, intramuscular, and intracisternal injections (Berkley 1991). It occurs mainly among people who inject drugs. However, HIV continues to be transmitted in health care settings through the use of contaminated injecting, surgical and other skin-piercing equipment, transfusion of blood and plasma products, tissue, organ and sperm donation and accidental occupational exposure such as needle-stick injuries. The cases of transfusion of blood or plasma products contaminated with HIV have pushed health authorities to impose the selection of suitable blood donors and testing of blood that is used for transfusions in most high-income countries.

In such countries, the implementation of safety measures has significantly reduced the risk of transmission of HIV during blood transfusion. However, HIV infection continues to be a risk associated with blood transfusions in resource-poor nations where routine testing of all blood used for transfusions is absent, inadequate, or of low quality. Nearly all the patients who receive infected blood develop post-transfusion HIV (WHO 2014a, 18–20).

Mother-to-child transmission of HIV is the most important mode of HIV acquisition in infants and children, but the exact mechanism of mother-to-child transmission of HIV remains unknown. As previously seen, transmission may occur during intrauterine life, delivery, or breastfeeding. The greatest risk factor for vertical transmission is thought to be advanced maternal disease, likely due to a high maternal HIV viral load (Garcia et al. 1999). Without prophylactic treatment, approximately 15–30% of infants born to HIV-positive women will become infected with HIV during gestation and delivery, a further 5-15% becoming infected through maternal milk during breastfeeding (De Cock et al. 2000). HIV infection of infants and children generates a lifetime chronic condition that potentially shortens life expectancy and contributes to significant human, social, and economic costs (WHO 2014b).

Epidemiological factors

Every Western country has tried to reduce the impact of HIV by implementing wide-reaching prevention programmes characterised by the promotion of new behaviour models. The basic idea of these initiatives was to compel each individual to act responsibly. In other words, once a person discovered they were HIV-positive, their only blame would be to have been negligent. In particular, refusing the use of condoms as a preventive measure has often been justified by the fact that it impairs intimacy and feeds a state of distrust in a couple's relationship (Schiltz and Sandfort 2000, 1574–1575). This refusal often occurs if one partner reveals that they are HIV positive; and, in the case of healthy heterosexual women, it can be accompanied by verbal and physical violence. This situation has produced a considerable increase in the number of couples in which both partners are HIV-positive (Ibid., 1579).

It must be stressed that along with the routes of infection, epidemiological factors assume a prominent role in the study of the HIV phenomenon. Epidemiology is a science which studies the frequency and distribution of diseases in human populations. It identifies the etiological agents of every disease and gathers and publishes the data required to manage, evaluate and plan prevention and treatment services for various pathologies (Bonita,

Beaglehole, and Kjellström 2006). There are three different kinds of research in the field of epidemiology: descriptive, analytical and experimental. In each research, incidence and prevalence are morbidity indicators[5]. More precisely, HIV incidence is expressed as the estimated number of new cases arising in a specified population over a given period. The Joint United Nations Programme on HIV and AIDS (UNAIDS) normally refers to the number of adults aged 15–49 years or children (aged 0–14 years) who have become infected during the past year. HIV prevalence instead quantifies the number of individuals in a population who are living with HIV at a specific point in time regardless of the time of infection and is usually given as a percentage of the population. UNAIDS normally reports prevalence among adults between 15 and 49 years old. In this analysis, risk represents one of the pivotal concepts of epidemiology and occupies a central position in Western culture. It can be defined as a "conceptual mechanism through which to determine the possible and/or likely outcomes of our actions in the face of the structural uncertainties thrown up by the social and natural world" (Dannreuther and Lekhi 2000, 575). It is a tool used for predicting and monitoring the future of the following events: weather, business management, environment protection, crime control, transport and promotion of health (Heyman, Henriksen, and Maughan 1998, 1296). This operation postulates that some individuals, groups and experts have or believe they have the necessary resources to obtain adequate measurements. As regards health, epidemiologists are researchers who investigate patterns and causes of disease in humans and make choices based on available, albeit imperfect, data.

In the past, one of the most important heuristic tools in analytical epidemiology was the concept of the risk group, which referred to a category of individuals whose behaviours favour the spreading of an infection (Brown 2000, 1276). The division of a population into categories was an expedient aimed at measuring the effects that can be ascribed to biological, environmental and social variables. The exposed categories employed in the case of HIV were the following: people who inject drugs, homosexuals, people who inject drugs and homosexuals, haemophiliacs and blood transfusion recipients, heterosexuals and mother-to-child transmission. It was particularly misinforming and improper to transfer the terms risk categories, or more simply risk groups, into the social context. Unfortunately, this happened and contributed to creating a sort of boundary between these groups and the rest of the population (Goldstein 1991). This distinction is incorrect and misleading, as the risk of infection does not depend on the membership to a specific social group but rather on behaviours that can lead

---

[5] In the language of epidemiology, morbidity refers to the state of being diseased or unhealthy within a population.

to being exposed to the risk. For example, within the homosexual social group, there are lifestyles which are diverse in terms of consistency and frequency of sexual behaviours at higher risk of HIV exposure. Moreover, these lifestyles have changed since the outbreak of the epidemic (Altman 1998).

Within the process of interpreting sexual behaviours that create, increase, or perpetuate risk, the use of models oriented towards an individual psychological dimension has been predominant for a long time. These models aim at explaining how individuals perceive risk according to an epidemiological definition used in prevention messages and the motivations which drive individuals to modify their behaviours. The perception of risk occurs on the basis of the information which protects the individual from being infected. This protection is simply an individual and intentional act partially influenced by the surrounding social environment. Implicit in this kind of approach is the hypothesis that the protection of one's health represents the fundamental priority of each individual. In recent times, a second model of the relational kind has emerged, according to which every sexual relationship is the result of interactive processes between partners. Here the act of the single person becomes meaningful only in relation to another individual. Hence, the interactions which make up the relationship take on meaning only if they are considered within the relational boundaries, while they lose meaning if they are taken into consideration separately. This perspective does not necessarily neglect or underestimate the single characteristics of the individual and the elements of the context, but simply recomposes them within the logical structure of the relationship (Bajos and Marquet 2000, 1533–1535). The application of this model can be well-represented by the management of behaviours that place individuals in situations in which they may be exposed to HIV, which does not comply with individualistic, rationalistic and functionalistic risk-management models. The problem is managing to protect oneself while involving the other person (Manning et al. 2012).

Prevention policy: A theoretical approach

A highly important objective of prevention interventions is the identification of so-called hidden populations or groups of individuals whose identification is especially difficult because their institutional perception is poor or, in some cases, inexistent. This can depend on many objective and subjective factors: their small size, their personal choice to maintain a low profile, their lack of communication with the social environment, their location and composition, and the presence of juridical protection that ratifies their right to maintain a low profile (Ellard-Gray et al. 2015).

The term hidden population can incorporate situations that are definitely diverse on account of the different meanings that the single terms can take on. These differences concern at least three closely interconnected aspects: in this field, the concept of population seems weak and uncertain as I can hardly consider it comprehensive of the characteristics of the individuals it comprises and on account of the criteria of inclusion, which are hardly ever univocal and self-excluding (for example, studies can be conducted on sexually-abused women, but in the course of her existence a woman will not be exclusively defined by this fact and could simultaneously be comprised in another hidden population, such as a group of people who use drugs); individuals can be part of a hidden population at different and more-or-less conscious levels (think of crime and drug use). An extreme case is that of people who are unaware of having specific diseases, and the degree of visibility can be greater or lesser depending on the particular case (murder vs gambling) and the observer (tax-evaders are unknown to the tax authorities, but are well-known by tax accountants). Moreover, it often depends on the individual's attitude towards the specific problem (think of homosexual pride versus those who hide their sexual orientation because they are perceived as deviant) (Sydor 2013; Duke 2007; Tortu, Goldsamt, and Hamid 2001).

An epidemic breaks out when an infection begins to develop outside the key populations at higher risk (both key to the epidemic's dynamic and key to the response). Certainly, the monitoring of the populations from which the infection originates has to be undertaken as the passing of the virus from these populations to healthy individuals is crucial to the spread of the disease. However, it is important to be aware that the infection has spread throughout society and that it can thus progressively spread via other channels. Social scientists have elaborated methods that can identify a submerged population deemed at higher risk, estimate its numerousness and suggest appropriate health-education strategies (Icard 2008).

The efficacy of the prevention strategy depends, to a large extent, on the communication of health-education models capable of promoting the implementation of healthy habits by convincing or, in any case, inducing people to take all necessary measures (Brown, Crawford, and Carter 2006). Traditional interventions are no longer seen as enough to prevent and control HIV effectively. Research shows that properly designed behaviour-based health communication activities can have a significant positive impact on health-related attitudes, beliefs and behaviours (Doyle et al. 2012).

Over the last 30 years, five principles have emerged as core components for effective prevention communication strategies. First, public health professionals, policymakers and HIV prevention practitioners must provide scientifically accurate, complete and current messages. Second, a successful information campaign relies deeply on the trust between recipient and sender, whether an individual, an organisation, or a public authority. Third, communication programmes should promote self-respect and empowerment by shared objectives that include a strong message of affirming the person's individuality with health-related objectives. Fourth, each communication strategy should primarily ensure the participation of key populations at higher risk and vulnerable populations in all its phases through community-centred, dialogic and participatory approaches that can alleviate possible negative responses (Sander et al. 2016, 5–7).

HIV epidemiology clearly demonstrates that having vaginal, anal or oral sex without a condom with an infected person is the main source of transmission of the virus (UNAIDS 2018a, 8). The people at whom the prevention intervention is directed must be stimulated to discuss how to avoid the risks of a possible infection effectively. Sex must not be considered exclusively as an urge to be satisfied, as this would make any kind of behaviour acceptable. It must be pointed out that the use of condoms is becoming increasingly common, also because tests have proved that it prevents the transmission of HIV and of sexually-transmitted diseases (Arkell and Harrigan 2018). Its diffusion, however, encounters significant difficulties in various areas of Sub-Saharan Africa, as diverse faith-based organisations are against the use of condoms because, in their opinion, this would promote infidelity and promiscuity (i.e. condoms are associated with sinful and immoral acts, such as casual sex). In particular, some religious leaders link HIV, condom use and immorality during their church sermons, hence suggesting that only non-believers are at risk of infection. This induces young church-goers to believe that they are immune to risk and, consequently, they do not adopt with any consistency appropriate protective measures. Other religious leaders share the views of many secular Africans who oppose condom use because they consider it as an unworkable prevention strategy that reduces sexual pleasure (Ochillo, Teijlingen, and Hind 2017). However, the church needs to limit its judgemental attitudes towards sexual behaviour by recognising the reality of sexual activity among the youth and the need to use protection (Mash and Mash 2013).

Several studies have demonstrated that many heterosexuals tend to label diverse minority groups, such as males who have sex with males, bisexuals, transgender persons and sex workers and their clients, as deviant individuals who are the most likely to be exposed to HIV or transmit it. This suggests that they are key to the epidemic and key to the response (Lewis et al. 2015; Fredriksen-Goldsen et al. 2014; Goh 2008; Samudzi and Mannell 2016; White Hughto, Reisner, and Pachankis 2015; Fauk et al. 2018; Pitpitan et al. 2013; Scambler and Paoli 2008). This attitude implies a separation between heterosexuals and the labelled minorities (Herek 2009). However, it also resurrects an old traditional religious idea according to which God can punish those who commit a sin such as sex outside marriage including same-sex intercourse, casual sex or commercial sex, with some physical or mental diseases (O'Mathúna and Larimore 2006, 59–60). In the course of history, some diseases, such as leprosy and the plague, have symbolised sin more than others as people associated them with immoral behaviour (Grigsby 2004). Social control called for the marginalisation and social exclusion of the sick person (Halasz 2018).

Most studies that have verified the extent to which HIV has modified the sexual habits of the population have indicated that only a minority has changed their behaviour (Noroozinejad et al. 2013; Berten and Van Rossem 2009; Odu and Akanle 2008; Ntozi et al. 2003). Individuals often choose their partners within their network of friends or acquaintances, and this choice is based on the certainty of evaluating their partner's health by their appearance (Hendrick and Hendrick 2000). Being aware of controlling the perception of risk is extremely important for the individual. The increased susceptibility to an infectious disease is strictly correlated to a reduction of the sense of personal control over one's health. An individual cannot increase or reduce the risk related to a specific event unless they are able to exercise specific control over the event itself by implementing appropriate behaviours, but if this does not happen, they risk contracting an infectious disease, including HIV (Carnaghi et al. 2011). It must be stressed that control is also exercised at a social level by both laws and ethical codes, which are important tools for preventing unwanted events (WHO 2017).

In light of the above, HIV prevention strategies designate the adoption of specific actions, suggested by health-information programmes aimed at preventing the spread of the HIV epidemic. These actions may be taken by individuals to protect their own health and the health of the people who live in their community (appropriate use of condoms, pre-exposure prophylaxis, post-exposure prophylaxis, adherence to antiretroviral therapy, and so on) or may be organised by governments or other institutions as public health policies (sex education, LGBT sex education, safe injection programmes, and so on) (UNAIDS 2018b). However, from a public health standpoint, HIV prevention can be articulated in the following three distinct phases. First, primary prevention focuses mainly on how to help persons protect themselves from contracting HIV (Kelly and Kalichman 2002, 626). It proactively seeks to build adaptive strengths, coping resources and health in populations and communities, and supports the use of appropriate diagnostic tools and antiretroviral treatments with apposite educational policies (including about the range of preventive tools available) and social/structural-level change (including changes in laws, policies and practices). This strategy also asserts that it is possible to only efficiently address problems before or when they occur when people have resources they need to thrive (including increasing the number of available therapeutic choices when people manage their own health) (Ayala et al. 2017, 7). Second, secondary prevention is sometimes used to refer to interventions designed to reduce risk-taking behaviours among people living with HIV (e.g. consistent condom use, reducing partners, abstinence, serostatus disclosure, and clean injection equipment) (Killianova 2013; Brown and DiClemente 2011; Fisher and Smith 2009). They intend to prevent the transmission of the virus to those who are HIV negative by educating HIV-positive people on how to reduce the risk of transmission of HIV to others (so-called positive prevention) and to support the patient's ability to adhere to their HIV medications to avoid complications (Veterans Health Administration 2008). Lastly, tertiary prevention aims to limit the further negative effects of HIV and increase the quality of life of people with chronic HIV infection (Cabassi 2004, 29). This includes reducing viral load and caring for the physical and psychological health of the patient by providing the essential foundation for maintaining safer behaviours and improving their daily living conditions (Knox and Chenneville 2006, 395). Most often, more than one approach for prevention is directed towards a target group since behaviours that may place it at a higher risk of HIV exposure are multidimensional and overlapping. A large number of interventional strategies can be applied at the micro-level (for example, individual-focused interventions on patients living with HIV and their family members or formal caregivers, such as health professionals, nurses, and social workers), meso (community) level, and macro (policy or structural) level with a certain efficacy (Sahasrabuddhe and Vermund 2007).

Conclusion

Infectious diseases emerging throughout the centuries have included some of the most terrifying epidemics of the past. New infections keep on developing, while many of the old plagues are still present (Morse 2001). The emergence of new infectious diseases, including not only HIV, but also coronavirus disease 2019 and new strains of influenza, indicates again that health issues have an international dimension and necessitate strategic global interventions (Sands, Mundaca-Shah, and Dzau 2016).

HIV, the virus that causes AIDS, is one of the world's most serious public health challenges, mainly in Sub-Saharan Africa. In this geographical area, the disease has dramatically reduced life expectancy but in particular among countries with large HIV epidemics (Gori, Manfredi, and Sodini 2019, 333). The international policy agenda of HIV has emerged gradually in parallel to its recognition as an international concern. As a result, there is a global commitment to preventing new HIV infections and ensuring that everyone with HIV has access to antiretroviral therapy (ART)[6] (WHO 2016a).

The use of ART is now a standard medical practice for stopping the progression of HIV because it reduces the viral load in the body (Chendi et al. 2019). In HIV-positive people, ART is highly recommended because it provides individual and public health benefits. A recent study published in *Lancet HIV* in 2017 examined the life expectancies of people by analysing data sets from 18 European and North American cohorts of people living with HIV. Specifically, the researchers observed data from 88,504 patients who started ART between 1996 and 2013. They found that life expectancy had risen since the advent of ART, in particular, between 1996 and 2010, with life expectancy in 20-year-old patients increasing by about nine years in women and ten years in men. Additionally, the estimated life expectancy for a 20-year-old patient who began treatment with antiretroviral drugs between 2008 and 2010 was 78 years, namely a life expectancy near to that of the general population (The Antiretroviral Therapy Cohort Collaboration 2017).

Antiretroviral treatment can also be prescribed as a prophylaxis for individuals at risk of exposure to HIV (pre-exposure prophylaxis [PrEP] and post-exposure prophylaxis [PEP]) (Saag et al. 2018). PrEP involves the use of antiretroviral drugs by HIV-negative people in order to prevent them from acquiring HIV. The World Health Organization recommends this prophylaxis for individuals who do not always wear condoms during sexual activity and are therefore at high risk of HIV infection. The decision to use PrEP rests with the individual, who must immediately stop the administration if he or she acquires HIV infection (Coombs and Gold 2019, 1). PrEP has been shown to be highly effective, reducing the risk of contracting HIV by up to 99% if taken correctly and consistently (CDC 2019). PrEP has produced a slight increase in life expectancy for key populations at higher risk of HIV exposure as confirmed by the following studies: the first was carried out in the United States of America on a cohort of men who had sex with men and with a mean age of 34 years. PrEP reduced lifetime HIV infection risk from 44% to 25% and increased average life expectancy from 39.9 years to 40.7 years (Paltiel et al. 2009). The second study examined the clinical effects of implementing a PrEP programme in a cohort of Brazilian men who had sex with men and transgender women and with a mean age of 31.4 years. PrEP reduced per-person lifetime HIV infection risk from 50.5% to 40.1% while it increased average life expectancy from 36.8 years to 41 years (Luz et al. 2018).

---

[6] Synonyms are combination ART and highly active ART (WHO 2014c, 3).

PEP is a short-term antiretroviral treatment to prevent the acquisition of HIV infection after potential exposure in either occupational or non-occupational situations, mainly for cases of sexual assault. The first dose should be offered as soon as possible following exposure, no later than after 72 hours (WHO 2013, 83). It has been estimated that PEP can reduce the risk of HIV infection in the order of 80% (Nambiar and Short 2019, 23), with consequent positive effects for longevity, physical and psychological health conditions and quality of life (Pinto et al. 2019).

The points made above supply additional elements for a better comprehension of the basic aspects of the HIV epidemic, which have been already concisely addressed in the chapter, and constitute a helpful information base to frame the disease sociologically in the next chapter.

Chapter 2

Normalcy, pathology and the 'sick role'[1]

Sociological organicism

The influence of the paradigms of natural science on the epistemology of social sciences is now clear to see. The present-day sociological literature expresses an almost absolute aversion for the nineteenth-century organicist sociology without even occasionally attempting to ascertain whether this school of thought has left a permanent legacy. An important contribution from the organicists was that of transferring some concepts and principles which belong to medical science into social thought. One of the pivotal principles adopted by Auguste Comte, who himself took it from François Broussais, involves normal and pathological social states representing the extreme stages of a single kind of condition (Foucault 1999). The insistence of these authors on this medical analogy is today echoed in expressions such as 'healthy society' (Wilkinson 1996).

Comte was the principal theoretical point of reference for most organicists. According to Comte, social disorders should be considered pathological cases existing within a specific social body, thus being akin to the illnesses that can be present in the human body. He held Broussais' ideas in high regard (Broussais was one of the great reformers of medicine) and widely used them. According to Broussais, there is no interruption between physiological and pathological phenomena; a physiological phenomenon becomes pathological when specific, measurable alterations from a qualitative standpoint can be observed. In other words, the phenomena of an illness basically coincide with those of good health, the only difference being their intensity. Each concept of pathology must be based on previous knowledge of the normal state, but at the same time, the scientific study of pathological cases becomes essential to every pursuit of the laws of the normal state. Comte stressed several times the need to determine the meaning of normalcy before methodically exploring

[1] The content of Section entitled "Children orphaned by AIDS and their deviant tendencies" was originally published in Meini, Bruno, and Mara Tognetti Bordogna. 2018. "The Impact of HIV-Related Stigma on Children Orphaned by AIDS or Living with Seropositive Caregivers." *International Review of Sociology* 28 (3): 541–555. Reprinted by permission of Taylor & Francis Ltd, http://www.tandfonline.com on behalf of University of Rome 'La Sapienza'.

pathological cases, but never suggested any criterion capable of recognising when a phenomenon is normal. Hence, with regard to this aspect, I am led to believe that he was referring to a common corresponding concept, given that he indiscriminately used the notions of a normal state, physiological state and natural state (Canguilhem 1966). Based on what has been previously represented, clearly Comte's intention was to refute any qualitative difference between the natural and pathological phenomena since he defined the pathological as a mere extension of the normal state beyond the common.

Unlike Comte and Broussais, Claude Bernard, the founder of modern physiology, did not work on general cases, but formulated a theory based on experimental observations (Bernard 1865). In the case of diabetes, for instance, the change from a normal to a pathological condition is due to a quantitative alteration which can be distinctly observed in the level of blood glucose normally produced in the body (Jörgens and Grüsser 2013). Based on these premises, the assumption of a scientific medico-biological approach to society can thus lead back to an organic unity of the social facts, which in principle were commonly attributed to ethical, political and juridical differences. The authoritativeness of social science is based on a metaphor, that is, on the organism metaphor, according to which every social organisation possesses internal balancing and control capacities. Hence, society becomes a unifying organism that can absorb global or local conflicts, which previous paradigms assigned to collisions between contrasting interests (Barberis 2003).

The organistic set-up of early sociological theories led to a misunderstanding of the nature of the existing relations between society and the boundaries of pathology. Auguste Comte in sociology and Adolphe Quetelet in his criminological and anthropometric studies arbitrarily identified the norm with the average. The concept of normalcy was not considered a criterion relative to the capacity of organisms to adjust to an environment, but a meta-social principle resulting from mathematical relations from which human characteristics were inferentially made to derive from (Udehn 2001, 29–30). Thereafter, Émile Durkheim (1895) identified one of the main rules of his method in the distinction between the normal and the pathological. Given that the fundamental characteristic of sociology is to consider social facts as things, the French sociologist wished to obtain an objective criterion relating to the facts themselves, which enables the formulation of a distinction. He solved the problem resorting to a criterion applied in biology, thus defining the facts that present the most general forms as normal, and as morbid or pathological those which assume exceptional forms. The normalcy Durkheim referred to is statistic normalcy, which underlies the identity distinction between the generic type, medium type and healthy type.

The 'sick role'

The importance given by Talcott Parsons to the interdependence of the various levels of reality, in the explanation of social phenomena, makes his approach a necessary point of reference in the analysis of health/illness issues. The concept of illness was already formulated in *The Social System* (1951), in which Parsons describes illness as a condition that upsets the normal functioning of the individual from an organic as well as personal and social standpoint. Illness does not simply represent an external threat from which the social system must defend itself, but is part of an integrating social equilibrium. Illness, indeed, intentionally or not, represents a reaction to the pressures of society; in other words, it is a way of evading social obligations. This set-up results from what Parsons considers the quintessential social problem, namely social order (Williams 2003, 181–182).

The analysis of the concept of illness and, more generally, of the medical profession is situated in the context of the social problem of order. Parsons poses the question of whether being sick constitutes a special role or whether it is simply a fact; in other words, a condition. The answer is that the individual who has fallen ill is not only physically sick but now adheres to the specifically patterned social role of being sick, while this role remains a mere condition of the organic system from a medical standpoint. The curative process which legitimises the function of the physician, along with the dependent nature of the sick person's role with their obligation to heal, suited Parsons' idea of a functionally balanced society (Weiss and Lonnquist 1997, 243). The division of social roles and the unbalanced power relationship serve the social aim of re-establishing social norms and re-equilibrating the social system (Young 2004, 4).

For Parsons, illness is an intrinsically social and role-structured phenomenon. When an individual becomes sick, he argued, there is available a social role, the 'sick role', which channels them to the doctor. Sickness is a temporary, medically sanctioned form of deviant behaviour, which frees the sick person from normal role performances and is dysfunctional to society. The equilibrium that society maintains can be disrupted when individual members, due to sickness, are not able to fulfil their routine responsibilities. Like crime, it is a problem of social order, and the physician is an agent of social control who regulates entry to the sick role and applies his or her specialist knowledge and skills with the aim of reintegrating the deviant into society. Reintegration does not involve punishment but treatment (Davis 2010, 214). However, it is logical to underline that people with HIV, despite advances in medicine, are not reintegrated into normal social relationships and the consequent fulfilment of their roles according to Parsons' model. They become permanent actors in the role of a sick person; a role from which they cannot escape, as they are victims of a chronic pathology. Consequently, the expectations relative to the sick role are more suited to describing situations such as those that come to fruition in the case of diseases in which the physical inability is temporary (Parsons 1978).

In Western societies, people are regarded as being sick when their behaviour complies with the four general expectations described hereafter. Firstly, sick people are exempted from their normal activities and responsibilities in virtue of the social role they normally have, and the exemption is related to the nature and seriousness of their illness. Secondly, sick people are not held responsible for their condition, given that they cannot be expected to recover by way of a simple intentional act. Their condition, as well as their behaviour, must change, but this is possible only by means of a mental or biological reorganisation process. While the first two expectations are in some way the rights of a sick person, the second two instead delineate obligations. Usually, a sick person is expected to acknowledge the undesirability of their condition and consequently of wanting to get well as quickly as possible, and then to seek medical advice and cooperate with doctors (Parsons 1951, 436–437).

Being sick means that the subject enters a role of sanctioned deviance which must, however, be distinguished from other deviant roles, since a sick person is not deemed responsible for their condition (Finerman and Bennett 1995). The sick role serves as a mechanism of social control that aids the system to guide deviant tendencies, in this case an illness, away from group formation (i.e. a deviant subculture of the sick), and the successful establishment of the claim to legitimacy (Scott and Marshall 2009, 687). Sick people are not tied up with other deviants to constitute a separate sub-culture, but each is connected with a group of non-sick people, his or her personal circle, and, above all, physicians. The sick thus become a statistical status class and are deprived of the possibility of forming a united and supportive community. Furthermore, to be sick is by definition to be in an undesirable condition, so that it makes absolutely no sense to uphold that the best way for everyone to deal with the most frustrating aspects of the social system is to get sick. These two functions of the sick role are active also when no therapeutic influence is exercised, and their weight with regard to the social system should not be underestimated (Parsons 1951, 477). However, the sick role is one of the few roles that requires certified diagnosis prior to both entry and exit. A symptomatic individual cannot enter the sick role unless a medical statement attests to his or her clinical condition. The condition constitutes illness until a doctor declares it to be sickness. While the family and members of one's social groups may provide temporary confirmation of the state of being sick, this will not allow the individual to be excused from work or school, nor will it allow the affected individual access to medical treatment, hospital admission, or drug prescriptions. At the same time, the patient remains in the sick role until formally dismissed by the doctor (Thomas 2003, 220).

Some diseases, like mental illness and AIDS, involve a high degree of stigma and sufferers may decide to conceal public knowledge of their pathology (Browne 2006, 122). They may therefore decide to adopt the role of a sick person exclusively within the boundaries of a medical subsystem, as the result of the diagnosis is confidential (Parsons 1975). Doctors can experience conflicts between maintaining the confidentiality of the doctor-patient relationship and disclosing information to a patient's parent or spouse. This raises the question of whether there are any circumstances in which a doctor at a clinic should disclose that a patient is seropositive or has AIDS, when this is against the patient's wishes. Such situations often pose dilemmas for doctors and raise questions regarding their main duties and responsibilities, as well as possibly presenting conflicts in relation to their own beliefs and values. However, there are good grounds for asserting that the maintaining of the confidentiality of the doctor-patient relationship is a priority. In particular, this allows to preserve patients' trust in doctors and their willingness to consult and discuss their problems freely in the future; destroying this trust undermines the very foundation of the relationship between these two actors (Morgan 2003).

There are moral implications to reporting that an individual is HIV-positive, as this means revealing behaviours that have led to this condition. This disclosure calls into question the identity of the individual before their social environment and represents an upheaval which disrupts the equilibrium of social interactions (Parsons 1964, 267–271). Research has focused more on the attitudes held by seronegative people towards people living with HIV than on the perspectives of those directly affected. Two significant dimensions associated with social interaction and identified by researchers as being of primary importance for understanding HIV-related stigma include fear of contagion and controllability of infection. People avoid interaction with those living with HIV because they fear becoming infected with it. On the other hand, negative attitudes towards seropositive people are also closely connected to other people's perception of how much control these seropositive people had over the infection. People that are perceived as having more control over their means of infection are more stigmatised and receive less empathy than those perceived as having less control. For example, attitudes could be more negative towards a seropositive sex worker than towards a housewife whose husband knowingly infects her without ever disclosing his positive status before or after marriage. The sex worker could be perceived as being guilty or responsible for her HIV-positive status, whereas the housewife is seen as an innocent victim (Varas-Díaz, Serrano-García, and Toro-Alfonso 2005, 171). In addition, those who are stigmatised are commonly both individuals who are truly ill and people who assume behaviours that place them in situations in which they may be exposed to HIV such as having sexual intercourse without a condom or using non-sterile drug injecting equipment. People with behaviours that may place them at higher risk of HIV exposure do not necessarily identify themselves with any particular group. In other words, just certain behaviours, rather than membership of a particular group, place individuals in situations in which they can be exposed to HIV. These individuals are sometimes erroneously identified as groups at risk and thus deemed infectious even though they are healthy (Israel, Laudari, and Simonetti 2008).

The argumentations set forth thus far highlight the central problem encountered when I apply the Parsonian concept of the sick role, which is the non-correspondence between the condition of an individual's organic system and their capacity to adjust on a personal and social level. The disfunctioning of an individual's organic system (disease) can be compared with the maladjustment of a person's personality system (illness), but not necessarily with a social maladjustment (sickness). One of the factors that regulate the degree of inconsistency is the personality system and especially its specific function, that of identity. In Parsons' view, identity becomes a subjective orientation function; in other words, a principle that regulates the action which, by guiding the individual in choosing among behaviour alternatives, preserves the internal coherence of the psychological system by means of its suitability to the value system. In point of fact, the formation of an identity relies on a process of internalisation of values and cultural symbols mediated by the social system. This process can be deemed accomplished and, in its fundamental features, irreversible immediately after adolescence. The consequence of this set-up is that a mature individual always tends to act coherently. It seems that the interior coherence of individual identity and social conformity cannot be considered separately without generating forms which are pathologically or theoretically connected to ambiguous categories of deviance. In this perspective, one can thus comprehend how the sociological analysis of the AIDS phenomenon has made the well-known interpretative limits even more noticeable (Sciolla 1983, 28-29).

The element of intentionality

The element of individual responsibility becomes central when a person contracts a disease. This problem was analysed by Edward Albert (1986) who examined the process of legitimisation of the sick person's status from a moral rather than medical standpoint. He builds on the assumption that every society is founded upon specific moral values, according to which the community tends to approve or disapprove the behaviours of its members. Like Parsons, he reveals that a similar distinction is institutionalised in every society and that the differentiation of the system of reference fosters the specialisation of social-control functions and of the organisational system required for their fulfilment. Moreover, he stresses that specific behaviours that can cause pathological manifestations identify the individual who carries them out as a deviant rather than a sick person. Albert structures his theory by resorting to the model of deviance suggested by Parsons. Two trajectories can be inferred from this theory: the first distinguishes deviance from a situational or normative standpoint, depending on whether a person's behaviour complies with a situation or normative models. In the first case, there are alterations in the performances of a role produced by an illness; while in the second, what is subsumed from a moral standpoint within the concept of sin is clear. The second trajectory distinguishes deviance according to the degree of the individual's involvement; therefore, it can concern their willingness to fulfil certain obligations connected to specific norms or deriving from particular roles they have in specific communities.

As previously seen, intentionality is not always involved in contracting an infection. This is the case in new-borns (Thisyakorn 2017), individuals who have received several transfusions and haemophiliacs (Evatt 2006), who fall within the Parsonian classification of illness as unintended deviance (Williams 2005). However, this classification becomes complicated for those individuals whose lifestyle places them at greater risk of being infected, as, in this case, the subject's motivations become determining and their placement within the typology is rather difficult. Consequently, it is logical to wonder how an HIV-positive sex worker or a seropositive people who inject drugs should be classified and how their deviance should be ranked. To answer these questions, Albert (1986) suggests that the Parsonian model be supplemented with Theodore R. Sarbin's theory (1967), which establishes a connection between nature and the severity of the sanctions associated with a deviating behaviour and the performance of role expectations. According to Sarbin, the existing expectation towards an acquired role implies a minimum tendency to sanction negative performances, while it provides a reward for deserving ones. On the contrary, the expectation towards assigned roles could give scant or no rewards to positive performances and heavily sanction to negative ones.

Michael D. Quam's (1990) dissatisfaction with the AIDS-related issues that the Parsonian interpretative scheme brought up drove him to adopt Eliot Freidson's situational theory, according to which, from a social standpoint, an illness is the significance that an actor or those who surround him attribute to a behaviour, and the sick person's attitude is regulated precisely by this significance. In this theory, an illness represents a social reaction that disregards any kind of premise of a medical nature. The definition of a sick person's role is based on two variables which define the illness as a specific social reaction to deviance; the attribution of individual responsibility and the degree of severity of the reaction (Freidson 1970). On the grounds of this argumentation, Quam concludes that when a disease is perceived as sufficiently serious, and the sick person is not responsible for his condition (deviation), they are ascribed with the legitimacy of their status and the sick role is unconditionally assigned. However, if the disease is seen as an intentional deviation from social norms, the sick person may be considered an offender. Based on this theory, sick people can be divided into innocent victims and guilty victims according to their social identity. Comprised in the former category are HIV-positive children, haemophiliacs and people who have received several blood transfusions. The latter category includes individuals whose lifestyle systematically breaches commonly-accepted social norms: men who have sex with men, sex workers and people who inject drugs. Therefore, in the latter case, it makes no difference whether an individual has intentionally exposed themselves to the risk of infection given that, in order to certify their intentionality, it is sufficient that they belong to a category which is in its own right defined as deviant. The personal characteristics of these categories of individuals are such that the boundary between unintentional deviance (disease) and deviance disappears, and this accounts for the social tendency to discriminate, stigmatise and criminalise HIV-positive people. This tendency is also worsened by interventions inspired by social control strategies likely to create unjustified social alarm (Quam 1990, 33).

Within the disease and deviance dichotomy, the concept of disability which Lawrence D. Haber and Richard T. Smith proposed during the 1970s is worthy of attention as something that is different from both the sick role and deviant behaviour. In their essay, disability is intended as a social process which indicates a behavioural model arising from the loss of a person's ability to fulfil their ascribed social roles due to chronic physical and mental impairments. Based on this model, the normalisation of deviant behaviours, accomplished within a reciprocal structure of roles, can be conceived as a means for facilitating the conservation of roles and social control. In other words, disability can be intended as social adaptation to inability, which organises an individual's behaviour according to a specific model of expectations similar to the behavioural adaptations defined by Edwin M. Lemert as secondary deviance[2] (Haber and Smith 1971, 88–89).

---

[2] Lemert made a distinction between primary deviance and secondary deviance. Primary deviance occurs when an actor engages in norm-violating behaviour without viewing himself as engaging in a deviant role, therefore with marginal consequences for their mental make-up (Lemert 1951, 75). By contrast, secondary deviance significantly affects the psychological structure of the subject and takes place when "a person begins to employ his deviant behaviour or a role based upon it as a means of defence, attack, or adjustment to the overt and covert problems created by the consequent societal reaction to him, his deviation is secondary" (Ibid., 76).

An issue of particular relevance is whether people who have HIV but appear asymptomatic can be considered disabled and therefore be protected by the law. This issue can be addressed by illustrating a specific case as an example. In 1994, Dr Randon Bragdon performed a dental examination on Ms Sidney Abbott and discovered a cavity. She had indicated on her intake form that she was 'asymptomatic' HIV-positive. Dr Bragdon told her that he could not fill her cavity in his office and that he would agree to do it only in a hospital setting. Abbott would have to pay for the expense of being admitted and using the facility. Abbott decided to sue Bragdon on grounds of discrimination, citing the Americans with Disabilities Act. On June 25, 1998, the United States Supreme Court in Bragdon v. Abbott addressed the Americans with Disabilities Act definition of an individual with a disability and ruled that Ms Abbott's asymptomatic HIV infection was a physical impairment. The Court also added that the HIV infection placed a substantial limitation on Ms Abbott's ability to reproduce and to bear children and that reproduction was a major life activity. Finally, after evaluating the medical evidence, the Court concluded that Ms Abbott's ability to reproduce was drastically limited in two ways: (1) an attempt to conceive would impose a significant risk on Ms Abbott's partner, and (2) an HIV infected woman risks infecting her child during gestation and childbirth (Jones 2003, 91).

As I have previously seen, the Supreme Court ruled that HIV-positive people have physical impairments that qualify them as individuals with disabilities who are protected by the Americans with Disabilities Act. However, not everyone considers HIV as a disabling condition, especially in its asymptomatic stage. HIV is an epidemic that can be stopped or at least minimised in its most debilitating effects, but it will continue to prosper until stigma and discrimination are reduced (Holloway 2014).

A high number of HIV-positive people, including those on antiretroviral therapy, experience different types of disability such as impairments (e.g. sensory, musculoskeletal, cardiovascular, mental), activity limitations (e.g. mobility, daily activities) and participation restrictions (e.g. work, social life). Consequently, healthcare practitioners are now expected to handle the augmented complexity of chronic HIV (UNAIDS 2017, 6) in agreement with the United Nations Convention on the Rights of Persons with Disabilities (2006) (Ibid., 2).

The analysis carried out has clearly illustrated that deviance no longer represents the only available investigation tool for studying the social scope of HIV and that the existence of an element of relationality implied in the concept of disability allows us to overcome the health/disease dilemma posed by HIV (Verbrugge and Jette 1994).

Children orphaned by AIDS and their deviant tendencies

The deviance issue related to health also arises when taking the children orphaned by AIDS into consideration. Despite a modest decline in HIV adult prevalence worldwide and increasing access to antiretroviral treatment, the number of children affected by or vulnerable to HIV remains quite high (Office of the US Global AIDS Coordinator 2012). Children orphaned by AIDS have limited life prospects and are without adequate affective and economic support. They are not only traumatised by the loss of parents, whose physical deterioration they may often have witnessed, but their loss and grief sometimes risk being aggravated by prejudice, stigma, discrimination and social exclusion processes (Wild 2001). Moreover, they could suffer additional emotional trauma caused by the fact that they may remain alone without any help from the traditional African safety net, the extended family. They may increase the already elevated number of street children present in many African countries. Many such children have been evicted by unscrupulous relatives, compelled to leave school because they have not been able to pay school fees and must sometimes take care of their younger siblings (Schönteich 2002, 30). In these pressured circumstances, street children may be more vulnerable to engaging in criminal activities, both against persons and property, or to becoming victims of a range of crimes such as assault, abuse and rape. In addition, an increasing number of them are being sexually exploited within commercial sex rings (Fourie and Schönteich 2001, 39).

Children orphaned by AIDS constitute a social group of disenfranchised young people devoid of parental guidance, supervision and care (Loeber and Stouthamer-Loeber 1986). In particular, orphaned young males mainly suffer from the untimely death of a father figure who could represent a positive role model during their growth and this will place children at greater risk of developing subsequent antisocial behaviours, including delinquency (Pharoah and Weiss 2005, 2). Furthermore, an experienced adult male figure provides secure attachment and emotional support to children to allow them to grow up serenely and demonstrate high levels of empathy and self-discipline. As a result, such an absence can produce a negative effect on a boy's capacity to develop self-control and can lead to an increase in violent behaviour (Harper and McLanahan 2004).

A further and emergent theme is that HIV has mainly contributed to modifying the demographic structure of Southern Africa (Heuveline 2004). In the worst affected countries, the median survival with HIV is estimated to be around ten years old. In these countries, the majority of HIV infections occur between 15 and 25 years of age for women and between 20 and 30 years for men. As a result, many men aged between 30 and 40 will die in the coming years, leading to an over-representation of young men between 15 and 29 years of age (UNAIDS and WHO 2005, 20–25); this is an age group in which people's propensity to commit crime is at its highest level (Schönteich 1999). Criminological theories suggest that this demographic change can imply an increase in the levels of crime and violence, which will negatively impact on the stability and security of the region (Pharoah and Schönteich 2003, 11). The fear is that the AIDS epidemic will exacerbate this phenomenon by creating millions of orphans. In fact, these distressed young people may provide a steady recruitment pool for individuals and organisations wishing to challenge the existing status quo (Loewenson and Whiteside 2001).

Randy B. Cheek (2000) argued that children orphaned by AIDS who are disconnected from social, economic and political support structures may constitute an extra-national population group, who could easily become a tool for ethnic warfare, economic exploitation or political opportunism. Boys would become child soldiers, and girls would become sex slaves to male fighters. Moreover, he added that uneducated, malnourished, and purposeless children can represent a potential army, which, if exploited, could effectively destabilise most countries in Southern Africa. Finally, Cheek reported the example of the conflict in Sierra Leone, where little boys were recruited into the Revolutionary United Front with promises of food, alcohol, drugs and girls.

The relationship between crime and age has been the main subject of several criminological investigations based on the main premise that crime is mostly committed by adolescents and young adults (Smith 1995, 395). The age factor crucially impacts offending rates, and this relationship is often designated as the age-crime curve. This curve indicates a specific tendency, namely, the propensity to commit crimes reaches its peak in the late teen years and declines as age advances (Farrington 1986). Robyn Pharoah questions Martin Schönteich's analysis highlighting how many of the arguments on parentless children are openly speculative in nature, based on limited empirical data and would seem to be part of a growing body of advocacy-oriented literature aimed at raising awareness of HIV as a potentially significant security (as opposed to health) problem (Pharoah 2004a, 5–6). She maintains that orphans and other children made vulnerable by AIDS may not represent a real threat to the stability of Southern Africa, and South Africa in particular, as some analysts have predicted, and adds that despite the fact that the number of children orphaned by AIDS is increasing, relatively few children presently seem to be living in situations of extreme poverty and without some sort of support (Pharoah 2004b, 121). In other words, although an increasing number of children orphaned by AIDS is beginning to place stress on traditional coping mechanisms such as the extended family, they are still remarkably intact (Mkhwanazi et al. 2018, 73).

As previously examined, the dynamics surrounding children orphaned by AIDS have been mainly the object of investigation by psychologists, security analysts and demographers till now. Only recently, sociologists have started studying this phenomenon as one of the most serious effects brought about by the HIV epidemic in African societies. Social control theories can provide a helpful theoretical support for sociologists interested in providing a general sociological explanation of the issue of children orphaned by AIDS who commit deviant or criminal acts (Meini 2008a, 51–52) whereas Edwin Sutherland's learning theory can give a valuable contribution to the analysis of the child soldier phenomenon. He asserts that criminal behaviour is learnable and learned through interaction with other deviant individuals. Through this contact, children learn not only techniques on how to perform certain crimes, but also specific rationales, motives and so on. The principal part of learning criminal behaviour occurs within intimate personal groups. A person becomes a delinquent due to an excess of definitions (or values) favourable to the violation of the law over definitions (values) unfavourable to the infringement of the law. In other words, criminal behaviour emerges when an individual is mainly exposed to social signals that favour criminal conduct rather than social messages that promote the observance of the law (Sutherland and Cressey 1974). According to the Coalition to Stop the Use of Child Soldiers (1999), two key factors have led to a steady increase in the use of child soldiers. Firstly, technological advances have made weapons, especially small arms, light enough for children to carry and use. Falling prices have contributed to the proliferation of these weapons. Secondly, the longer a war goes on, the more likely children are to be recruited, as the shortage of manpower due to casualties and escalating conflict leads to a search for more recruits.

Conclusion

This chapter has explored sociologically the nature of the HIV epidemic seeking to highlight how sociological theory can positively contribute to explaining the multifaceted socio-criminological dimensions of the virus (Watkins-Hayes 2014; Akers and Lanier 2009). It thus represents an outstanding contribution to the ongoing sociological debate on infectious diseases (Dingwall, Hoffman, and Staniland 2013).

Parsons conceptualises illness as an undesirable and unintentional form of deviance within a social system that functions normally until its members perform their roles adequately. He explains that the behaviour of a sick person is deviant because it deviates from the normal performance of their social roles. This deviation (sick role) can become a pervasive threat to the stability of society unless appropriate social control mechanisms intervene (Heidarnia and Heidarnia 2016; Varul 2010; Arluke 1988).

In this context, Parsons' description of the sick role represents a theme of fundamental importance when one intends to illustrate the dichotomous relationship between health and illness within a social system that constantly looks for stability. In fact, as specifically formulated by Parsons in *The Social System* (1951), illness is not only an external threat from which the social system must defend itself, but, as mentioned above, can also be seen as a state of deviance, or dysfunctionality, whose pressure creates conditions for returning to a state of functionality. This new social equilibrium is practically achieved thanks to the therapeutic action exercised by the physician on the ill (Bury and Monaghan 2013, 91–93; Ziguras 2004, 77).

The deviance issue related to health also emerges when examining the children orphaned by AIDS. Most researchers argue that children who have lost their parents to AIDS could experience social isolation, discrimination, and stigmatisation, which could, in turn, lead to antisocial or violent behaviours. Policy initiatives should support a separate justice system, which channels children who are in conflict with the law away from the formal court system into reintegrative programmes (Meini 2008b).

In the subsequent chapter, starting from the analysis of children orphaned by AIDS or made vulnerable by AIDS, who are ostracised, discriminated against, and isolated due to the shame associated with this disease, the author thoroughly illustrates the impact that stigmatisation and discrimination processes can have in the expansion and maintenance of the HIV epidemic (Meini and Tognetti Bordogna 2018).

Chapter 3

The impact of HIV-related stigma and discrimination against children orphaned by AIDS[1]

HIV as a human rights issue

The protection of human rights is an effective way to protect the public's health, including a successful response to HIV (Jürgens and Cohen 2009). There are two aspects of public health that are important from the human rights perspective. On the one hand, protection of public health is one of the universally accepted grounds for limiting individual rights and freedoms. Preventing the spread of communicable diseases may cause deprivation of liberty, intrusion into private and family life, and the limitation of different types of freedom (freedom of movement, freedom of worship, and so on). One the other hand, such restrictions have to be specifically defined by law and can be judicially reviewed if they unreasonably restrict human rights. Thus, from a health viewpoint, human rights offer a set of principles that public health policies are obligated to protect and uphold (Tomasevski 2006, 72).

The right to health is a fundamental component of the human rights approach to HIV (Patterson 2004, 9). The HIV epidemic is not just a medical problem, but one that includes issues regarding gender, development and human rights (Viljoen and Precious 2007, 4). The latter are, in fact, inextricably connected to the spread and impact of HIV on single individuals and communities around the world. A lack of respect for human rights fuels the spread and aggravates the impact of the disease, while at the same time HIV undermines progress in the realisation of human rights (Roseman, Gruskin, and Banerjee 2004, 10). The relationship between HIV and human rights stresses the

---

[1] The content of Sections entitled "HIV-related stigma" and "Orphans and other children made vulnerable by HIV" was originally published in Meini, Bruno, and Mara Tognetti Bordogna. 2018. "The Impact of HIV-Related Stigma on Children Orphaned by AIDS or Living with Seropositive Caregivers." *International Review of Sociology* 28 (3): 541–555. Reprinted by permission of Taylor & Francis Ltd, http://www.tandfonline.com on behalf of University of Rome 'La Sapienza'.

ways in which people vulnerable to human rights violations and neglect are more vulnerable to HIV infection. Moreover, if infected, such people do not have access to appropriate quality services, care and treatment, especially antiretroviral therapy as the most important human rights achievement in their HIV responses (Levi et al. 2016; Gruskin and Tarantola 2008).

Human rights are relevant to the response to HIV in at least three ways: first, a lack of human rights protection increases vulnerability to HIV, especially among populations who are the most likely to be exposed to HIV such as gay men and other men who have sex with men, sex workers and their clients, transgender people, people who inject drugs, and prisoners, but also certain vulnerable groups such as women, young persons and children, including orphans and other children made vulnerable by AIDS. Second, a lack of human rights protection fuels stigma, discrimination, and violence against people living with and affected by HIV. These negative and harmful attitudes are often generated by a misunderstanding about the routes of HIV transmission as well as by the false perception that links the HIV virus to socially disapproved behaviours such as sex outside marriage, sex between men, and drug use. Lastly, a lack of human rights protection hinders effective strategies against HIV. Discriminatory, coercive and castigatory approaches to HIV increase vulnerability to infection and aggravate the impact of the epidemic on the population of each country (e.g. ideologically and morally driven restrictions on information and education about the prevention of HIV, including safe sex and condom use, HIV testing without informed consent, and HIV-related immigration restrictions on entry, stay and residence) (Duger et al. 2013, 102-103).

The Human Rights Council, in its resolution 16/28 on the protection of human rights in the context of HIV and AIDS, requested the Office of the United Nations High Commissioner for Human Rights to engage actively with the 2011 General Assembly High-Level Meeting on AIDS, providing a human rights-based perspective, and to inform the Human Rights Council thereon. In December 2011, the report of the United Nations High Commissioner for Human Rights (UNHCHR) on the protection of human rights in the context of HIV and AIDS was submitted pursuant to that request. This report provides (a) a general idea of the context and objectives of the 2011 *Political Declaration on HIV and AIDS: Intensifying our Efforts to Eliminate AIDS* adopted at the United Nations General Assembly High-Level Meeting on AIDS, including information on the role that the Office of the High Commissioner for Human Rights (OHCHR) played in supporting a human rights-based perspective; and (b) an analysis of the above-mentioned political declaration from a human rights perspective (UNHCHR 2011). The 2011 political declaration reaffirms the 2001 declaration of commitment on HIV and AIDS and the 2006 political declaration on HIV and AIDS and the urgent need on behalf of the member states of the United Nations to considerably increase efforts towards the goal of universal access to comprehensive prevention programmes, treatment, care and support. In particular, it includes a specific chapter on human rights and is especially important as it is an affirmation of the recognition by the United Nations General Assembly of the key role of human rights in the HIV response (United Nations General Assembly 2011).

Countries that have placed juridical principles relative to human rights at the centre of their HIV-related policies have seen epidemics averted or slowed. They include the following: the right to non-discrimination on the basis of HIV status; the right to appropriate treatment as part of essential healthcare; the right of HIV-positive people to participate in the development of AIDS policies and plans (Jürgens and Cohen 2009); the right to privacy, among other rights, which protects and defends the right of the individual to self-determination, integrity, informed consent, patient-doctor confidentiality and right to know (Burke 2015); the right to life implies that the government must guarantee the full enjoyment of life to all human beings, whether they are HIV-positive, have AIDS or not (UNAIDS and European Commission 2013); and the prohibition to torture, abuse and carry out medical experiments establishes the precise guidelines which a government should abide by in order to prevent torture, abuse and medical experiments taking place (OHCHR and WHO 2008, 3). Consequently, specific actions aimed at defending the rights and dignity of certain key populations at higher risk of HIV exposure, such as detainees (Jürgens, Nowak, and Day 2011) or the homeless (Bagheri Amiri et al. 2018), could be called for (Dingake 2018).

The enactment of laws to protect and preserve the human rights of people living with HIV and key populations at higher risk of HIV is of primary importance in order to create an enabling environment for effective HIV responses. For realising this, it is desirable to enshrine human rights principles in national HIV laws that should have a basis in international human rights law (UNDP 2013; African Commission on Human and Peoples' Rights 2018). This body of law should inspire interventions related to three distinct areas seeking to address the HIV epidemic: first, human rights law supporting states to respond effectively to the challenges of the HIV epidemic by assuring a framework on the basis of which they can organise policies capable of integrating public health objectives and human rights standards. Second, human rights also constitute a sort of compass useful for the orientation of non-governmental organisations and advocacy groups when monitoring the performance of every single state in their programmes and strategies and to intervene for redress if these public health policies violate human rights. Lastly, human rights empower public health practitioners to take action for the protection and promotion of health at the societal level (Patterson and London 2002, 967), eliminating structural barriers to biomedical prevention, health education, and engagement with healthcare services (Enoch and Piot 2017, 119).

However, although no global human rights treaty explicitly addresses HIV, there is a multiplicity of non-binding instruments that affirm human rights and public health recommendations in the context of HIV. Among these play a central role the *International Guidelines on HIV/AIDS and Human Rights* developed during the Second International Consultation on HIV/AIDS and Human Rights in light of the need for guidance for governments, international organisations, non-governmental organisations and civil society groups on how to best promote, protect and fulfil human rights in the context of the HIV epidemic. The Second International Consultation on HIV/AIDS and Human Rights was organised by UNAIDS, in cooperation with the Office of the High Commissioner for Human Rights (OHCHR), in Geneva, from 23 to 25 September 1996. These international guidelines were revised in 2002 (Guideline 6), and a consolidated version was jointly published by UNAIDS and OHCHR in 2006 (Eba 2015, 228–229). This last version aims to assist more effectively policymakers and others in complying with international human rights standards regarding law, administrative practice and policy (OHCHR and UNAIDS 2006).

Aggleton et al. (2005, 7–10) define stigma as a process of devaluating an individual based on certain attributes (for example, skin colour, manner of speaking, or sexual preference) deemed discreditable or unworthy by others. Discrimination, in turn, occurs when stigma is acted on and consists of actions or behaviours directed against those who are stigmatised. In the context of HIV, stigma reinforces negative connotations through the association of HIV and AIDS with already-marginalised groups such as sex workers, people who inject drugs, gay men and other men who have sex with men, transgender people, prisoners and migrants. The HIV-positive individuals of these groups are often believed to deserve their health status because they are engaged in behaviours judged morally wrong. At the same time, discrimination can also relate to HIV status itself. People with actual or suspected HIV-positive status may be denied the right to healthcare, employment, education and freedom of movement, including limitations on international travel and migration.

Social research suggests that the underlying determinants of stigma and discrimination are consistent across different contexts and epidemics and comprise the following: lack of consciousness of stigma and discrimination and their harmful consequences; fear of HIV infection through casual contact; and social judgment linking people living with HIV to behaviours considered inappropriate or dissolute (UNAIDS 2007). These determinants can be effectively addressed through measures that ensure the advancement of human rights in their HIV response. The current UNAIDS strategy (2016–2021) aims to ensure that these measures are implemented by removing, on the one hand, punitive laws, policies and practices around sex work, drug use, same-sex sexual relations and, on the other hand, encouraging people to cooperate with service providers in healthcare, workplace and educational settings to eliminate HIV-related stigma and discrimination, including against people living with HIV and other key populations (e.g. gay men and other men who have sex with men, sex workers and their clients, and people who inject drugs) and orphans and children made vulnerable by HIV (UNAIDS 2015a, 18, 89).

HIV-related stigma

The concept of stigma is the process of perceiving an attribute of another, as deviant from the social expectations that are held by the majority (Australasian Society for HIV Medicine and National Centre in HIV Social Research 2012, 9). In other words, a trait is deemed stigmatising when it is considered deeply discrediting by the vast majority of people (Goffman 1963).

In recent years, the concept of stigma has received significant attention in the public health debate, especially in relation to mental illness and HIV (Parker 2012). The prevailing perspective is that stigma damages health and should be combated by policymakers and public health agencies. Such arguments, for example, have been persuasive in addressing the stigmatisation issue of HIV-positive people. Public health officials were conscious of the negative consequences of stigmatisation for public health namely that the stigmatisation of key populations at higher risk of HIV exposure such as men who have sex with men, people who inject drugs, and sex workers only serves to make them more vulnerable to HIV infection (Stuber, Meyer, and Link 2008, 355). Stigma contributes to the burden of illness and influences the effectiveness of case finding and treatment that are the main concerns of disease control (Weiss, Ramakrishna, and Somma 2006). There are a number of diseases that are stigmatised, such as mental illness, AIDS, venereal diseases, leprosy, and certain skin pathologies. People who suffer from these diseases are discriminated against in the health care system, they often receive much less social support than those who have a non-stigmatising illness, and they can also have serious difficulties in daily activities if their disease is highly disabling (Sartorius 2007). Stigma can affect health both through a micro-level psychological mechanism (downstream) and through structural-level mechanisms (upstream). The former can impact on mental health directly and indirectly through stress responses while the latter involve the unequal distribution of resources. Upstream mechanisms operate in several organisational environments. For example, when healthcare professionals hold stigmatising beliefs and attitudes, they are more likely to provide unequal and discriminatory medical treatment (Clair, Daniel, and Lamont 2016, 224). Stigma appears to increase the risk of adverse health outcomes, mainly through disruption and alteration of the following systems: institutional and communal (material resources and conditions), interpersonal (social relationships), and intra-psychic (self-worth, coping behaviours) (Hatzenbuehler, Phelan, and Link 2013). Nieweglowski and Corrigan (2017) illustrate the relationship between stigma and health as follows:

> Stigma is a complex process that results from the interaction of stereotypes, prejudice, and discrimination. When applied to health conditions (e.g., mental illness, HIV/AIDS, diabetes, obesity), stigma can contribute to a lack of recovery and resources as well as devaluation of the self. People with stigmatised health conditions may be too embarrassed to seek treatment, and others may not provide them with equal opportunities. This often results in discrimination in employment, housing, and healthcare settings.

In summary, health-related stigma is a complex process which is the fruit of the interaction of negative attitudes such as stereotypes and prejudices held by some in relation to health conditions (e.g. disabilities, mental disorders, sexually transmitted diseases, obesity) of specific groups (Parker 2012).

HIV is perhaps one of the most stigmatised global medical conditions. HIV is a virus that people are afraid of contracting. The various misconceptions associated with HIV have also contributed to the perception of it as a life-threatening infection that affects 'others', especially those already stigmatised by their sexual behaviour, gender, race, or socio-economic status, and has resulted in some individuals denying that they could be at risk or affected by it (Amuri et al. 2011; Loutfy et al. 2012; Parker et al. 2002, 3; Smit et al. 2012). In particular, it weakens the social ties that unite people (i.e. organisations, institutions, key individuals, events, customs, and rituals) in a community (Decosas 2002, 8–10). Currently, HIV remains one of the world's most serious health challenges, particularly in low and middle-income countries (UNDP 2016).

HIV-related stigma normally refers to negative and harmful attitudes and beliefs directed against people who are living with, affected by, or associated with HIV and its spread (Husbands et al. 2012, 2), and may result in discrimination based on actual or perceived HIV-positive serostatus (UNAIDS 2007). This unjust consideration and/or treatment has as its main object those social groups which are already socially excluded because of their risk-taking behaviours (Keetile 2014; Vian et al. 2012; Zhu et al. 2012), and can lead to suspicion of any individual who comes into contact with these groups (Mawar et al. 2005). The stigma associated with HIV should not be considered as a singular entity. The stigma of the infection is layered with other specific stigmas, such as those associated with the routes of transmission (e.g. unprotected sexual intercourse with an infected sex worker and sharing of needle injection equipment with someone who is infected) and personal traits (e.g. gender, race, and religion) (Reidpath and Chan 2005). This co-interaction of layers of stigmas (Herek 1999; Scheper-Hughes and Lock 1991) has almost certainly contributed to the spread of HIV rather than retarded it (Husbands et al. 2012, 2) as it represents one of the greatest barriers to HIV prevention, testing and treatment efforts (Parker and Aggleton 2003).

HIV-related stigma specifically can be portrayed as the process of the devaluation of people living with, affected by, or associated with HIV (Herek 1999, 1106; Lawson et al. 2006, 56). For example, individuals and groups who are in close relationship with HIV-positive people (caregivers, family members, lovers, and relatives) may experience stigma by proxy. People may also be the object of stigmatisation because they are associated with people with behaviours that may place them at a higher risk of HIV exposure and that are frequently described as suspect, immoral, or as the main vectors of HIV transmission (e.g. men who have sex with men, sex workers, and people who inject drugs). This form of stigma has been defined as symbolic stigma (Husbands et al. 2012, 2–3). Herek (1986) argued that HIV-related stigma usually has both symbolic and instrumental components. Herek and Capitanio (1998) use the term symbolic stigma to describe discriminatory attitudes toward people living with HIV based on moralistic value judgments. For example, a private Christian school decides not to hire an HIV-positive teacher because he or she is judged as immoral. Herek (1986, 2002) and Herek and Capitanio (1998) use the term instrumental stigma to represent intentional discrimination based on an exaggerated fear of contracting a lethal virus such as HIV, as well as deliberate discrimination based on concerns regarding the financial impact of HIV or AIDS on personal taxes and health care costs. This might include, for example, refusing to care for or support financially an HIV-positive family member. The distinction between instrumental and symbolic stigmas is based on two diverse individual psychological attitudes: evaluative based on instrumental concerns about personal risk for infection and expressive based on a need to affirm one's self-concept by expressing personal values. HIV-related stigma identifies and connects the presence of a biological disease agent (or any physical signs of a disease) to negatively-defined behaviours or characteristics or certain groups of people, and often results in discrimination (what people do to disadvantage HIV-positive people unjustly). However, stigma does not always have to imply a process of discrimination to produce a negative effect, because people may internalise stigma or presume they will be stigmatised or discriminated against, and may decide not to offer themselves for testing or treatment and cure, or enjoy a good quality of life as a result (Deacon, Stephney, and Prosalendis 2005; Goffman 1959). Internalised stigma is the extent to which those negative characteristics and beliefs about people living with HIV are backed and accepted internally (Simbayi et al. 2007; Earnshaw and Chaudoir 2009; Rueda et al. 2012).

HIV-related stigma impacts negatively on the quality of life, self-image, self-esteem and behaviours of people living with HIV, who often choose not to disclose their HIV status because they fear losing their homes and jobs and being discriminated and rejected by family and friends (Florom-Smith and De Santis 2012; Cohen, Mugavero, and Hall 2017, 8). HIV-related stigma can also represent a significant barrier to HIV prevention, diagnosis, and cure (Churcher 2013; Mbatha 2013) because it plays a significant role in HIV disclosure decision-making. Consequently, interventions aimed to reduce internalised stigma can aid in efforts to increase HIV disclosure and thus decrease the secondary transmission of HIV (Lee, Kochman, and Sikkema 2002; Okello et al. 2015). People living with HIV who ignore, conceal or deny their status are less likely to take steps to prevent spreading the virus to others because they often decide to perpetuate risk behaviours (Valdiserri 2002).

The ways in which HIV is transmitted contribute to the stigma associated with the disease (Fishman 2013, 208–210). Accordingly, and based on this premise, the health care sector should be one of the first places where concrete interventions against stigma and discrimination should be undertaken, especially towards key populations at higher risk of HIV exposure such as sex workers, males who have sex with other males and people who inject drugs (Australasian Society for HIV Medicine and National Centre in HIV Social Research 2012, 16–18). Health care personnel have an ethical duty to avoid engaging in stigmatising behaviours and a legal duty not to discriminate (Anderson 2009, 1000) because these conducts could push patients to conceal their status. Concealment of the disease from health professionals may cause a rise in the number of infected people and disease prevalence (Saki et al. 2015).

HIV-related stigma is an important risk factor associated with health conditions in exposed populations such as men who have sex with other men, sex workers, orphans and children made vulnerable by AIDS (Pulerwitz et al. 2010). It reinforces existing prejudices and social stereotypes, which, in turn, significantly contribute to vulnerability to HIV infection among members of the above-mentioned populations (Cairns 2008).

Orphans and other children made vulnerable by HIV

Children orphaned by AIDS are often victims of negative attitudes such as ostracism, discrimination, and social, affective and economic marginalisation due to the shame associated with the deadly disease or irrational fear that children made orphans by AIDS could spread HIV to other children

(Interagency Coalition on AIDS and Development 2006, 3). An orphan may also decide to leave school because they have to take care of their family. Education is tremendously important because it teaches children how to look after their own health, but also because it can provide them with the professional skills that are necessary to raise them out of poverty (UNAIDS Interagency Task Team on Education 2004).

HIV seriously damages the affected households, especially women and children. The latter are often traumatised because of the loss of one or both parents to AIDS. Loss of a parent may result in a significant worsening of life conditions; it also potentially increases the probability of this group being exploited by unscrupulous individuals (UNAIDS 2008, 164). In particular, where both parents have died, the oldest child sometimes becomes the head of the household and looks after siblings because there is no one else capable of assuming this role (i.e. grandmother or another relative) (Laurie 2015, 131). Without the care of parents or an appointed caregiver, children risk malnutrition, poor health, insufficient education, migration, homelessness, rape and abuse (Ogunbodede 2004, 358). There is, therefore, a need to pay particular attention to children in vulnerable situations, such as orphans, street children, and children in humanitarian crises (UNAIDS 2016, 45).

Children are in particular more vulnerable to stigma than adults because of their fragility (Cree et al. 2004). HIV-related stigma impacts on children in many different forms. Some examples include: children may be blamed for their parents' behaviour if they die from AIDS (this is a strong belief in Ethiopia where orphans are seen as being born 'unlucky'); children may be excluded from school, from families and from communities because of the fear of infection if HIV is present in their family; many orphans are treated differently from other children in a new family and accused of continuing to misbehave like their parents did; some orphans do not accept living in a new family and run away to live on the street because the atmosphere at the hosting home is very bad (Kidd and Clay 2003, 110–117).

HIV-related stigmatisation remains a potent stressor for HIV-positive people and their family members, including children (Vanable et al. 2006). The psychological vulnerability of children affected by HIV is generated from multiple AIDS-related stressors such as the loss of a parent or living with a dying parent to AIDS, stigmatisation from parental HIV, and the emotional and economic challenges of orphanhood (Lin et al. 2010). In particular, parental HIV negatively impacts on children's psychological well-being in the early stage of parental HIV-related illness and persists through the course of parental illness and after parental death. Individual coping skills, trusting relationships with caregivers, and social support are interventions suggested to mitigate the negative effect of parental HIV towards children (Chi and Li 2013).

Despite some decline in HIV adult prevalence worldwide and increasing access to antiretroviral treatment, the number of children affected by or vulnerable to HIV remains quite high (Office of the US Global AIDS Coordinator 2012). Since 2002, at least 10 million children (aged 0–17) worldwide have lost one or both parents to AIDS. This number peaked in 2009, when there were an estimated 15 million children worldwide who had lost one or both parents to AIDS. Although this number had progressively fallen, there were an estimated 13,4 million children in 2015 who were living without one or both parents due to AIDS globally. More than 80% of these children (10.9 million) lived in Sub-Saharan Africa (UNICEF 2016a, 26–28, 89).

The expression 'AIDS orphans' is inappropriate because this term contributes considerably to the stigmatisation of children whose parent or parents have died from AIDS, but it also labels them as HIV-positive, which may be false. Contrary to traditional usage, UNAIDS suggests the use of the expression 'orphans and other children made vulnerable by AIDS' in its guidelines regarding the preferred terminology. The term 'orphan' describes a specific typology of orphans, namely those who have lost either one or both parents to AIDS (UNAIDS 2015b, 4) whereas the term 'other vulnerable children' (or simply 'vulnerable children') is an expression referring to minors who are HIV-positive, live without adequate adult support (i.e. in a family environment in which one or both parents are sick, a household that has recently lost a loved one due to a chronic illness, and/or a child-headed family), live outside of family care (i.e. in residential care facilities and orphanages or on the streets), or are marginalised, stigmatised, or discriminated against (Institute of Medicine et al. 2007, 233–234).

The vulnerability of a child made orphan by AIDS begins well before the death of their parent or parents. The effects commence when he or she lives with an HIV infected parent or parents, who are not able to provide adequate care for him or her, and may include economic deprivation, inadequate schooling, psychological and emotional distress, neglect and increased burden of responsibility associated with a parent's illness (UNICEF 2006, 18). Zaba et al. (2005) show that HIV impacts on child mortality directly through the transmission of HIV to newborns by infected mothers and indirectly through higher child mortality rates associated with maternal death. Specifically, researchers indicate that children (ages 0–3) are 3.9 times more likely to die in the year before or after their mother's death whereas the excessive risk of death correlated with having an HIV-positive mother declines to 2.9 times; moreover, this effect lasts throughout childhood. In addition, based on a comprehensive review of published and unpublished literature on the intern-generational impact of AIDS, Cluver and Operario (2008) found that orphaned children may be at a heightened risk of HIV infection compared with non-orphaned children (control group). They identified five potential pathways by which orphans of parents who have died of AIDS face an increased risk for HIV. These pathways were triggered by the following five contributing factors: poverty, mental health problems, characteristics and dynamics of sexual behaviour, care-giving stressors and family violence, sexual abuse and rape. The evidence on each was limited, and additional research was necessary.

HIV-positive adults feel stigmatised or fear for the future of their children once they are dead because the extended family is sometimes unable to take care of them adequately (Ngige, Ondigi, and Wilson 2008, 224–225). Within an extended family, the quality of the relationship between the new caregiver and the child strongly influences his or her development. Several studies have shown that the closer children remain to their biological family, the more likely they are to be well cared for (UNICEF 2006, 20). Geary (2000), for example, observed that partial results of some studies were consistent with the view that children who lived in stable family environments with both biological parents enjoyed a more healthy state than those who lived in different situations. On the basis of these results, he concluded that home stability impacted positively on the survival rates of the offspring. Orphans, however, may also choose not to live with extended family members for the following reasons: first, they fear maltreatment; second, they do not want to be exploited for work; third, they want to continue to study; and fourth, they think that they are better off on their own (Lloyd 2008, 24–25).

HIV discrimination

Discrimination refers to the prejudicial treatment of individuals because they are part, or are perceived to be part, of a particular group or category (Nöstlinger et al. 2014, 155) and is based on a particular personal characteristic such as race or sexual orientation, or specific physical attributes. Discrimination often results in some form of rejection or exclusion (Giddens et al. 2009). The concept of discrimination, as indicated by Goffman (1963), is strictly connected to that of stigma. Consequently, it cannot be conceptualised as being separate from stigma, but it is the ultimate result of the process of stigmatisation—in effect, 'enacted' stigma. Discrimination (or enacted stigma) devalues and reduces the life chances of the stigmatised (Nyblade and MacQuarrie 2006, 2, 6, 8). For example, stigma can lead to prejudice and active discrimination towards persons who are actually, or are simply perceived to be, HIV-positive, and the social groups and persons with whom they are associated (EngenderHealth 2004, 15; Brown, BeLue, and Airhihenbuwa 2010; Li et al. 2008).

Almost 40 years after the onset of the HIV epidemic, HIV stigma and discrimination persist and continue to be fuelled by the general lack of knowledge about basic modes of HIV transmission and groundless fears of contagion, as well as moral judgment and pre-existing biases against certain populations (e.g. men who have sex with men, people who inject drugs, sex workers and their clients) (Anderson 2009; Stangl, Brady, and Fritz 2012). Specifically, HIV-related discrimination, also known as enacted HIV stigma, refers to any measure entailing an arbitrary differentiation among people depending on their real or presumed HIV serostatus (Caraël et al. 2000).

It seems that for people living with HIV, or for those assumed to be HIV-positive, any area of their life can be touched by stigma and subjected to discrimination (National AIDS Trust 2003). The United States National Association of Social Workers recognises that people living with HIV, and sometimes even those who are tested for the virus, continue to face discrimination in employment, military service, housing, access to health care, education, social and community programmes, and fundamental civil and human rights (Tomaszewski 2012). Discrimination can be institutionalised through laws, policies, and practices (Boulton et al. 2017; Harsono et al. 2017; Lehman et al. 2014; Burki 2011).

HIV-related stigma and discrimination limit the success of HIV prevention, treatment, care, and support programmes because they discourage people living with the disease from disclosing their status even to family members and sexual partners and undermine their ability and willingness to access and adhere to treatment. Thus, stigma and discrimination put at risk the state of health of both individuals and entire communities (UNAIDS 2014, 2). This requires that policymakers and public health institutions incorporate stigma reduction strategies into HIV programmes and enable individuals and communities to better understand how stigma undermines their well-being (Husbands et al. 2012, 5).

Children in households affected by HIV witness, or in several cases care for, their parents or other caregivers dying of AIDS. This painful process is frequently compounded by the stigma and discrimination attached to HIV and being an orphan. Most of these children also suffer the emotional trauma caused by ostracism by their peers and relatives and/or by disapproval and rejection by the community at large (Todres 2007, 425–430; UNICEF 2006), including neighbours, guardians, teachers, and other children of the care-taking family. Consequently, community-based and governmental initiatives should aim to reduce stigma and discrimination against children orphaned by AIDS by helping victims (Delva 2010). Furthermore, it is at this point of heightened vulnerability that the orphan is at higher risk of bad health, nutrition, dropping out of school, mental problems, faulty development, involvement in risky behaviours such as alcohol and drug misuse, illegal or hazardous activities (e.g. petty crimes, vandalism), sexual promiscuity and being subject to all forms of exploitation like prostitution, beggary, and forced labour (Lata and Verma 2013, 456).

Parental HIV status negatively impacts on the psychological well-being of children and makes them more prone to stigma and discrimination (Chi and Li 2013; Mishra and Bignami-Van Assche 2008). Specifically, Fleming (2015) points out that orphans and other children made vulnerable by AIDS experience discrimination in accessing education and healthcare. Few orphans are able to enrol in schools because they cannot afford the cost of education materials on the one hand and then have to take care of their siblings on the other. Educational institutions serve as a place of socialisation for young people whose homes can be destroyed, but these institutions might also be a sad setting for learners such as children orphaned by AIDS who suffer discrimination and rejection there (Moletsane 2013, 297). Consequently, these institutions must establish a supportive learning environment for orphans and other children made vulnerable by AIDS so that they can find a job and live with dignity. Education is an effective form of protection against HIV to which these children may be susceptible (Mwoma and Pillay 2016).

Orphans and other children made vulnerable by AIDS are often burdened with the ensuing collapse of their family structure but, as the experience of numerous Sub-Saharan countries proves, traditional support systems are unable to effectively assist the growing number of children in need of help and protection. The HIV epidemic tends to have a negative impact on young people as a whole, even if their family structure remains largely intact, because it puts a strain on communities and erodes opportunities for education and development (Utan 2005, 61).

It is important to note that poor households are often limited in their choices regarding resource allocation because they have little income or wealth available. Under these harsh economic conditions, non-biological children may, therefore, experience discrimination (Gillespie 2006, 7) at home (for example, being the last to get food) or within the community (for example, ostracism and social marginalisation) by adults and other children (Smart 2003, 4). By contrast, in non-poor households, resource allocations of biological and non-biological children do not differ considerably so that these families are more likely to host non-biological children and allow them to attend school (Gillespie 2006, 7). Children who are not at school risk being forced to work in a multiplicity of often exploitative environments, including as domestic servants, agricultural and factory workers, and child prostitutes. Children orphaned by AIDS are at greater risk of being exploited both in formal and informal work settings because they cannot count on parental support (Todres 2007, 428–429).

Orphans and other children made vulnerable by AIDS are sometimes prevented from accessing health services (Bejide 2014, 323). Healthcare providers refuse to treat not only orphans and vulnerable children but also their HIV-positive parents. Even where children and their families are not subjected to discriminatory treatment, family resources are very limited (Todres 2007, 429). Consequently, only the availability of low-cost or free antiretroviral drugs, together with the greater willingness of healthcare workers to assist orphans and children made vulnerable by AIDS, can decrease discrimination against these groups of individuals (Thi et al. 2008).

Discrimination at schools, in health services and in other institutions compromises the rights of orphans and other children made vulnerable by AIDS and often limits their opportunities (Smart 2003, 4). These children have difficulty understanding why they are treated differently from other children. This treatment can trigger a sense of exclusion which negatively influences the self-esteem of orphans and other children made vulnerable by AIDS (International HIV/AIDS Alliance and Vasavya Mahila Mandali 2004, 7). In addition, discrimination of orphans and other children made vulnerable by AIDS with respect to care and protection issues, including access to food, can take three main forms: 1) Public ostracism and social exclusion as a result of the stigma attached to the disease. This is still, partially, the result of a lack of knowledge and misunderstandings regarding modes of transmission. Many people refuse to accept a child into their family if the parent has died of AIDS because of fear of HIV spreading into the family. 2) Taking in orphans and other children made vulnerable by AIDS for exploitative purposes. Members of the extended family may exploit these children as cheap sources of labour and sometimes deny them their inheritance rights by taking away their property. 3) Intra-household discrimination occurs when caretakers treat orphans and other children made vulnerable by AIDS differently than their biological children, including having heavier workloads and being served less food (Greenblott and Greenaway 2007, 10–11).

Although a remarkable diversity of cultures, mentalities, social perspectives, languages and history of human rights are present within societies, a common front should be organised against the HIV epidemic. Governments should review laws and policies that support discrimination and enforce new ones that protect people living with HIV from various forms of HIV-related stigma and discrimination (Kontomanolis et al. 2017, 116). In South Africa, for example, the Equality Court was created to promote rights and to guarantee access to justice for vulnerable groups and focuses specifically on complaints related to cases of unfair discrimination that can be based on a number of factors, including HIV status. The Labour Relations Act also protects employees from being dismissed because of their HIV status and being discriminated against in terms of employee benefits, promotions, staff training, and other work-related aspects. Lastly, the Employment Equity Act explicitly includes HIV status as a forbidden ground for discrimination and discrimination on this ground is actionable (Ahonsi et al. 2014, 19).

Orphans and other children made vulnerable by AIDS should have a right to protection, confidentiality and privacy, and access to basic services such as education and health without any discriminatory treatment (Interagency Coalition on AIDS and Development 2006, 3). Governments need to ensure that the right of orphans and other children made vulnerable by AIDS to non-discrimination in access to basic services is clearly recognised in national laws (Moletsane 2013, 303). Practically, this means that governments should implement national HIV and child protection plans which include mechanisms to address children's HIV-related stigma and discrimination in HIV and child protection standards and operating procedures (e.g. alternative care guidelines, HIV testing protocols, paediatric HIV care, treatment and support guidelines) (UNICEF 2016b, 8), and a social safety net for orphans such as child support grants and foster care grants (Hall and Sambu 2018, 137–143). However, the problems faced by orphans and other children made vulnerable by AIDS can be solved only if all levels of society, from international donor agencies and national governments to community-based organisations and individual families, work together to provide a safe, empowering environment (Utan 2005, 66). In other words, it is essential that medical care, socioeconomic support, human rights and legal support, psychosocial support, and counselling services are mutually implemented (Family Health International 2001) through well-resourced national and international aid plans (UNICEF 2016a, 28).

Conclusion

Populations more likely to be exposed to HIV or to transmit it include both key populations at higher risk of HIV exposure and vulnerable groups. Stigmatisation and discrimination of these two distinct social groups with time created a witch-hunt climate that has made the implementation of an effective social-inclusion programme increasingly difficult (Meini 2013, 193).

Key populations at higher risk of HIV exposure are said to be those that have the highest risk of contracting and transmitting HIV as a result of what they are doing or of what they could do if placed in a situation with HIV–related predisposing factors. Examples of those population groups are men who have sex with men, transgender persons, people who inject drugs, male and female sex workers and their clients, offenders in prisons, and seronegative partners in serodiscordant couples. Vulnerable groups are said to be in a state of vulnerability if their living conditions contribute significantly to placing them at risk of acquiring HIV. Examples of these groups are adolescents, orphans, street children, mobile workers, migrants and displaced populations and others (WHO Regional Office for the Eastern Mediterranean, n.d.).

The key populations and vulnerable groups are both important to the dynamics of HIV transmission and essential partners in an effective response to the epidemic (WHO 2016b). The reduction of stigma and discrimination can dramatically improve the lives of people living with, affected by, or associated with HIV and their families and make easier investments in HIV prevention, care and treatment programmes (Carr et al. 2010).

This chapter has looked in-depth at how stigmatisation processes make it much more complicated to protect the basic rights of children orphaned by AIDS or made vulnerable by HIV. Additionally, it has revealed that many of them are at higher risk of being exploited by criminal gangs or becoming victims of abuse, especially in Sub-Saharan Africa. Consequently, the author suggests putting in place a policy that involves orphans and other children made vulnerable by HIV and AIDS being placed into social protection schemes and programmes (Meini and Tognetti Bordogna 2018).

Shame and stigma are integral parts of the male logic of using sexual violence as a tool to gain power and control over victims, especially young women and children (Kalra and Bhugra 2013). For centuries, violence on women remained a hidden, invisible problem without a name. This invisibleness was undoubtedly dictated by the lack of real power on behalf of women, who have always been subjected to male power (Fox 2002). This is what still happens today in many Sub-Saharan African states where gender violence is a national emergency (Medie 2019). In particular, several victimological studies have focused not only on sexual violence in itself, but also on the inherent risk of HIV infection (Ellsberg and Heise 2005). In Chapter 4, in light of the above, the author analyses the impact that violence against women and children has on the HIV epidemic by taking into consideration South Africa as a case study.

The dual health burden of intimate partner violence and HIV in South Africa

The capital of sexual violence

It is not easy to distinguish exactly the term 'gender' from the closely related term 'sex'. The World Health Organization defines sex and gender as follows: sex 'refers to the biological and physiological characteristics that define men and women', while gender 'refers to the socially constructed roles, behaviours, activities, and attributes that a given society considers appropriate for men and women' (WHO 2014d). Sex and gender constitute important determinants of health and form a complex interrelationship. Specifically, sex is often conceptualised either as wanted and consensual or as unwanted and non-consensual, reflecting a one-dimensional and dichotomous model. Wanted sex is treated as consensual while unwanted sex is treated as non-consensual and/or forced (Peterson and Muehlenhard 2007).

For centuries, violence on women remained a hidden, invisible problem without a name. This invisibleness was undoubtedly dictated by the lack of real power on behalf of women, who have always been subordinated to male authority (Fox 2002), a relationship that has resulted in sanctions only when it has broken the traditional honour code (Schwerhoff 2013; Gill 2008). This is what still happens today in many states of Sub-Saharan Africa in which gender-based violence represents a social, cultural and health emergency (Sanjel 2013). Gender-based violence can be intended as a physical and/or psychological coercion of women (or of those who can represent a functional substitute in the economy of relationships), which can generally be comprised in the sexual sphere and is more or less socially stigmatised. This kind of coercion is typical of patriarchal societies (or those that are partially such); that is, of moderately or strongly male-dominated societies (Bimbi 2000, 52–53).

As regards sexual relationships, expectations are determined by culturally-transmitted clichés that can tolerate violence and thus encourage men to feel superior and legitimise sexual aggressions on women, who are considered prey (Crowell and Burgess 1996). This phenomenon reveals the existence of some myths regarding rape, which comprise denying the existence of rape (for example, believing that most reports of rape are false or that women generally lie about rape), the motivations for rape (e.g. 'she asked for it', 'he was unable to control himself'', 'these things happen to women who provoke men', etc.) and the minimisation of the seriousness of the event. The study of the myths regarding rape, carried out in many research projects, has brought out the existence of significant associations between the acceptance of the myths themselves and the admission on behalf of men of being sexually aggressive (Murphy, Coleman, and Haynes 1986). I am looking at a biologising approach in which male sexual impulses not only seem uncontrollable, but are broadly legitimated from a Pavlovian standpoint. The result is the deresponsibilisation of the rapist and the attribution of fault to women's behaviour (Akins 2004).

One of the contributions of the feminist analysis was that of severely criticising those explicative models centred on individual pathologies. The psychopathological model would be credible if rape represented a marginal, numerically-small phenomenon; but, its incidence has taken on truly alarming proportions in many countries. In particular, the official data on sexual crimes show that the aggressor's personality can be defined as disturbed only in a few cases. Therefore, the psychopathological model does not help us explain the causes of rape; that is, of a phenomenon whose incidence varies according to the culture and organisation of each society (Jewkes and Abrahams 2000, 18).

In African countries, questioning a prevalently patriarchal relationship system makes women especially vulnerable, as men feel threatened by their possible loss of power and implement aggressive and violent strategies (Namy et al. 2017; Decker et al. 2015; Mookodi 2004). Violence on women (sexual, physical and psychological) therefore represents a way to exercise a form of control that re-establishes a dominion that must be certain and absolute for the purpose of defending a manliness in crisis (Giddens 1992). Rape violates the physical safety of the victim as well as their sexual and psychological integrity. It can be considered as an invasive and humiliating form of sexual terrorism (Smith 2001, 73). This crime is one of the least-reported, as many victims tend to conceal it. The reasons are embarrassment, fear of retaliation or of not being believed, and lack of trust in the judicial system. The trial can indeed become a further act of violence on the victim, from which the term secondary victimisation stems (Tamarit, Villacampa, and Filella 2010).

The South African Police Service (SAPS) released the country's crime statistics for 1 April 2017 to 31 March 2018 at the beginning of September 2018. Crime statistics analysis covers all major categories of crimes, such as contact crimes (crimes against the person) (e.g. murder, sexual offences, attempted murder, assault with the intent to inflict grievous bodily harm, common assault, common robbery and robbery aggravated including the following TRIO crimes:

house robbery, business robbery and carjacking), contact-related crimes (e.g. arson and malicious damage to property), property-related crimes (e.g., burglary at non-residential premises, burglary at residential premises, theft of motor vehicles and motorcycles, theft out of or from motor vehicles and stock-theft), other serious crimes (e.g. all types of theft not mentioned previously, commercial crimes and shoplifting) and crimes detected as a result of police action (e.g. illegal possession of firearms and ammunition, drug-related crimes, driving under the influence of alcohol and/or drugs and sexual offences detected as a result of police action) (SAPS 2018).

In general, violent crime remains an ever-present threat in South Africa. Armed robbery is the most widespread major crime, mainly involving handguns and/or knives. Of particular worry are home invasion robberies. These crimes are generally violent and can occur at any time. Criminals prefer to commit these crimes when the occupants are at home or arriving/leaving because they can identify where valuables are kept, and the residential alarm is deactivated. Financial and identity theft crimes, including debit/credit card and advance-fee scams, are also common (e.g. card cloning, ATM fraud) (Overseas Security Advisory Council 2018, 1). Furthermore, the prevalence of sexual assault and violence has led to South Africa being dubbed 'the rape capital of the world'. This is mainly attributed to the pervasive rape culture that permeates the country. There is a widespread belief that many victims are to blame for being raped because of the fact that they dress in a provocative way, are intoxicated, or even for their sexual orientation. Of course, this belief is without any foundation because the victim is never at fault (Nagtegaal 2018).

All the definitions of rape, sexual aggression, and related terms incorporate the idea of non-consensual behaviour. Many data archives and some researchers go by the legal definition of rape, which however changes according to the country and sometimes changes with time (UN Women 2012, 24–25). In South Africa, the Criminal Law (Sexual Offences and Related Matters) Amendment Act No. 32 of 2007 reformed and codified the law relating to sex offences. It expanded the definition of rape, previously limited to vaginal sex, to include all non-consensual penetration. Moreover, it equalised the age of consent for heterosexual and homosexual sex to 16 years. Rape falls under the broad category of sexual offences, which include sexual assault, incest, bestiality and flashing, among other crimes. In particular, it makes a significant distinction between rape and sexual violation. Rape is when a male or female individual coercively or forcefully penetrates the vagina or anus of another male or female individual. From this definition I can infer that, for the first time, the law recognises male rape, which was previously classified as a mere indecent aggression. Instead, the legal definition of sexual violation is when an individual violently penetrates a genital organ or anus with an object. This penetration is oral-genital when the rapist introduces his penis forcefully into the mouth of the victim (Vetten 2007; Machisa et al. 2017, 11–12). Prior to 16 December 2017, the definition of rape was much more limited; namely, rape was defined as an intentional and unlawful sexual intercourse with a woman without her consent. This means that rape statistics from before this date only referred to the vaginal rape of women by a man. In addition, because of this change, rape statistics from before 2008/2009 should not be directly compared to statistics released after this date (Wilkinson 2016).

The statistics presented here are based on the official figures for police-recorded rapes in South Africa between 2008/2009 and 2017/2018 and are included in the broad group of sexual offences. Although rape makes up the majority of cases, this category cannot be used in place of disaggregated rape statistics. The histogram shows that rapes appear to have progressively decreased between 2012/2013 and 2016/2017, and slightly increased in 2017/2018. Rape rates offer further information on the level of sexual violence in South Africa. The rape rate defines the number of rape incidents per 100,000 citizens. Figures do not take into account rape incidents that go unreported to the police (SAPS 2018).

Figure 4.1: Trend in rape, 2008/2009 - 2017/2018

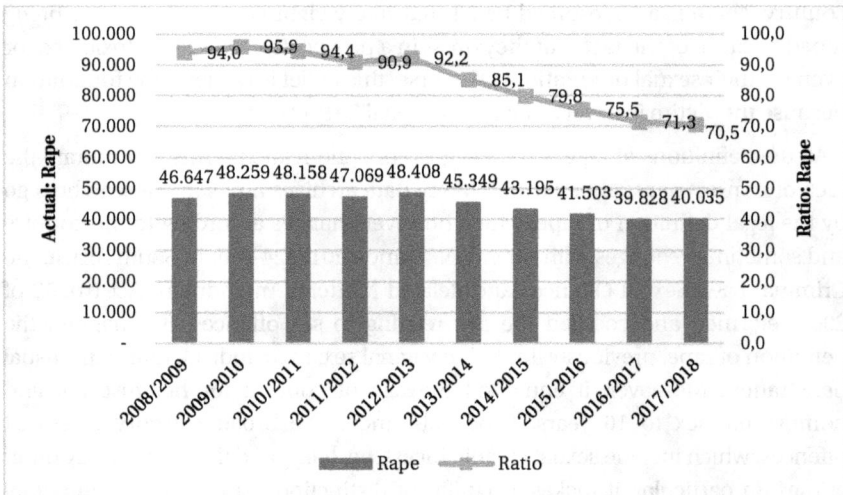

Source: SAPS 2018, 81

The annual Victims of Crime Survey (VOCS) report released by Statistics South Africa focuses on eleven types of household crimes and seven types of crimes against individuals, including sexual offence and assault for both dimensions. The household crime section deals with crime incidents reported by household heads, while the individual crime section focuses on crime experienced by a randomly selected person in the household aged 16 years and older (Statistics South Africa 2018, 15). In particular, the estimates provided by the section that deals with sexual offences and assault at the family level are different to those arising from individual interviews reported in the section that deals with sexual offences and assault at an individual level. It is expected that the numbers provided for households are smaller than those provided for individuals because household heads may not be aware of all of the crime experiences of members of their households. VOCS uses a narrower definition of sexual violence, which is limited to the intentional sexual violation of individuals through grabbing, touching or rape, because of the limitation of the survey methodology. The SAPS definition of sexual offence is broader and includes bestiality, a sexual act with a corpse and other unlawful sexual acts. Therefore, quantitative data collected by these two institutions do not measure the same thing but produce crime statistics that complement each other (Ibid., 46).

Statistics currently available show that violence against women has reached epidemic proportions in South Africa (Sibanda-Moyo, Khonje, and Brobbey 2017). In 2017/2018, more female-headed households (19,116 → 65.9%) experienced sexual offences than male-headed households (9,870 → 34.1%), while more male-headed households (72,528 → 53.1%) experienced assault than female-headed households (64,079 → 46.9%). Specifically, it is estimated that the number of people who experienced sexual offences in 2017/2018 was 36,451, namely 32,881 females (91.2%) and 3,570 males (9.8%). Sexual offence is a crime that mostly affects women and girls. Conversely, more males than females had household experiences of assault in 2017/2018. It is estimated that the number of persons who experienced assault was 172,270, namely 104,399 males (60.6%) and 67,872 females (39.4%). Assault is a crime that affects men and boys to a greater extent (Statistics South Africa 2018, 46–47). It is estimated that 22,694 individuals experienced 28,596 incidents (mostly women aged 16 and above) as victims of sexual offences in 2017/2018. VOCS also estimates 277,397 victims of assault in 2017/2018 who experienced 377,739 incidents. Assault is defined as an attack, physical beating or threat of attack without taking anything from the victim, and includes domestic violence. The VOCS definition of assault excludes sexual assault and combines SAPS common assault and assault with intent to inflict grievous bodily harm (Ibid., 56–58).

Figure 4.2: Number of sexual offence incidences and sexual offences reported to the police, 2013/2014 - 2017/2018

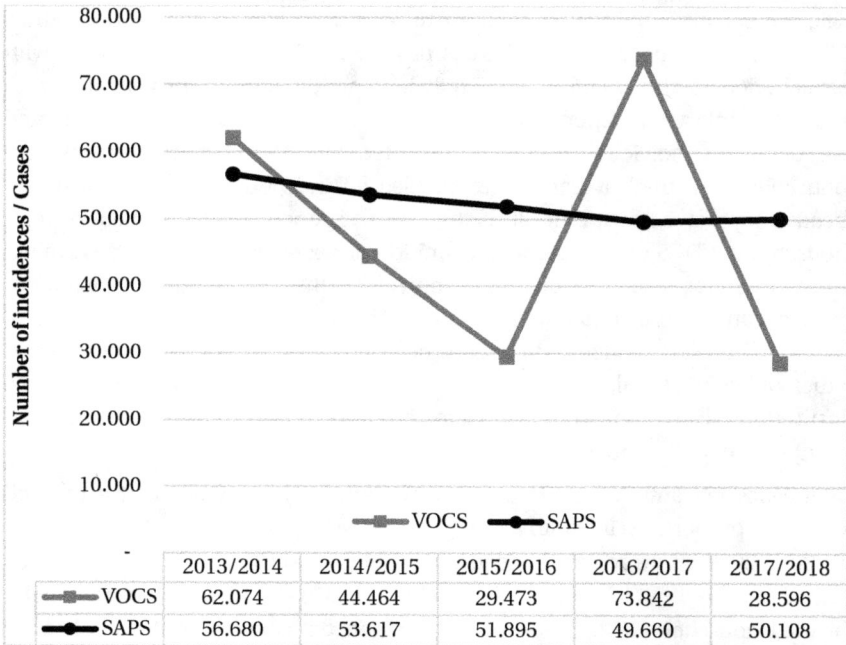

	2013/2014	2014/2015	2015/2016	2016/2017	2017/2018
VOCS	62.074	44.464	29.473	73.842	28.596
SAPS	56.680	53.617	51.895	49.660	50.108

Source: Statistics South Africa 2018, 57

As I have previously illustrated, rape, targeting women and girls, has become a serious problem in South Africa (Harrisberg 2019). The 2016/2017 Victims of Crime statistical release reported that 250 out of every 100,000 women were victims of sexual offences compared to 120 out of every 100,000 men. Using the 2016/2017 South African Police Service statistics, in which 80% of the reported sexual offences were rape, together with Statistics South Africa's estimate that 68.5% of the sexual offences victims were women, we obtain a crude estimate of the number of women raped per 100,000 as 138. This figure is among the highest in the world. For this reason, some have labelled South Africa as the 'rape capital of the world' (Statistics South Africa 2018, 8).

South Africa's rape crisis

Nicholson (2016, 121) considers Pumla Dineo Gqola's volume *Rape: A South African Nightmare* a brilliant work where the author wonders how the language and cultural practices of past and contemporary South Africa have produced a social context in which gender-based violence is endemic and routinely excused. Gqola (2015) traces the origins of the violent South African machismo to white systems of colonial oppression during which women slaves were at risk of being raped by their masters and other male slaves. She highlights how rape was a core feature of colonial rule in Cape society where British soldiers at war with the Xhosa were recorded as having committed rape. Rape was used as a weapon of war against the conquered (black slave women). Colonial obsession for African sexuality led to the creation of a stereotype of black women as hypersexual, perpetually unsatisfied and therefore deemed impossible to rape. This stereotype is still at play today, but it does not make black women immune from the risk of abuse. Vernal (2011, 11) adds that slave women took advantage of the opportunity to improve their social status when they married white men. The opportunity costs of this type of supposed advantage were high: vulnerability to rape and sexual exploitation. Slave owners energetically promoted this discourse by engaging in sexual relationships with subordinate women over whom they exercised almost absolute power. The Dean of Research at the University of Fort Hare and prominent feminist theorist, Pumla Dineo Gqola, argues that "we have to accept that something in our country enables it to happen. Something makes it acceptable for millions to get raped on a regular basis. That something is patriarchy" (Gqola 2015, 6). But the Head of the Institute for Gender Studies at the University of South Africa, Professor Deirdre Byrne, criticises this idea of considering patriarchy as the single cause of South Africa's unacceptably high prevalence of rape as it is not able to explain why in all other patriarchal societies, which is to say almost all human societies, this does not happen. She specifies that when patriarchy is coextensive with a potent urge towards hegemonic masculinity as well as impressive economic disparities, then a toxic and explosive situation arises in which socio-economic desperation becomes predisposed to violence against easy targets. She concludes that the multidimensional problem of rape requires a multi-pronged solution that should address all stakeholders (Byrne 2018).

The underreporting of rape represents one of the most persistent patterns in law enforcement (Allen 2007). Therefore, it is not surprising that the African continent's best-known fact-checking organisation, Africa Check, specifies that it is very difficult to estimate the real number of rapes committed each year in South Africa (Africa Check 2017). Police data not only under-reports the extent of sexual violence but also provides no information regarding the context of where rapists attack victims or the relationship between perpetrators and victims. In addition, there are some particular categories of rapes that have attracted a good deal of public attention, but little research or have not been well documented (e.g. the rape of very young children or older women, the deliberate and selective rape of lesbians and other gender non-conforming women, the sexual victimisation against people with intellectual disabilities, and the sexual violence against men and sex workers). Consequently, official data needs to be employed carefully because rape statistics recorded by the police represent only a minor part of the phenomenon. Moreover, these data need to be cross-checked with other types of sources such as community-based surveys and small-scale qualitative studies (Vetten 2014). Victimisation surveys, for example, can be a great tool for gathering detailed information on certain offences, including rape. Usually, the main objectives of these surveys are to estimate the prevalence (i.e. how many people were victims of a crime) and incidence (i.e. how many times the same crime happened to the same person) of various types of property and violent crimes (Vriniotis 2015, 2). This occurs by interviewing a representative sample of a particular population and asking them a series of questions about their experiences as victims (Koon-Magnin 2014, 457–458), though the formulation should consider the fact that most of them prefer not to depict their incidents as rape even though what they have experienced would fit its legal definition. Such a method is generally used to estimate the gap between reported and unreported crimes (Vetten 2014, 4–5). These surveys are fundamentally critical tools for estimating the dimensions of the dark figure of unreported crime, but also they can provide information about the experiences of victims, nature of crimes, fear of crime and other responses to crime and victimisation and can also be used to assess crime prevention effects of particular initiatives, including the response of the criminal justice system if the crime was reported (Newburn 2017, 56). Several victimological investigations carried out in many South African cities demonstrated that over 50% of rapes were not reported (Masuku 2002, 7–8). In addition, in her book *Rape Unresolved: Policing Sexual Offences in South Africa*, Professor Dee Smythe, Director of the Law, Race and Gender Unit in the Faculty of Law at the University of Cape Town, South Africa, points out that approximately only one-seventh of rapes of women are reported to the police in South Africa on a daily basis (150 in 1,000), with fewer than 30 of the cases being prosecuted and no more than ten resulting in a conviction. This translates into an overall conviction rate of 4–8% of reported cases (Smythe 2015).

There is little information on the percentage of males who commit rape or on the percentage of females who have been raped in South Africa. Data from two regional studies have tried to fill this gap (Wilkinson 2016). The first was *The War at Home: Gender Based Violence Indicators Project. Gauteng Research Report, South Africa*. This study was the first comprehensive community-based research study on the prevalence of gender violence in the smallest, most populous and richest province of South Africa, namely Gauteng. It covered the period from April 2009 to March 2010. Unlike police data that relies on reported cases, the study involved self-reported behaviour and experiences obtained through in-depth interviews with a representative sample of 511 women and 487 men (90% black and 10% white) reflecting the demographics of the province. 8% of the women and 5% of the men interviewed were foreigners. Researchers found that 51.3% (263) of all women recruited in the study had experienced some form of violence (emotional, economic, physical or sexual) at least once in their lifetime and 75.5% (370) of men in the province admitted to having perpetrated some form of violence against women at least once in their lifetime. 13.8% of women experienced, and 13.3% of men perpetrated, all four forms of gender-based violence, namely economic, emotional, physical and sexual violence. About one in five (18.13%) women experienced and more than a quarter (29.0%) of men said they perpetrated gender-based violence in the 12 months previous to the study. More than one in three men confessed to having committed a rape (37.4%) in their lifetime, while one in four women (25.3%) said they had been raped in their lifetime by a man, whether a husband or boyfriend, family member, stranger or acquaintance. Overall, 18.8% of women experienced intimate partner rape on one or more occasions. In all, 12.2% of women were victims of a non-partner, while 31.0% of men admitted to having raped a woman who was not their wife or girlfriend. The prevalence of disclosure by women of rape in the year previous to the study was at 7.8%, in other words, nearly one in 12 women said they had been raped in that time. The proportion of men disclosing perpetration in the year previous to the study was lower at 4.7%. This study confirmed the terrifyingly high prevalence of violence against women in Gauteng, but also the inadequacy of official statistics because much crime is unreported to the police and so never ends up in the statistics (Machisa et al. 2011).

The second was *The Gender Based Violence Indicators Study: Western Cape Province of South Africa* that provided the first comprehensive baseline data on violence against women in the province. It was inspired by the Southern African Development Community Protocol on Gender and Development, which aimed to halve gender-based violence by 2015. Researchers used a mixed-method approach that combined both qualitative and quantitative approaches. They conducted a cross-sectional household survey of women and men by selecting a representative target sample of 1,500 household members. Researchers collected data from 14 July to 6 September 2011. From each household, the researchers recruited only one randomly-selected eligible person (750 women and 742 men from different demographic and socio-economic backgrounds from across the province). This study showed that 39% of women had experienced some form of violence in their lifetime, and that the same proportion of men admitted to perpetrating violence. The highest proportion of violence is the kind for which there is no category in police records, namely emotional, verbal and economic abuse. Most of this violence took place where citizens would feel safest, namely in the home and in communities, undermining women's ability to participate fully and meaningfully in social life. Violence against women has negative effects on women's health and wellbeing. These effects include physical injury, poor mental health, unplanned pregnancies, stigmatisation and ostracism, absence from work, sexually transmitted infections and increased risk to HIV. In particular, 13% of women experienced, and 5% of men perpetrated, sexual intimate partner violence. 13% of women that had been pregnant reported abuse during at least one of their pregnancies. In most cases, women and men reported multiple incidents of physical or sexual intimate partner violence. Although data showed that violence against women is endemic in Western Cape, only 1% of abused women reported the crime to the police, and 2% of the victims reported their violence to medical providers. From this, one can conclude that there is an urgent need to explore factors that hinder women from reporting (Musariri-Chipatiso et al. 2014).

The relationship between sexual violence and HIV among young women

In 2011, United Nations Member States officially recognised the link between violence against women and HIV. Specifically, they committed to reducing women's vulnerability to HIV through the elimination of all forms of violence against women and girls, including harmful traditional practices, abuse, rape and other forms of sexual violence, battering and trafficking in women and girls (United Nations General Assembly 2011, 12).

Violence against women is both a cause and a consequence of HIV and as such is a driving force behind the epidemic that negatively impacts on women's health and wellbeing (UNESCO 2013, 4–5). There are four potential ways to clarify the linkages between violence against women and HIV. First, gender inequality is a common risk factor for both violence against women and HIV (e.g. societies where laws and policies perpetuate women's submission to men have a higher risk of women experiencing intimate partner violence and HIV infection). Secondly, violence against women is an indirect factor for increased HIV risk (e.g. women who were sexually or physically abused either during their infancy or adolescence are more likely to have behaviours that may place them at higher risk of HIV exposure such as engaging in commercial sex or having unprotected sex with multiple sex partners, especially when those sex partners are concurrent). Thirdly, sexual violence is a direct risk factor for HIV transmission (e.g. women are often injured during a rape, with lacerations or tears in the vagina. These genital traumas increase the risk of being infected with HIV). Lastly, violence against women is an outcome of HIV status and disclosure (Amin 2013, 4–14).

In almost all cases, the cause of transmission of HIV is unprotected sex, whether consensual or not. In a situation of non-consensual sex, women play a subservient role to men. This means that women's sexual negotiation skills are strongly limited in a situation of abuse, a situation in which men are expected to exercise a dominant sex role within intimate relationships. A lack of empowerment, however, compromises the efficacy and effectiveness of HIV prevention interventions, thus encouraging the spread of the virus (Samson 2008, 17–18; Dunkle et al. 2004).

The circumstances underlying the correlation between sexual violence and risk of infection are a complex set of biological, social, cultural and economic factors (Erb-Leoncavallo et al. 2004, 45–46; Outwater, Abrahams, and Campbell 2005; Krishnan et al. 2008; Samuelsen, Norgaard, and Ostergaard 2012). Forced or coercive sex with an HIV-positive partner is one of the principal routes of transmission for HIV and sexually transmitted infections (STIs) to women. The risk of exposure to HIV is also increased both by the presence of other STIs and by contact with sexual secretions and/or blood. This biological risk of exposition is also amplified by the fact that the majority of these victims suffers from severe vaginal haemorrhages caused from traumatic genital injuries resulting from a violent sexual encounter (WHO Department of Gender, Women and Health and Global Coalition on Women and AIDS 2004, 2). Moreover, all of this will facilitate the entry of HIV into the bloodstream (Stockman, Campbell, and Celentano 2010; Burgueño et al. 2017). In particular, girls and adolescents have a greater risk of being infected with HIV because of the frailty of their vaginal tissues which are still in development and, thus, tear easily during sexual intercourse (Aranda 2008, 28; Birungi et al. 2011). Cultural and social norms are highly influential in shaping individual behaviour, including the use of violence. Rules can protect against violence, but they can also support, encourage or tolerate its use. In the latter cases, often they are norms that legitimise male authority over women, including gender norms that promote female subordination to male partners in intimate relationships (WHO Department of Violence and Injury Prevention and Disability and Centre for Public Health, WHO Collaborating Centre for Violence Prevention, Liverpool John Moores University 2010, 98–99). In this context, women are not able to adopt safe and protective conducts in the sexual sphere such as negotiating condom use (Madiba and Ngwenya 2017; Shannon et al. 2009; Choi and Holroyd 2007) or refusing to engage in risky sexual behaviours (e.g. early sexual debut, having concurrent sexual relationships, unprotected anal sex, engaging in commercial sex, having a partner who adopts behaviours that may place him at higher risk of HIV exposure and harmful use of drugs or alcohol) and, as a result, the risk of HIV transmission from a male partner is significantly higher (Shrestha, Karki, and Copenhaver 2016; Stöckl et al. 2013; Do and Meekers 2009; Kalichman et al. 2007; Jenness et al. 2011; Kalichman et al. 2011; Shannon et al. 2014; Chemaitelly et al. 2019; Chen et al. 2010; Azim, Bontell, and Strathdee 2015; Mburu, Limmer, and Holland 2019; Schneider et al. 2014).

The male idea of dominant masculinity is often identified in the family environment as the ability of the man to become or remain the single economic provider in the family. In the face of threats of job instability or unemployment, feelings of frustration, rage and impotence are sometimes used as good reasons for violence against women (Kabeer 2014, 17), including forms of sexual coercion and HIV–related risks (Zablotska et al. 2009; Lichtenstein 2005). In this situation, economic insecurity forces a certain number of women into relationships with men who engage in dissolute sexual behaviours, including frequenting sex workers, which increase women's vulnerability to HIV infection (Dunkle et al. 2004; Gomes do Espirito Santo and Etheredge 2005; Macia, Maharaj, and Gresh 2011; Chapman, do Nascimento, and Mandal 2019). But, this economic fragility can also push some women to become sex workers themselves to survive despite serious risks that this activity implies for their health (Onyeneho 2009; Reed et al. 2010; Jadhav et al. 2013; Namey et al. 2018; Steen et al. 2019). The power imbalance between men and women within couples can be further distorted by a significant age disparity between partners, a disparity that is often considered as a potential risk factor for HIV among young female partners in Sub-Saharan Africa. Older men are more sexually experienced and therefore more likely to pass on HIV to their younger intimate partners, especially if these young women or adolescent girls are not able to negotiate safer sex with their partners because of unequal power dynamics with men (Fustos 2011).

The 'age-disparate relationship' is a particular type of relationship in which the age difference between sexual partners is generally five years or more, but for a non-conjugal sexual relationship between partners with at least a 10-year-age difference the literature uses expressions such as 'inter-generational relationship' and 'cross-generational relationship' (UNAIDS 2011, 6). Different studies describe intergenerational sex as an issue of primary concern because intergenerational sexual partnerships may increase the risk of HIV acquisition among adolescent girls and young women, mostly twentysomethings, who have sex with older men (Luke 2005; Hope 2007; Drakes et al. 2013; Dana, Adinew, and Sisay 2019; Stoner et al. 2019). This concern has been frequently labelled as the 'sugar daddy syndrome', the 'sugar daddy trap', or the 'sugar daddy phenomenon'. Specifically, in the literature, a sugar daddy is the name given to an older man who offers financial and material support (e.g. food, housing, and clothing) to younger women from poor backgrounds in exchange for companionship and sex (Maphagela 2016).

In 2015, South African girls started posting photos of luxurious shoes, clothes, and piles of money while tagging the pictures #blessed. What these pictures showed was a wealthy, older man (a 'blesser') spending money lavishly on a younger woman (a 'blessee') in exchange for friendship and sexual favours (Garsd and Crossan 2017). The 'blesser-blessee' relationship is another brand for the sugar daddy relationship in South Africa in which blessers are married men who secretly engage in extramarital affairs with young women usually aged between 15 and 24 (Mampane 2018). Blessers often use Blesser-finder, a dating website on social networks whereby they describe how they want their blessees to look. It markets itself through slogans such as #UPGRADEYOURWORTH and #YOURPUSSYISNOTCHARITY in an effort to show itself as a source of female empowerment through their intimate parts (Thobejane, Mulaudzi, and Zitha 2017). Blesser-blessee relationships can be therefore portrayed as a form of transactional sex which brings together technology (e.g. Instagram, Facebook, and Twitter), sexuality, and economics within a consumerist milieu. They originated in the online environment, making it easier for old rich men (blessers) to meet young women (blessees), but its function has been more than merely instrumental (Moodley and Ebrahim 2019).

Apart from the physiological reasons that make women more vulnerable to HIV, scholars frequently blame sugar daddies (or blessers) for the many HIV infections among young women (Leclerc-Madlala 2008, 11). Sugar daddy relationships (or blesser-blessee relationships) are believed to be a major contributing factor in the spread of HIV because social norms permit (and even encourage) married men to engage in condomless sex outside of marriage with multiple younger female partners in Sub-Saharan Africa (Population Services International 2005; Fallon 2018). Men frequently refuse to wear a condom because it is believed they prevent sexual pleasure, and the young women sometimes risk violent actions by their partners, who believe they are entitled to sex in exchange for material and financial benefits. Both can result in women and girls contracting HIV (Madiba and Ngwenya 2017).

So, to recap, exposure to intimate partner violence can increase women's risk of HIV infection through the following three main ways: forced or coercive sexual intercourse with an HIV-infected partner, limited or compromised negotiation of safer sexual practices, and tendency to engage in sexual behaviours that create, increase, or perpetuate risk (Maman et al. 2000).

According to UNAIDS, in high HIV prevalence settings, women experiencing intimate partner violence are 50% more likely to be infected with HIV than those who have not (UNAIDS 2018c, 4). South Africa has one of the highest levels of both HIV and gender-based violence in the world. The analysis so far conducted on the link between these two epidemics has highlighted the importance of addressing gender-based violence in the fight against HIV (Ghanotakis, Mayhew, and Watts 2009; Hassen and Deyassa 2013). South Africa remains the principal epicentre of the global HIV epidemic as it is home to the largest HIV epidemic in the world. Specifically, 20% of all seropositive people are South African citizens, and almost 60% are women over the age of 15 (Allinder and Fleischman 2019).

Jewkes et al. (2010a) assessed whether intimate partner violence and relationship power inequity increased the risk of incidence of HIV infection in young South African women. To do this, they completed a longitudinal analysis of data from a previously published cluster-randomised controlled trial carried out in the Eastern Cape province of South Africa in 2002–2006. 1099 women aged 15–26 years who were HIV negative at baseline and had at least one additional HIV test over two years of follow-up were included in the analysis. The results showed that 51 of 325 women with low relationship power equity at baseline acquired HIV compared with 73 of 704 women with medium or high relationship power equity. 45 of 253 women who reported more than one episode of intimate partner violence at baseline acquired HIV compared with 83 of 846 who reported one or no episodes. These data suggested that intimate partner violence and low relationship power equity increased the incidence of HIV in young women in rural areas of South Africa, on the one hand, and risk of the incidence of HIV infection was not associated with rape by a non-partner, on the other hand. In addition, the research established that men who raped were more likely to become infected with HIV.

Claudia Garcia-Moreno, lead specialist of Gender, Reproductive Rights, Sexual Health and Adolescence at WHO and one of the authors of the report *Global and Regional Estimates of Violence Against Women: Prevalence and Health Effects of Intimate Partner Violence and Non-Partner Sexual Violence* (Garcia-Moreno et al. 2013), has suggested that physical and sexual violence against women cause a tremendous impact on the health of women. Specifically, she added that, in some regions, women who experience intimate partner violence are 1.5 times more likely to become infected with HIV compared to women who have never experienced such violence (Schlein 2013). This claim finds support in the cross-sectional study of 1366 women presenting for antenatal care at four health centres in Soweto, South Africa, who accepted routine antenatal HIV testing. Women with violent or controlling male partners were 1.5 times more likely to acquire HIV compared to women who had never suffered violence by their partners. Researchers postulated that abusive men were more likely to be HIV-positive and impose risky sexual practices on partners (Dunkle et al. 2004). Further evidence was provided by a systematic review that included 28 studies involving 331,468 individuals from 16 countries, including eight studies from the US, four from South Africa, ten from East Africa, three from India, one from Brazil, and two from multiple low-income countries. This study showed that intimate partner violence was associated with a 1.2-fold increased risk of HIV infection among women aged ≥15 years (Li et al. 2014).

Médecins Sans Frontières' report, entitled *Untreated Violence: The Need for Patient-Centred Care for Survivors of Sexual Violence in the Platinum Mining Belt*, illustrated the findings of an in-depth survey conducted in November-

December 2015 among approximately 900 women aged 18-49 living in Rustenburg Local Municipality, South Africa. Rustenburg Municipality is the platinum mining capital and one of Africa's fastest-growing cities, with a population of 301,795 men and 247,780 women living in informal settlements near the mines where the health consequences of sexual violence remain largely unaddressed and require immediate interventions. The survey found that one in four women living in the Rustenburg area have been raped in her lifetime, and approximately half have been subject to some form of sexual violence or intimate partner violence, horrific but not unusual statistics in South Africa (Médecins Sans Frontières 2016). Further analysis of data showed that sexual and physical intimate partner violence and forced sex or sexual acts (rape) by non-partners contribute to a large disease burden, specifically one-fifth of HIV prevalence (6,765 cases) and more than one-third of clinical depression cases (7,034 cases). But, few sexual violence survivors sought health care services after the incident, namely 5% told a health care professional, 4% a counsellor, and 3% a social worker. These shocking findings were presented in Seattle at the annual Conference on Retroviruses and Opportunistic Infections (February 13–16, 2017) (Zhang et al. 2017).

Gang rape, also known as 'jackrolling', has become an alarming youth cult practice in South Africa (Stuijt 2009). Originally, the word 'jackroll' was coined to indicate the forceful abduction of young women under 26 in black townships by a specific gang of around ten members called the 'Jackrollers' which operated in the late 1980s in the Diepkloof area of Soweto (Mokwena 1991). Jackrolling is almost always committed in the open, with the rapists not having any intention of concealing their identity because they want to earn respect and esteem from other members of the gang. Most jackrolling incidents occur in public spaces like shebeens (informal township bars), taverns, picnic spots, schools, nightclubs, and on the streets, sometimes in the presence of boyfriends and husbands who are forced to watch jackrollers rape their partners (Vogelman and Lewis 1993).

Participation in violent games such as jackrolling is used as a way of reasserting male dominance over women (McGhee 2012), especially in the sexual sphere (Bloom 2013). The ultimate purpose of this horrible form of entertainment is not so much to satisfy the sexual appetites of jackrollers but more to cement a bond among them within a social environment impregnated with camaraderie and machismo (Anderson 2000, 811–813). These gang rapes occur without any kind of lubrication and without condoms so that the brutal abrasions cause mucosal tearing and bleeding, making HIV virus transmission through vaginal walls a certainty (Stuijt 2009). Such conditions of unprotected, unlubricated sex with multiple partners have fuelled the rapid spread of HIV in South Africa (Armstrong 1993). Specifically, unprotected sexual intercourse and multiple sexual partnerships have been identified as behavioural factors which significantly contribute to the spread of HIV in countries with a generalised epidemic because they connect people to a sexual network in which HIV is spread more quickly, and the whole community can be adversely affected (Shayo and Kalomo 2019; Mutinta 2014).

Child rape and risk of HIV infection

Some of the forms of violence on minors fall within gender violence and cannot be separated from it analytically, politically or from the standpoint of prevention and defence interventions. At a macro level, the more socially and economically discriminated women are in a society, the more diffused and serious are the situations of violence that children experience. At a micro level, violence in parent-child relationships is primarily a functional interrelation or substitution of the violence between partners; and, although it is carried out by women, it tends to reaffirm the man-woman gender hierarchy. Moreover, there is continuity between the denial of child sexuality and denying women control over their bodies, which generate the reification and materialisation of the desires and wills of both. The social permissiveness relative to the use of a woman's or a child's body as the prosthesis of male autoerotism stems from this (Bimbi 2000, 53–54).

In South Africa, millions of citizens live in crowded informal settlements, and such living conditions force numerous children born outside of marriage to share rooms and beds with adults who are not their biological parents, making sexual abuse more likely to occur (Luthy-Kaplan 2015). The growing incidence of child rape has been often linked directly to a profound lack of parental supervision and after-school programmes and the lack of necessary emotional, social and financial support and protection. For many adult men, sex is an absolute right which responds exclusively to a logic of personal pleasure without any affective connotation, including sex with minors (Meinck et al. 2015; Shields 2010; Jewkes et al. 2009, 1).

In June 2018, the Minister of Police, Bheki Cele, revealed specific numbers for child murders and child rapes during a parliamentary debate. Of the 124,526 total rape cases reported in the three financial years mentioned below, children were the victims of a shocking 41% of these cases. In 2014/2015, there were 15,520 child rapes reported, but only 1,799 ended up in successful convictions. In 2015/2016, 16,389 were reported, and just 2,488 were convicted. In 2016/2017, there was a rise both in the number of child rapes and the number of convicted rapists (19,071 and 6,366 respectively). In the same period, 2,600 children were also murdered. For Cele, this means that at least 46 children are raped every day, and at least two of these are murdered in South Africa.

However, he added that only one in five child rape cases and only one in three murder cases resulted in successful convictions (Andersen 2018).

As previously indicated, child protection statistics in South Africa paint a disconcerting picture: 41% of all reported rape cases from the financial years 2014/2015, 2015/2016, and 2016/2017 involve children. The data highlights the child protection issue as a national emergency for South African society. As a result, each year the government and organisations across the country organise a week of initiatives designed to raise awareness about children's rights, in particular on their safety and security. The National Child Protection Week aims to sensitise all sectors of South African society to the care and protection of children, the most vulnerable and valuable members of our society (Nwaneri 2019). Despite good policy intentions and improved service delivery in specific areas of the country, numerous South African children remain at risk of sexual abuse (Jamieson, Berry, and Lake 2017, 91). In 2016, a national prevalence study was designated to estimate the yearly incidence and lifetime prevalence of child sexual abuse and maltreatment in South Africa. The study is based on two data sources: first, a population survey that had been conducted with a sample of adolescents aged between 15 and 17 who were recruited from schools (4,086 participants) as well as households (5,631 participants), and secondly a series of focus group discussions with social workers, on the one hand, and in-depth interviews with social workers, social work supervisors, and other management-level staff providing investigation, protection and placement services, on the other hand, servicing the communities or geographical spaces identified through the sampling process. Together these two different, but complementary, typologies of interviewing provided a comprehensive range of qualitative information about the child protection system in South Africa. The study results revealed that 35.4% of adolescents interviewed in schools had experienced some form of sexual abuse at some point in their lives, whilst the percentage obtained from the household portion of the sample was slightly lower, but confirmed a rate of 26.3% that is still worryingly high. This meant an estimated total of at least 784,967 young people in South Africa who had been sexually abused by the age of 17 years (Artz et al. 2016).

From the above account, it can be deduced that sexual abuse among children and adolescents in South Africa is quite widespread. Rapists seek out increasingly younger victims, so little girls in particular are at risk of contracting HIV from violent sex attackers (Stuijt 2009). The mistaken belief that sex with a virgin will cure an HIV-infected person, AIDS sufferer of his illness, or other sexually transmitted diseases offers an explanation for why child rape occurs (Groce and Trasi 2004; Meel 2003). This false credence that is still today extremely popular among the African community resident in black

South African townships originated historically from a long-running myth that a person suffering from venereal diseases (e.g. syphilis and gonorrhoea) could be cured by having sexual intercourse with a virgin. This myth was particularly rampant in Scotland in the late nineteenth and early twentieth centuries and in various parts of Eastern Europe in the late eighteenth century, and is currently still prominent in HIV-ravaged Sub-Saharan Africa (Blank 2007, 62). Epstein and Jewkes (2009), however, question the idea that the 'virgin rape myth' drives either HIV infection or child sexual abuse in today's South Africa because they assert that this claim is predicated on racist assumptions regarding the presumed amorality of African men and is extremely stigmatising towards HIV-positive people.

As a supplement to what I have already mentioned above, there is little evidence to advocate that the virgin rape myth is one of the most important sources of child sexual abuse (Heiberg 2005, 128). Instead, often childhood adversities and socio-cultural factors such as patriarchal conceptions of male domination and manliness, and especially the perpetrators' beliefs about sexual entitlement, are cited as the main causes. The demand for immediate sexual satisfaction is the triggering factor of many child rape cases. Rapists are mostly motivated by the need to affirm their sexual power on vulnerable objects which their young victims are seen as being (Fraser 2015).

A quarter of new infections in South Africa are caused by sexual violence (Hlatshaneni 2019), with an estimated number of new infections among children aged between 0 and 14 still remaining significantly high (UNICEF 2019). There are numerous ways in which the HIV epidemic and sexual abuse interact: first, access to social security is almost impossible for children orphaned by AIDS because they are devoid of an adult caregiver, and this situation makes them even more vulnerable to sexual exploitation in exchange for the satisfying of basic needs. Secondly, rape and sexual abuse increase children's risk of contracting HIV-infection, given the infrequent use of condoms during sexual assault incidents. Specifically, the violent nature of rape causes genital abrasions and bleeding that augment the risk of HIV transmission. Thirdly, teenage girls aged between 15 and 19 are particularly vulnerable to HIV infection as the high prevalence rates among them demonstrate. Differences in HIV rates between girls and boys indicate that the former are more probable to be infected by older men than by their male peers, and these age differences increase the likelihood of sexual violence too. Fourthly, adolescent girls and children have limited ability to negotiate safer sex when they are in an abusive relationship, thus increasing the risk of being infected by an HIV-positive abuser. Fifthly, in a social context where there has been a revival of customary practices such as virginity testing (e.g. in KwaZulu-Natal, a coastal South African province), girls who are deemed virgins may become prime targets for sexual violence or abuse due to jealousy or a presumed HIV-negative state (Heiberg 2005, 128–129). Lastly, the practice of abducting a young girl in order to force her family to give permission for marriage is known as *ukuthwala* (forced marriage) in South Africa. It occurs mainly in rural parts of South Africa, especially in Eastern Cape and KwaZulu-Natal. This traditional practice, which is permitted by customary law but against the South African constitution, places immature South African brides at far greater risk of HIV infection than their peers who marry later because a good number of them have sexual relationships with husbands who work far away from home and sometimes engage in condomless casual sex, including sexual intercourse with sex workers (Banwari 2011, S119). In addition, these abducted girls are often married to older and more sexually experienced men with whom it is difficult to negotiate safer sex, refuse sex or avoid sexual abuses, thus making them vulnerable to sexually transmitted infections, including HIV. These girls get married before the age of 18 (early marriage) without having the minimum level of sexual health information because, once married, they are often taken out of school where they would have attended sex education programmes, which further increases their risk of contracting HIV (Bailey-King 2018). Consequently, prevention of child abuse needs to be included as part of the HIV prevention agenda in South Africa (Jewkes et al. 2010b).

As previously seen, the victim of sexual aggression can contract HIV as a result of the violence suffered. The risk of exposure to the aforementioned virus is further increased when sexual violence is carried out by a group of aggressors (e.g. gang rape) (Schleifer 2004, 11). Consequently, it is desirable both to provide an education that aims to protect rape victims from HIV (Basile et al. 2016) and to investigate the efficacy of post-exposure prophylaxis if rape occurs. This last strategy draws attention once more to the topic of crime as a public health problem (Green, Gilbertson, and Grimsley 2002).

There is a strict connection between the epidemic of rape and the epidemic of HIV in South Africa; thus if governmental authorities do not address this odious crime energetically, HIV will continue to proliferate across the country (Barday 2017). The Criminal Law (Sexual Offences and Related Matters) Amendment Act No. 32 of 2007 aims to prevent secondary victimisation of a victim (adult or minor) of sexual crime through the criminal justice system (Bougard, Booyens, and Ehlers 2015). The law provides few social-support and medical-aid measures. One of the main ones is the free provision of post-exposure prophylaxis (PEP) in cases of sexual violence. PEP is a 28-day course of antiretroviral medicines aimed at protecting the health of victims of sexual assault soon after possible exposure to HIV. It can reduce the risk of HIV infection by about 80% as long as the medications are taken within 72 hours of the occurrence of a rape (WHO 2014e; Nare 2013). By law, the victim or the investigation officer is entitled to a court sentence that obligates the alleged culprit to undergo HIV testing within 90 days of an assault taking place. However, these testing provisions regarding the forced disclosure of the accused's HIV status have fed an animated debate among South Africa's jurist community on the constitutionality of this measure (Naidoo and Govender 2011).

Conclusion

As previously described, violence against women and children is an epidemic which is infecting South Africa. Gender-based violence is pervasive in South Africa because violence has been rooted in the foundation of South African society. Every year, official statistics reveal disturbing truths that increasingly shock and dismay South African civil society. South Africa has one of the highest rates of violence against women in the entire world (Smith 2019).

South Africa's criminal justice system needs to work harder in its fight against the scourge of rape in the country so that many perpetrators can be arrested and condemned harshly. However, the statistics reveal that over 90% of rapes still go unpunished because of an inefficient investigation system. Consequently, most rape victims decide not to report their aggressors because they do not trust the criminal justice system and want to avoid being victimised again by their vengeful rapists (Qukula 2019).

Many victimological studies have focused not only on sexual violence in itself, but also on the inherent risk of HIV infection. It is a reality that heterosexual transmission is, epidemiologically, at the heart of the HIV epidemic, and African women appear to be disproportionately vulnerable to infection. There is no doubt that between gender-based violence and HIV exists an almost symbiotic linkage in much of Sub-Saharan Africa, namely the two threads of the relationship tend to be mutually reinforcing in this developing area (Flint 2011, 53).

Another form of violence caused by rooted unequal power relations between females and males is represented by harmful customary practices that are often enforced as a way of strengthening male domination and impact negatively on the health and safety of girls and women (OHCHR 1995). The next chapter investigates the potential association between the harmful aspects of widow inheritance, virginity testing, female genital mutilation, and HIV transmission in adolescent and adult females in Sub-Saharan Africa.

Chapter 5

A victimological analysis of the link between harmful traditional practices and HIV[1]

Polygyny, widow brides and cleansing rituals

Research has identified sexual concurrency as a leading cause of high prevalence rates in Sub-Saharan Africa, but few studies have openly examined the contribution of marital concurrency. Utilising a multi-level model of Demographic and Health Surveys (DHS) with HIV-biomarkers for 16 African countries, Fox (2014) assessed the relationship between an individual's HIV serostatus and rates of formal marital concurrency (polygamous unions) and informal marital concurrency (extramarital sexual relationships) among married men and women. Compared with monogamous unions, both formal and informal marital concurrency was positively associated with HIV infection at the individual level. However, the odds of having HIV were higher among individuals living in regions with more informal marital concurrency, but lower in regions with more polygamy (protective effect), even accounting for individual-level sexual behaviour. Much of the understanding of the effect of concurrent sexual partnerships on the spread of HIV derives from mathematical models, but the empirical evidence is limited. In "Polygyny and the Spread of HIV in Sub-Saharan Africa: A Case of Benign Concurrency", the authors focus on polygyny, the most common form of polygamy that designates a marital practice in which a man has more than one wife simultaneously, and study its relationship with HIV prevalence at the ecological level. Specifically, they tested the relationship between HIV and polygyny at the country as well as sub-

---

[1] The content of this chapter was originally published in Meini, Bruno, and Mara Tognetti Bordogna. 2019. "The Contribution of Harmful Traditional Practices to HIV Transmission among Adolescent and Adult Females in Sub-Saharan Africa: A Victimological Approach." *International Journal of Gender Studies in Developing Societies* 3 (1): 37–59. Re-used with permission by Inderscience Publishers, Geneva, Switzerland.

national level using data from 19 African DHS and AIDS Indicator Surveys (AIS)[2] with individually-linked survey and HIV serostatus data. The ecological association between polygyny and HIV prevalence was negative at both levels, and polygyny was labelled as a case of benign partnership concurrency. HIV prevalence was lower in countries where the practice of polygyny was widespread and was also lower in areas within countries with higher levels of polygyny. The researchers emphasised the fact that the negative statistical relationship between polygyny and HIV observed in this study could not be explained by the sexual network structure alone; two other features of polygyny which influenced the spread of HIV over and above the structural network effect were found. The first feature is the disproportionate recruitment of HIV-positive women into marriages with a polygynous husband. Specifically, the addition of new wives (mainly divorcees and widows) was likely to introduce the virus into what might have been an HIV-free monogamous marriage. The second feature is the lower average coital frequency in conjugal dyads of polygynous marriages. A polygynous man divides his time between two or more wives, which unavoidably leads to a reduction in the coital frequency with each of them (Reniers and Watkins 2010). The lower the average coital frequency, the slower the sexual spread of HIV, since there are fewer sex acts by which infection can propagate into the polygamous system (coital dilution effect) (Sawers, Isaac, and Stillwaggon 2011). This second effect was able to counterbalance the first effect, reducing HIV incidence in serodiscordant couples within a polygynous union. The reduction in coital frequency might arise from three principal reasons: resource constraints on a polygynous husband's coital budget, relative old age of husbands in polygynous unions, and an awareness to reduce the risk of HIV infection (e.g. the new husband of an inherited spouse might be conscious of the cause of death of his wife's previous husband). The two mechanisms mentioned above produce together a mixing pattern whereby HIV-positive women are disproportionately recruited into polygynous marriages where the coital frequency is lower. Consequently, seronegative individuals in polygynous marriages are at higher risk of HIV than those in a monogamous marriage, but the population-level effects of polygyny on the transmission of the virus are beneficial on average (Reniers and Watkins 2010, 5–6). Two years later, Reniers and Tfaily (2012) restated the relationship between polygyny and HIV using a multilevel analysis. At the individual level, they found that polygyny correlated positively with HIV status, particularly for junior wives

---

[2] The AIS was introduced to provide countries with generalised HIV epidemics with a standardised tool designated to monitor andevaluate national HIV and AIDS programmes (ICF Macro 2010).

of polygynous men. At the aggregate level, however, the correlation was negative, suggesting that polygyny inhibited the spread of HIV. Researchers investigated four explanations for the divergent individual and ecological-level associations. These were connected with

1   the adverse selection of HIV-positive women into polygynous marriage systems
2   the sexual network structure produced by polygyny (gender-asymmetric partnership concurrency)
3   the coital dilution
4   the restricted access to sexual partners for younger men in populations where polygynous men presumably monopolised the women in their community (monopolising polygynists).

The investigation by Reniers and Tfaily found evidence for some of these mechanisms so that they supported the proposition that polygyny impeded the propagation of HIV. Similarly, Mtenga et al. (2015) found that being in a polygamous marriage does not increase women's vulnerability to HIV as the characteristic structure of sexual networks in polygamous marriages and the coital dilution effect may help prevent or delay HIV transmission between spouses. They analysed a sample of 3,988 married or cohabitant individuals, aged 15 years and older from the town of Ifakara in the Kilombero district of the Morogoro region in Southern Tanzania. The data concerning the relationship between polygamous marriage and HIV status resulted in being questionable because the number of study participants who were living in official polygamous marriages was only 104 (2.61%). Consequently, it is necessary to develop further research based on larger samples of individuals in polygamous relationships in Tanzania in order to provide more accurate information about the association between polygamy and HIV. Concurrent partnerships have been suggested as a risk factor for transmitting HIV, but their impact on the epidemic depends upon how prevalent they are in populations, the average number of concurrent partnerships an individual has, and the length of time they overlap (Beauclair, Hens, and Delva 2015). As I have previously seen, polygyny is the classic example of long-term concurrency, and Reniers' studies suggest that it impedes rather than accelerates the spread of the epidemic. This conclusion, however, is not confirmed by the study conducted by Eaton et al. (2014) who explored changes in reported multiple partnerships, non-marital concurrency, and polygyny in eastern Zimbabwe during a period of declining HIV prevalence from 1998 to 2011. Trends were reported for adult men (aged 17–54 years) and women (aged 15–49 years) from five survey rounds of the Manicaland HIV/STD prevention project, a general-population open cohort study. The study population consisted of 12 geographically distinct communities in Manicaland Province (four subsistence farming areas, two roadside trading settlements, four large-scale agricultural estates, and two rural commercial centres) with a total current population of around 57,000. The cohort was established from 1998 to 2000 and completed five survey rounds, each occurring over two-three years. At the baseline, 34.2% of men reported multiple partnerships, 11.9% reported non-marital concurrency, and 4.6% reported polygyny. Among women, 4.6% and 1.8% reported multiple partnerships and concurrency, respectively. All three partnership indicators declined by similar relative amounts (around 60%–70%) over the period. Polygyny accounted for around 25% of male concurrency. After adjustment for age group, survey round, socioeconomic stratum, and religion, polygynous men were 2.92 times more likely to become divorced and 1.63 times more likely to have casual partners than monogamously married men. Twelve incident HIV infections were observed among polygynous men, for an incidence rate of 2.2 cases per 100 person-years, compared with 1.3 cases per 100 person-years (106 infections/8,165 person-years) for monogamously married men and 1.1 (86 infections/7,548 person-years) for unmarried men. After adjustment for age group, survey round, socioeconomic level, and religion, polygynous men had a risk of HIV infection that was 1.46 times that for married men. From this analysis, it is clear that polygyny was surprisingly unstable and should not be considered a safe form of concurrency separate from non-marital concurrency in eastern Zimbabwe; rather, it is recommendable to include polygynous men as a population for further HIV prevention. Widow inheritance (also known as wife inheritance) is a cultural practice whereby a widow has the duty to marry a kinsman of her late deceased husband, often his brother (inheritor). The son of this union is considered to be the son of the first husband who continues the genealogy of the deceased, not the genetic father, and inherits what was legally the property of his late father. This custom aims to preserve the relationship between the families of the two spouses that was previously initiated in the original marriage as upon the death of the husband the marriage is not dissolved but the widow remains, legally, the owner of the home and a member of her deceased husband's family unless her family repays the bride price or *lobolo* (Ogolla 2014). Traditionally, an inheritor was prohibited from having sexual relations with an inherited widow, but, gradually, this taboo was replaced by an expectation of sex in an inheritance relationship. Unfortunately, as Buckley (1997) notes, the sexualisation of the widow inheritance system occurred substantially when HIV infection rates in central and East Africa first began to increase. As more and more AIDS widows were inherited, this sexualisation exposed inheritors, and their own wives, to the disease, which helped HIV infection rates to increase very rapidly (Conroy 2011). Widow inheritance is common in certain patriarchal communities of Kenya (Agot et al. 2010; Gunga 2009), Nigeria (Research Directorate of the Immigration and Refugee Board of Canada 2006a), Malawi (Muula and Mfusto-Bengo 2004), South Sudan (Beswick 2001), Zimbabwe (Research Directorate of the Immigration and Refugee Board of Canada 2006b) and Uganda (Mujuzi 2012). In addition to window inheritance, widows may be subjected to widow cleansing. This is a traditional practice in which a widow must have unprotected sex with a brother of her husband or another relative, or with a designated village cleanser, in order to exorcise her husband's spirit. While women can theoretically refuse to participate in these activities, in practice there is great pressure to comply. Women who refuse risk losing their land and property, banishment from their communities, and other forms of social ostracism (Gable et al. 2007, 146). A sexual cleansing rite is therefore observed before the window can be reintegrated into society (Ayikukwei et al. 2008). Customary rules require that ritual sex be penetrative, namely that the cleanser's sperm must be deposited in the vagina of the widow for the cleansing to be successful (Loftspring 2007, 255–256). After a widow has been cleansed, she is expected to be inherited by a man, traditionally a brother-in-law or cousin (Abong'o 2014). With the number of HIV-positive people continuing to climb in the Luo community, the practice of hiring a professional cleanser to perform the sexual cleansing ritual is common. The men who specialise in this practice have been known to move from one widow to another, putting both themselves and the widows that they have unprotected sex with at great risk of contracting HIV (Abubakar and Kitsao-Wekulo 2015, 398).

Virginity testing

Virginity testing is a practice involving a physical inspection of the genitalia of girls and women to verify that their hymen is still intact, providing evidence that they have not yet had sexual intercourse with a man (Maleche and Day 2011, 12). In most cases, this practice is often ineffective because the hymen is not a reliable indicator of virginity as it differs from woman to woman and sometimes is not present. The hymen can also remain intact after penetrative sex or be broken over time through exercise, insertion of tampons or even fingers. Other signs that show that a young woman is still a virgin, according to the inspectors, include tight muscle tone, firm buttocks and breasts, and a flat abdomen (Mojapelo 2016). However, the tests are often unreliable because they are done by people who are not medically trained (Barrett-Grant et al. 2001, 202).

The custom of virginity testing may be viewed as being unfair and unhealthy because it is a gross violation of fundamental women's human rights, such as privacy, dignity and health (Dlamini 2016). In South Africa and Uganda, virginity tests have been justified in terms of HIV prevention because it ensures abstinence in girls and proves to the new husband that she is still a virgin. This practice has also been documented in Libya, Egypt, Indonesia, Macedonia,

Afghanistan and Iraq, although not for the purposes of HIV prevention (Maleche and Day 2011, 12–13).

Despite the fact that virginity testing is legally banned in South Africa for children under the age of 16 (Behrens 2014), it is still largely practised in KwaZulu-Natal, a coastal South African province, where groups of Zulu have carried out virginity testing campaigns since the 1990s, both in the form of large movements including celebrations for several days with the Zulu King at the centre, and in the form of smaller-scale local initiatives, where girls are tested under simple and everyday circumstances. The initiator is often the headman of a community or a female *isangoma* (traditional healer) who works in different parts of the province. Some women practised in examining girls' hymens have been engaged as examiners while local women and men have arranged the events (Wickström 2010, 532–533). The restoration of the practice of virginity testing has been explained by the process of revitalisation of the indigenous traditional knowledge systems suppressed during the apartheid era (Vincent 2006, 27).

In 1991, King Goodwill Zwelethini reintroduced the Royal Reed Dance Festival, or as it is still best known in the Zulu dialect, *Umkhosi woMhlanga.* This ceremony takes place annually during the month of September at the king's royal residence, Kwa-Nyokeni Royal Palace in Nongoma, KwaZulu-Natal, and is attended by thousands of people from all over the world. The festival takes its name from the riverbed reeds and the symbolic part they play in the four-day event. The reeds are carried by more than 25,000 maidens who have been invited to the king's palace to participate in the traditional ceremony, which celebrates their virginity and their preparation for womanhood. In some cases, girls are taught traditional craft skills, cultural performances, agricultural practices and the preparation of customary dishes. Most of them are grateful for the opportunity to learn new skills, meet other girls and become part of a supportive network of women encouraging one other to avert pregnancies and HIV infections. The virgins come from all parts of Zululand, and in recent years there are also small groups from Swaziland, Botswana and Pondoland (Zululand District Municipality 2015, 186).

The royal reed dance festival has been mainly reintroduced as a means to prevent HIV spread by encouraging young Zulu girls to delay sexual activity until marriage. Thus, the reappearance of the practice of pre-marital virginity testing of maidens in KwaZulu-Natal is explicitly justified by ritual experts in terms of the epidemic (McNeill 2011, 27). Virginity testing is represented as a preventive ritual more than a diagnostic measure, an effort to celebrate, defend, and promote virginity to prevent young girls from contracting HIV (Wickström 2010, 536). Yet another concern is that virginity testers may encourage the spread of HIV and other sexually transmitted diseases as they touch and inspect several girls during these mass ceremonies (Hugo 2012). Consequently, in response to this concern, the KwaZulu-Natal Health Department has started providing rubber gloves to virginity testers and has trained them on how to use them appropriately (Leclerc-Madlala 2001, 538–539).

Virginity testers are aware that "the human body is more than just a physical organism fluctuating between health and illness. It is also the focus of a set of beliefs about its social and psychological significance, its structure and function" (Helman 2007, 19). The testers use standards that derive from indigenous knowledge rather than biomedical science in their chastity assessments (Leclerc-Madlala 2001, 539–540) and if a girl passes the virginity test, then she brings honour to her family (Amy 2008). This certificate of purity is also an economic document that may be used in negotiations on lobola or bridewealth (Wickström 2010, 546). Nevertheless, it should not be forgotten that there are girls who choose to have anal sex rather than vaginal sex with their partners because they fear failing a virginity test. This choice carries a higher risk of HIV transmission than unprotected vaginal intercourse (Leclerc-Madlala 2003).

Virginity testing has been declared an act of sexual violence against women by the World Health Organization and has been criticised as a patriarchal belief which nourishes gender inequality (Robatjazi et al. 2016), even if it has been often depicted as a risk-free indigenous response to HIV (Jewkes 2004, 138). Most of the girls are sent to be tested by their mothers. The question of whether or not these girls are coerced against their will is of primary concern to members of the South African Human Rights Commission who condemn the practice. Additionally, in some communities, the girl's father is fined by the chief for discrediting the community if his daughter is found to have lost her virginity (Leclerc-Madlala 2010, 415).

Girls who refuse virginity testing often are assumed to be non-virgins, and it is likely that a girl would prefer to undergo virginity testing than risk her reputation (Lasco 2002, 10). In 2000, during the hearings of the commission for gender equality, a serious concern was raised about virginity testing given that the certification of virginity may also expose girls to rape and sexual abuse, namely the possibility that men who wanted to be cleansed of HIV could rape virgin girls. This virgin cleansing myth is a mistaken belief that is widespread in South Africa, but also in some communities of Zambia, Zimbabwe and Nigeria. In these countries, this myth (also referred to as the virgin cure myth, virgin rape myth, or simply virgin myth) is blamed for being the principal cause of high rates of child rape (Flanagan 2001; Govender 1999; Meel 2003). In Zimbabwe, for example, some people believe that the blood produced by raping a virgin will cleanse the virus from the infected person's blood (Vickers 2006). Consequently, virginity testers have presumably become more reluctant to publicly identify virgins (Jewkes 2004, 138).

Thobejane and Mdhluli (2015) explored the perceptions of virginity testing among a group of six young girls selected by snowball sampling in a rural area in KwaZulu-Natal and how this practice could help in reducing the spread of HIV. The study draws on qualitative data, using mixed methods of data collection, such as in-depth interviews and focus group discussions with girls aged 12 to 21. In total, three focus group discussions were conducted and in-depth interviews were used to integrate the information collected during these discussions. The findings of this study in KwaZulu-Natal were consistent with the practice being associated with the original intention to demonstrate the purity of the bride before marriage. However, since the advent of HIV, the study revealed that girls who were virgins were in a much better position to receive greater respect and conduct a life free of this serious virus. Win (2004, 14) added that the relationship between HIV and virginity is a false myth. While virginity is an effective protection strategy for HIV up to the point of marriage, it does not save you from harm once you are married. Research has shown that most women are infected with HIV from their husbands despite being faithful. In reality, married women are at a higher risk of HIV infection than single women. The latter have a much greater ability to negotiate safer sex with their partners while the former have very limited autonomy of choice.

Traditional healers think that virginity testing is a valuable cultural practice that should be preserved (Van Dyk 2008, 456) and maintain that with its emphasis on total abstinence from sexual intercourse by girls, the practice is being revived to prevent HIV infection, to detect incest and abuse, and to re-instil and promote lost cultural values. Traditionalists view the revival of virginity testing as a signal of going back to basics, and it enjoys a lot of support from those communities that practise it (Thobejane and Mdhluli 2015). In contrast, most gender activists argue that virginity testing does not help to stop the spread of HIV but, in some areas, it is causing an increase in HIV infection because girls and young women are having anal sex (which has a higher risk) to avoid vaginal penetration (Barrett-Grant et al. 2001, 202). They add that virginity testing is a violation of a woman's rights to privacy and dignity because it is often involuntary, strongly discriminatory, and highly invasive. The girls do not have the freedom to decline the procedure without social sanction in traditional communities where parental persuasion amounts to coercion (George 2008, 1461). This difference of opinion represents an instructive example of the conflict that often explodes between the Western paradigm of HIV prevention and African values and customs (Green and Ruark 2011).

Female genital mutilation

Female genital mutilation, also known female genital cutting and female circumcision, is defined by the World Health Organization (WHO) and the

United Nations agencies as "the partial or total removal of the female external genitalia or other injury to the female genital organs for non-medical reasons" (WHO 2011, 1). WHO has subdivided female genital mutilation into four types depending on the extent of tissue removed (WHO 2008a, 4). In the first type, a clitoridectomy, part, or all, of the clitoris is amputated (Rodriguez 2014), while in the second, excision, both the clitoris and the inner labia (lips that surround the vagina) are completely or partially removed, with or without removal of the labia majora (larger outer lips) (Ahmadu 2000; Thomas 2000). Infibulation, the third type, is the most extreme form of female genital mutilation that involves completely sewing up a girl's vulva, leaving a small pea size hole for the purpose of menstruation and urination (Hicks 1996; Grassivaro Gallo, Livio, and Viviani 2004). The last category includes all other harmful procedures to the female genitalia for non-medical purposes, for example, pricking the clitoris with needles, piercing, incising, scraping, and burning of the genital area (UNICEF 2013, 7).

In 2016, the United Nations Children's Fund (UNICEF) estimated that at least 200 million girls and women had undergone female genital mutilation in 27 African countries as well as in areas of the Middle East such as Iraq and Yemen, in some Asian countries like Indonesia, India, Malaysia, Oman, Saudi Arabia, and the United Arab Emirates and in some places in South America such as Colombia. The practice was also found in immigrant communities in Europe and in North America and Australia (UNICEF 2016c).

Throughout the 1990s and 2000s, governments in Africa and the Middle East passed national legislation outlawing female genital mutilation. With the exception of Egypt and Eritrea, 25 countries in Africa where female genital mutilation is concentrated have ratified the Maputo Protocol, which prohibits and condemns all forms of the practice. Despite this, female genital mutilation remains pervasive in numerous countries that have ratified the Maputo Protocol, suggesting that the Protocol's standards have not been met (Muthumbi et al. 2015). Legislation prohibiting female genital mutilation has also been adopted in 33 countries outside Africa and the Middle East, mostly to protect children with origins in practising countries. Nevertheless, this legislation should be accompanied by measures capable of influencing cultural traditions and expectations to effectively address the practice within its broader social milieu (UNICEF 2013, 8–9).

Female genital mutilation practices are mostly performed on girls from birth to the age of 15. However, occasionally, adult and married women are also subjected to the procedure. The age at which amputation takes place varies with local traditions and circumstances (WHO 2008a, 4). Similarities are often seen within certain ethnic groups rather than within countries. For example, people originally from Somalia, mostly refugees from the war zones in the

Horn of Africa, live in many countries and usually carry out the same practice (Solnes Miltenburg 2010, 6).

Despite the fact that female genital mutilation causes harm to girls, it is performed in order to prepare girls for adulthood and marriage, to ensure virginity until marriage, to prevent promiscuity and promote conjugal fidelity, to maintain genital cleanliness and purity, to preserve cultural and religious identity, and to maintain family honour. Specifically, in certain communities, it is seen as a rite of passage or an initiation into a secret women's society; in others, it is thought to increase fertility and enhance male sexual pleasure (Perron et al. 2013).

Female genital mutilation can be found in all religious groups, despite the lack of any holy text prescribing this practice (Solnes Miltenburg 2010, 9). As confirmed by ethnographic studies, in certain Muslim communities, female circumcision is widely held to be a religious obligation, a cleansing rite which enables women to pray in a proper manner. The practice, however, is also found in Christian societies. In some countries where a particular religion is almost universal, as is the case with Islam in Sudan, the extent to which people of other religions practise female genital mutilation have little influence on overall prevalence. Clearly, variations in prevalence among people of different faiths reveal that female circumcision is a challenge for all religious groups in affected countries (UNICEF 2013, 69–72).

In 2010, WHO published a document titled *Global Strategy to Stop Health-Care Providers from Performing Female Genital Mutilation* in which female genital mutilation is described as a traditional practice that functions as a self-enforcing social norm. Families and individuals continue to practise it because they believe that their community expects them to do so. They further expect that if they do not respect the social norm, they will suffer social consequences such as derision, social exclusion, stigmatisation and loss of status. Health professionals, who typically have status in communities, can promote the abandonment of female genital mutilation by providing correct information on the negative health consequences of this harmful practice (UNFPA et al. 2010, 2).

In addition to social norms, there are legal norms that states may enact to discourage the practice and moral norms evoked by internalised values of right and wrong which suggest doing what is best for one's daughter. These norms may act in harmony, reinforcing one another, or they may be in conflict. However, it should be acknowledged that where the social norm of female genital mutilation is in place, the fear of social exclusion for not conforming may be stronger than the fear than legal sanctions such as citations, fines, and imprisonment. If families continue to allow their daughters to be mutilated and believe that this is expected by their community, the law may not serve as an effective enough deterrent to stop the practice. Conversely, among groups that have abandoned female genital mutilation, legislation can serve as a tool to strengthen the legitimacy of their actions and as an argument for convincing others to do the same (UNICEF 2013, 14–17).

Female genital mutilation is an age-old practice that implies immediate and long-term health consequences. Immediate complications include excessive bleeding, shock, severe pain, genital tissue swelling, fever, infections (including sepsis), difficulty urinating and retention of urine, problems with wound healing and sometimes death (Berg and Underland 2014). Long-term consequences include chronic pain, excessive scar tissue formation, development of cysts, abscesses and genital ulcers, dysmenorrhea, recurrent urinary tract infection, bacterial vaginosis, dyspareunia (painful sexual intercourse), sexual dysfunction and obstetric complications (Berg et al. 2014; Kaplan et al. 2013; Reisel and Creighton 2015) as well as psychological traumas (Behrendt and Moritz 2005; Knipscheer et al. 2015). Sporadic research data over the past ten years has correlated dirty and unsterilised cutting equipment, haemorrhages requiring blood transfusions and injurious sexual intercourse, causing vaginal tearing and lesions, with rising rates of HIV transmission among women and girls in countries where female genital mutilation is still widely practised. A few reports have described the potentially high risk of HIV transmission among mutilated girls and children since the beginning of the HIV epidemic (Keown 2007; Diouf and Nour 2013).

The Nigerian ex-Senator Iyabo Obasanjo-Bello, who chaired the senate's health committee, attributed the partial spread of HIV to female genital mutilation, especially when it is done to a group of girls at a single time. She explained that when the same surgical instrument (often a razor or a very sharp knife) is used by non-medically trained practitioners (traditional birth attendants, traditional healers or elderly woman of the village) to cut several girls on the same day during a rite of passage, this can increase the risk of HIV transmission (Karanja 2003, 64–65; Monjok, Essien, and Holmes 2007; Ogbebo 2010). This hypothesis was mainly confirmed by three studies. The first reported a plausible mechanism of HIV transmission during the *fanado*, an initiation ritual by which dozens of girls (generally aged 8–12 years) were excised on the same day by an elderly woman (*ngamanos*) with the use of a non-sterilised ceremonial knife on a highly vascular organ. HIV could have been introduced into these groups of girls infected through non-sexual mechanisms such as occupational, parental or vertical transmission before undergoing mutilation (Pépin et al. 2006).

The second was carried out by a team of researchers led by Devon D. Brewer, director of the American research firm Interdisciplinary Scientific Research. The researchers analysed data from the Demographic and Health Surveys of Kenya, Lesotho and Tanzania, which were based on nationally representative samples of adolescents and adults aged 15–49 years old, and assessed the relation between male and female circumcision and prevalent HIV infection in Kenyan, Lesothan, and Tanzanian virgins and adolescents. In these countries, circumcision is typically performed in adolescence or early adulthood and often in unhygienic circumstances where many individuals are circumcised with shared, unsterilised cutting instruments. They found that circumcised male and female virgins in a nationally representative sample of Kenyans, Lesothoans, and Tanzanians were substantially more likely to be infected with HIV than their uncircumcised counterparts. Among adolescents, regardless of sexual experience, circumcision was just as strongly associated with prevalent HIV infection. However, the relation between circumcision and HIV infection changed direction in adults, namely uncircumcised persons, were more likely to be HIV positive. The self-reported sexual experience was independently related to HIV infection in adolescent Kenyan females but was unrelated to HIV infection in adolescent Kenyan, Lesothan, and Tanzanian males. This research concluded that unhygienic male and female circumcision practices in eastern and southern Africa might transmit HIV (Brewer et al. 2007).

Maslovskaya, Brown, and Padmadas (2009) investigated the potential association between female genital mutilation and HIV by using the 2003 data from the Kenya Demographic and Health Survey (KDHS). The 2003 KDHS provided a unique opportunity to link the HIV test results with the many demographic, social, economic and behavioural characteristics of women in the reproductive age group (15–49 years), including women's female genital mutilation status. They hypothesised that female genital mutilation increased the risk of HIV infection if HIV was present in the community. The results showed that girls that had undergone female genital mutilation with a younger or the same-age first-union partner had higher odds of being HIV-positive than women with a younger or same-age first-union partner that had not undergone female genital mutilation; in contrast, girls that had undergone female genital mutilation with an older first-union partner had lower odds of being HIV positive than those women with an older first-union partner that had not undergone female genital mutilation.

For some scholars, the correlation between HIV and female genital mutilation is not as direct as some studies have previously demonstrated (Klouman, Manongi, and Klepp 2005; Morison et al. 2001). Yount and Abraham (2007) used data from 3,167 women aged 15–49 who participated in the 2003 KDHS to test the direct and indirect associations of female genital mutilation with HIV. Their adjusted models suggested that female genital mutilation was not associated directly with HIV, but was associated indirectly through several pathways. These pathways included a sexual debut before 20, being in a relationship with an older partner, having at least an extra-union partner, divorce and being widowed, and engaging in risky sexual behaviours (for example, frequent anal intercourse without a condom).

Although both research and theoretical speculations reveal the existence of a plausible association between female genital mutilation and HIV, epidemiologic assessment of this association is rendered difficult by many challenges in design, data collection, and analysis, especially given the heterogeneity in the practice being studied. It is evident that better insight into the question will require large cohort studies in areas with a high prevalence of both female genital mutilation and HIV and with rigorous data collection tools (Diouf and Nour 2013, 49).

Victimological remarks

The concept of victim and the scope of victimology should not be restricted to the scientific study of victims of crime alone (Doerner and Lab 2015; Fattah 1991; Mendelsohn 1976), but should cover all victims of human rights violations, including victims of conventional crimes and victims of harmful traditional practices, because human beings suffer from a variety of casual factors (Elias 1986; Garkawe 2004).

This chapter proposes a theoretical framework that integrates two interrelated ideas on victimisation processes in several African contexts. The first idea represents harmful traditional practices as the primary source of victimisation because they constitute violence against women and girls and violate their personal dignity and human rights. This concept derives from an understanding of victimisation as reflected in relevant international instruments (victimology of human rights) (Ndahinda 2007). The second idea considers the usual ways through which these harmful customary practices are performed as potential causes of secondary victimisation because they may expose female victims to HIV. This reflection originates from a comprehension of victimisation as described in numerous medical books (health victimology) (Battin et al. 2009).

The aforementioned theoretical framework may also be used to explain the processes of victimisation experienced by certain migrant and ethnic minority groups in some areas of Western Europe. Transnational migration over the past decades has contributed to the 'import' of ways of living, cultural and religious traditions and values from formerly colonised nation-states, including certain harmful traditional practices such as early marriages, female genital mutilation or honour killings. In addressing harmful customary practices in multicultural environments, the peculiarities of migration processes and the impact of different forms of oppression, abuse and violence that women and girls face in their everyday lives should not be underestimated or simply neglected (Longman and Coene 2015).

In Sub-Saharan Africa, the state and local governments should make laws that help discourage harmful cultural practices (Oriji and Ekechukwu 2015, 59). Laws are necessary, but not sufficient to stop these practices or enhance women's rights. The use of the law should be one component of a multidisciplinary approach aimed at empowering women and girls against harmful traditional practices and reducing their vulnerability to HIV infection. It is obvious that girls need to be empowered, above all through education, because they will be the women and mothers of tomorrow. Professionals designing programmes should employ the following key strategies in a human rights approach: first, promote a culture of opposition to all harmful traditional practices against females by using the media and involving males in addressing gender stereotypes and discriminatory values and norms which increase the risks faced by females; second, organise public education campaigns on the rights of women and girls and encourage the public to report cases of harmful traditional practices and gender-based violence to law enforcement agencies; third, enact laws and policies which make harmful traditional practices illegal and promote the rights of women to property, inheritance and a minimum age of marriage (Gbadamosi 2008, 3); fourth, eliminate harmful gender norms and practices through the engagement of men and boys in constructing alternative, non-violent masculinities oriented towards equality and respect by working with male role models and local leaders who promote healthy male sexuality and address male sexual entitlement, and by developing psychosocial support and counselling programmes for young boys who display early signs of sexually harmful behaviour (Fulu et al. 2013); and fifth, involve tradition-keepers (i.e. traditional healers, community and political leaders, faith-based leaders, and family elders) in implementing effective HIV prevention programmes that help harness negative local cultural practices into positive health practices which promote human rights and reduce the risk of HIV (Loosli 2004, 3–4). Thus, the international community must adopt these strategies to effectively challenge the sinister implications of such practices that violate the rights to health, life, dignity and personal integrity of many African women and girls (OHCHR 1995). If little is done in this regard, however, pervasive gender inequality, patriarchy and discrimination will undermine the progress in the HIV response for at least a generation (Cabal and Eba 2017).

Conclusion

This chapter has highlighted the growing concern within the international community regarding harmful customary practices as they violate the human rights of children and young women (Winter, Thompson, and Jeffreys 2002).

These rights include the right to life and health and the right to liberty and security (Special Representative of the Secretary-General on Violence against Children and Plan International 2012; Wadesango, Rembe, and Chabaya 2011). The right to security of the person comprises the right not to suffer any form of violence and in particular, recognises the need for children to receive appropriate protective measures (OHCHR 1995), but also it brings to light the need to ensure health security (WHO 2007). The World Health Report 2008 addresses, for example, the individual dimension of health security, concentrating on the role of primary health care in providing services that are centred on people's needs and expectations (WHO 2008b). On the other hand, the World Report 2007 is dedicated to promoting public health security at the global level by reducing the danger and impact of acute public health events that put at risk people's health across the world (WHO 2007).

In today's global society, professional experts and policymakers in the fields of public health, security studies, foreign policy and international relationships, development studies of United Nations agencies and others should work together because infectious diseases are spreading faster than ever before, being fuelled by the rapidity with which people travel across borders and continents. Therefore, international measures to prevent the spread of potential pandemic infectious diseases continue to be a priority in the twenty-first century (Aldis 2008; Quinn and Kumar 2014; WHO 2007). HIV is included in this priority as it is not only a health issue, a social issue, a development issue, an economic issue but also a security issue because it undermines the social, political and economic stability of entire countries and regional areas. These destabilising effects have been observed with particular intensity in developing countries, especially in Sub-Saharan Africa (Elbe 2006).

In the next chapter, crucial attention is given to better understanding the disease-security nexus and, in particular, the author addresses the challenges that HIV poses to the security and stability of the Sub-Saharan African region.

Chapter 6

The risk-security nexus

HIV, risk and social cohesion

Global health issues are often neglected as areas of interest in international relations around which the languages of risk and security have lately converged, particularly in the case of the HIV epidemic (Elbe 2008, 177). According to Ulrich Beck, risk can predict a future catastrophe, a perception that often ignores the very conditions that cause it; HIV is one such modern catastrophe. He defines risk as "a systematic way of dealing with hazards and insecurities induced and introduced by modernisation itself" (Beck 1992, 21). This definition considers the notion of risk as a synonym of hazard, danger or insecurity and then relates it to one specific set of historically novel dangers, those associated with modernisation. The concept of risk thus becomes analytically useful for Beck as a means of emphasising the existence of new global dangers such as environmental degradation or nuclear technology which are not caused by random acts of nature, but which are instead the fruit of human modernisation itself (Elbe 2008, 181). Beck notes that modern society is a risk society, namely a society which has become aware and apprehensive about the existence of these dangers, not only a society in which these dangers are present (Beck 1992, 21).

Within public health and policy debates, the notion of risk has come to dominate how the HIV epidemic is interpreted as a public health crisis in three important ways: as a hazard for individual lives, as a force with potentially negative or even devastating impacts on national economies and the management of the population in its demographic properties, and as a threat to institutions and organisations. From the perspective of risk management, one of the main aims is to keep under control the allocation of resources in order to make the strategies of prevention more effective (Burchardt 2007, 7). One of the most frequent observations in this context is that the epidemic affects the young and economically most productive generations (Heuveline 2004).

HIV undermines the cohesion of the social fabric which should capture the worth of intra-community dynamics. It weakens the social ties that unite people (i.e. organisations, institutions, key individuals, events, customs, and rituals) into a community, with the quality and strength of these ties determining the cohesiveness of the community (David and Li 2010). The HIV epidemic has developed in phases, each with its own peculiar impact on livelihoods, and each requiring diverse prevention and impact-mitigation strategies. In the initial phases, the impact is mainly felt at the family level and within specific populations. In a later phase (prevalence >5% in antenatal clinics) the healthcare system becomes overwhelmed, and community social cohesion is affected. When antenatal clinic levels surpass 20%, coping with problems at the community level becomes severe, social and economic effects are perceived in all areas of society, and national stability may be jeopardised (Farrington 2003).

HIV as a security issue

On 10 January 2000, the United Nations Security Council held its first-ever debate on a public health issue as a potential menace to international peace and security. This historic meeting was entitled: *The Situation in Africa: The Impact of AIDS on Peace and Security in Africa* (United Nations Security Council 2000a). Subsequently, among security specialists, especially in the United States of America, the conviction emerged that the stability of entire societies was threatened by the rapid growth of the HIV epidemic. An influential report compiled by the experts of the United States National Intelligence Council and entitled *The Global Infectious Disease Threat and its Implications for the United States* predicted a dark future for affected countries due to the following issues: the impact of HIV will likely aggravate and even provoke social fragmentation and political polarisation in the hardest-hit countries in the developing world; the relationship between infectious diseases and the political dimension is indirect but real. Infant mortality is correlated strongly with political instability, especially in countries that have achieved a certain extent of democratisation. The severe social and economic impact of HIV and the infiltration of the epidemic into the ruling political and military elites and middle classes of emerging countries will likely intensify the struggle for political power over the control of scarce state resources. The impact could hamper the development of a civil society and increase pressure on democratic transitions in Sub-Saharan Africa. This anticipated scenario, considered imminent in southern and parts of eastern Africa, was viewed as a serious danger to American national security (Gordon 2000).

A second scenario expanded the fear to a second group of countries: China, India, the Russian Federation, Ethiopia and Nigeria. It predicted a course of events similar to the first scenario, namely widespread epidemics and potential socio-political crises that, in turn, would threaten the security of the United States (Gordon 2002). Both scenarios did not unfold as predicted. HIV has threatened social stability only in the region of southern Africa where the epidemic is most advanced, and the fall in life expectancy is, in itself, a demographic tragedy (de Waal, Klot, and Manjari 2009, 27). In fact, state security, in most of southern Africa, is not only threatened by external dangers, but also by more insidious internal menaces, including diseases, many of which derive from the very weakness of the state and its lack of control over its own territory (Cilliers 2004). However, since the end of the Cold War, policymakers and scholars have increasingly begun to think about security as something more than an exclusive military defence of state interests (Pharoah and Schönteich 2003).

Taking into consideration the international debate on the effects of HIV on international peace and security and the aforementioned National Intelligence Council reports, the Clinton administration in 2000 declared HIV a national security threat. This crucial pronouncement pushed the United Nations Security Council to unanimously adopt, on 17 July 2000, historic resolution 1308: *The Responsibility of the Security Council in the Maintenance of International Peace and Security: HIV/AIDS and International Peacekeeping Operations*. Recognising for the first time the security implications of HIV, the resolution highlighted the potential threat the epidemic poses for international security, particularly in conflict and peacekeeping settings (United Nations Security Council 2000b).

The process of securitisation

The aforementioned events contributed in a decisive manner to starting the process of securitisation of HIV. Securitisation can be intended as a process-oriented conception of security which examines how a certain issue is transformed by an actor into a matter of security. The term was coined in 1995 by Ole Wæver who stated that the "use of the security label does not merely reflect whether a problem is a security problem, it is also a political choice, that is, a decision for conceptualisation in a special way" (Wæver 1995, 55). In the case of HIV, politicians can decide whether to depict the epidemic as a health issue (as human security theorists prefer), a development issue, or an international security issue (as national security experts prefer). If HIV is successfully securitised, then it is possible to legitimise extraordinary means to provide urgent and unprecedented responses. Surely, the fear and the anxiety climate of the post-9/11 period contributed to the securitisation of innumerable discourses. HIV did not elude this tendency, and as a result it received amplified attention and more international resources (Gündüz 2006, 56–57).

The process of securitisation is mainly promoted by the language of risk which it draws upon in at least three ways. Firstly, risk plays a constitutive role in making HIV a security issue. The epidemic is articulated as a long-term security risk, rather than as an immediate security threat. Thus, immediate action is necessary in order to avoid that the epidemic develops serious national and international security implications in the future (Elbe 2008, 180). HIV remains an actual menace to the life opportunities of millions of citizens. Future scenarios, African and global, must consider protracted risks such as new, adaptive and more dangerous strains of HIV. The capacity of HIV to assume new forms and develop resistance to current therapies should be cause for enduring vigilance. This is also due to peculiar long-term features of the human immunodeficiency virus which will produce significant health, social, political and economic effects for generations to come (de Waal, Klot, and Manjari 2009, 28).

Secondly, the language of risk and security is used for identifying a population at special risk of exposure to STIs, including HIV. In most regions, international peacekeeping personnel are recognised as a key population at higher risk of HIV exposure. Such personnel are also viewed as significant partners for responding to HIV and addressing sexual violence in armed conflict. However, the rate of HIV infection among peacekeepers tends to mirror the one present among young men of analogous age groups in their countries of origin. HIV prevalence among uniformed services (including police) does not significantly diverge from that of the rest of the population, with the exception of some countries in Sub-Saharan Africa, but not, as was claimed in 2000, two to five times higher than in comparable civilian populations. The incidence of HIV infection tends to increase in relation to the duration of deployment in a mission area. This relationship makes the strengthening of HIV prevention strategies necessary when troops are deployed. The success of certain HIV prevention schemes in the military is due to strategies which assign the responsibility to the military command for implementing the HIV policy as well as to the health and social services. Both carry out their tasks under the supervision of the United Nations Department of Peacekeeping Operations (DPKO), which is charged with the planning, preparation, management and direction of UN peacekeeping operations (UNAIDS and DPKO 2011a, 59–60). Peacekeeper induction training on HIV awareness grew about sevenfold between 2005 and the end of 2010. In the same period, the number of peacekeepers in field missions increased from 69,838 to almost 100,000. The interventions have focused on reducing risks for peacekeeping missions but also for host communities. Special training modules have been provided on gender and sexual violence, sexual exploitation and abuse, and children and women protection and support issues. These modules are also incorporated into the mandatory United Nations Standardized Generic Training Modules for United Nations Peacekeeping for nations contributing troops and police. More than 1,500 peacekeeping officers were trained as HIV peer educators in 2010 (Ibid., 25–27).

Lastly, military personnel, and peacekeepers in particular, could themselves become vectors of transmission both to host populations and from host populations to troop-contributing nations (de Waal, Klot, and Manjari 2009, 28). There are a number of factors exclusive to the military setting which could raise the risk of HIV infection among troops, especially during wartime: being extremely mobile, being young and sexually active, being away from home and partners for long periods of time, being indoctrinated into a military culture which encourages aggressiveness and risk-taking behaviours (i.e. sex without a condom, sex with multiple partners, coercive sex) as significant characteristics of effective combat soldiers, being violent actors because of the consumption of high levels of alcohol and drugs, and being richer than the local population as a structural condition which allows soldiers to buy sex on an on-going basis (Fourie and Schönteich 2001, 36–37). Moreover, military forces sometimes use rape as a weapon of war as well. During times of conflict, sexual violence is abetted by high levels of alcohol and drug use by soldiers far removed, both physically and psychologically, from the commonly accepted social norms. Mass rapes can facilitate the outburst of HIV epidemics (Chowdhury and Lanier 2012).

In this situation, it is logical that policymakers from lower-incidence countries (Western countries) might be reluctant to deploy their troops in the areas of high incidence, fearing that these military forces not only risk being infected but also that they might spread HIV once they return home. In addition, there is indeed a risk that infected peacekeeping troops (mainly African) will not be accepted by international agencies such as the United Nations and the African Union or that the country in need of these troops refuses to welcome them. These decisions can compromise the establishment of any process of stabilisation in a conflict area (Chemical and Biological Arms Control Institute and Center for Strategic and International Studies 2000).

As mentioned, the contribution of wars to the spread of STIs is well documented. Military conflicts lead to risky behavioural patterns which can abet the spread of epidemics, including HIV. However, what is less analysed is the reverse, the potential contribution of HIV to the spread of wars. HIV can be considered as an accelerant factor to the social, ethnic and political tensions which, in turn, have historically led to intrastate and interstate conflicts in Sub-Saharan Africa. Theoretically, HIV can facilitate warfare in three different ways. Firstly, HIV erodes the social, economic and political fabric of countries in transition, increasing thus instability and unrest at all levels of society. Secondly, HIV generates political constituencies whose demands cannot be met by leadership, thereby fuelling political disorders. Lastly, the HIV epidemic has resulted in the development of new scarce medical aid of vital importance (i.e. antiretroviral therapy) whose unequal distribution can exacerbate existing social and/or ethnic tensions. Consequently, the overlapping of all three of these situations is an overwhelming burden which can feed resentments and hatreds and push fragile societies into conflict and long-term disputes (Cheek 2001).

Human security approach

The unprecedented meetings of the United Nations Security Council have proved crucial in terms of placing the global HIV epidemic on the international security agenda. This tendency was confirmed by Resolution 1983 (2011) in which the Security Council reaffirmed its previous commitment to address the HIV epidemic as a threat to international peace and security. In particular, through the resolution, the Council underlined several aspects. First, the necessity of an urgent and concerted international action in order to curb the impact of the HIV epidemic in war and post-conflict situations. Second, the need for a coordinated programme at local, national, regional and international levels to lessen the HIV impact and the necessity of the UN's intervention to support Member States to address this issue. Third, the encouragement to incorporate HIV awareness, prevention, treatment, care and support; including voluntary confidential counselling and testing schemes and policies in the implementation of peacekeeping mandates. These policies are provided in the context of assistance to national institutions, security sector reform and disarmament, demobilisation and reintegration processes, with particular regard to vulnerable people, including women and girls. Fourth, the Council also underlined the need to strengthen HIV-prevention strategies within United Nations missions and encouraged constant mutual aid among Member States through their significant national bodies and uniformed and civilian personnel engaged in UN peacekeeping operations. Lastly, the Council stressed the implementation of a policy of zero tolerance towards sexual exploitation and abuse in missions (United Nations Security Council 2011).

This last resolution reaffirms the tangible interconnections between health, conflict and security issues. HIV poses a serious threat to the operational abilities of armies and across the uniformed services in humanitarian emergencies, conflict and post-conflict situations (Heinecken 2001; Ostergard Jr. 2002). Nevertheless, the HIV epidemic cannot be treated like a traditional security threat, which is an integral part of a strategic and military domain, but must be interpreted as a menace which goes beyond the traditional, including economic, environmental, health and political dimensions. This tendency emerged as a consequence of the United Nations Development Programme (UNDP) report, which advanced the new concept of human security (de Waal, Klot, and Manjari 2009, 29). The report defined human security as "safety from such chronic threats as hunger, disease and repression" as well as "protection from sudden and hurtful disruptions in the patterns of daily life – whether in homes, in jobs or in communities" (UNDP 1994, 23). This concept includes a departure from a traditional international relations security notion, where the state is the main referent object to a holistic vision, where people and their interrelated social and economic milieu obtain pre-eminence over states (Thomas 2001, 161). As a result, in the notion of human security, the focus is on the security of individuals and communities, and the state has the duty to defend people and their rights. Jennifer Hadingham, a South African pedagogy expert of the University of Witwatersrand (Johannesburg), confirms this interpretation asserting that HIV poses a "pervasive and non-violent threat to the existence of individuals, as the virus significantly shortens life expectancy, undermines quality of life and limits participation in income-generating activities. The political, social and economic consequences are equally detrimental to the community, in turn undermining its security" (Hadingham 2000, 120). The innovative people-centric concept of human security changed the basic idea of security, connecting security itself with citizens rather than territories and with sustainable human development rather than weapons (Tadjbakhsh and Chenoy 2007). The two principal components of human security were "freedom from fear" and "freedom from want" (UNDP 1994, 24). These twin ends of protection and empowerment symbolise the core principles of guaranteeing survival, basic human needs and human dignity (Gündüz 2006, 53).

The intention of human security is to capture the post-Cold War peace dividend and redirect those resources in the direction of an agenda of development (Department of Foreign Affairs and International Trade 1999). Hubert expands this conceptualisation, stating that, like other security ideas (domestic, economic and food security), human security concerns protection. This implies the adoption of precautionary measures to reduce vulnerability and contain risk, but also the implementation of corrective actions where prevention fails. In his conceptualisation, Hubert cites two out of seven threats to human security: economic security (poverty, unemployment, homelessness), food security (undernourishment, famine, hunger), health security (disease, infections, ineffective healthcare), environmental security (degradation, pollution, natural disasters), personal security (physical torture, war, crime, aggression, violence), community security (ethnic and race tensions, oppression, discrimination) and political security (repression, torture, ill-treatment, human rights abuses) (Hubert 1999, 25–33).

However, although the human security approach has contributed to placing HIV on the global agenda, the traditional national security issue still appears to be most significant in worldwide security plans and funds. There are persistent and strong doubts about HIV as a real danger to national security (except in southern Africa countries), thus the focus is always on state stability and democratic governance (Bedeski 1999). A number of scholars have examined the potential impact of HIV on security and democracy, asserting that the HIV epidemic can be considered as a destabilising factor in heavily-affected regions, as well as the impact of insecurity and anti-democratic forces on accelerating the spread of HIV or of democracy and governance on slowing that spread. Very little literature contains substantive proof of these predictions while the vast majority of sources are theoretical or conceptual speculations. The latter are based on the available epidemiological data and knowledge of political regimes, democratic theory, international relations and related issues (Manning 2002, 1).

The impact of AIDS on democratic processes

Alan Whiteside (1998) lists a number of ways that AIDS could impact democracy. He emphasised how the illness and death of young adults will impact negatively on society because these events generate a loss of human capital, or a waste of resources invested in education, training and experience. The increasing number of children orphaned by AIDS, he argues, will be a potential long-term threat to stability and development, while illness and death within military and police ranks may endanger order and security. Without a clear and effective political leadership, and in the face of an economic crisis, the epidemic, with its related stigma, could cause social instability, lead to blame and anomie in society, and infringe human rights. He also adds that it will result in government inefficiency and economic stagnation.

Another detailed analysis of the impact of AIDS on democracy and governance is provided by Samantha Willan (2000), who attempts to address the potential impact of AIDS on democratic governance. She emphasises five areas which together might lead to the collapse of democracy. The first of five categories is the increase in budget demands, stemming from growing demands on health and welfare systems and connected to a crowding-out of non-healthcare related spending. The second is a concurrent diminution in the tax base, as AIDS decimates the economically-productive sectors of society. The third is the imminent crisis of leadership because young political and economic leaders are being wiped out by AIDS. The fourth category is the significant lessening of citizen support and participation in democratic governance due to the fact that more people develop terminal diseases and are taken out of the public sphere. The last category concerns a progressive decrease in citizen compliance (i.e. payment of taxes) as the consequence of diminishing incentives for the observance of rules and expanding conditions of poverty and desperation.

Jeremy Youde (2007) underlines a theoretical link between disease and democratic stability and legitimacy in Sub-Saharan states. AIDS, he argues, can aggravate social cleavages and group tensions, and also undermine the state capacity to efficiently manage power and contribute to institutional fragility.

The paper's principal topic focuses on three ways by which AIDS could undermine democracy: by hindering the organisation and administration of elections and undermining their legitimacy, delaying economic development and weakening civil society.

Kondwani Chirambo (2004) notes that the disease may reduce the capacity of African governments to strengthen their often fragile democratic systems, attacking economic growth and reducing the responsiveness of governance institutions. Robert Mattes (2003) deepens this second aspect emphasising that the epidemic is likely to devastate large portions of policy-makers, national legislators, local councillors, election officials, soldiers and civil servants including doctors, nurses, teachers, ambulance drivers, firefighters and the police. He continues to point out that besides killing an increasing number of public servants and elected officials, the epidemic could harshly impact on the process of political institutionalism. A shrinking proportion of civil servants, policymakers, and legislators will have been at their positions long enough to acquire the necessary skills, experience and professionalism. It will be even more complicated for parliaments, ministries and government agencies to effectively perform their tasks. There will only be fewer qualified bureaucrats available to instruct younger staff on key formal skills (such as planning, budgeting, cost-benefit analysis, monitoring and assessment and staff management) or pass on more informal standard operational procedures or norms such as administrative accountability, bureaucratic neutrality and impartiality, and ethical conduct. Furthermore, Mattes calls attention to the fact that the epidemic could also have a deleterious effect on national, regional and local law-making procedures given that AIDS causes rapid turnover both among elected members as well as among parliamentary researchers, administrative assistants and clerks.

HIV prevalence and state weakness

Previous studies highlighted the existence of a strict relationship between high rates of HIV infection and state fragility. Fragility is a condition produced by certain casual factors that can be seen as both causes and characteristics of it. In the literature, the following four groups of factors are the most widespread: structural and economic factors, political and institutional factors, social factors and international factors. Structural and economic factors include poverty, low income and economic crises, violent conflict, the existence of armed rebels, natural resource wealth or lack thereof, interstate tensions and demographic pressure. Political and institutional factors embrace legitimacy and authority crises, bad governance, suppression of political freedom, weak institutions, political transitions and neo-patrimonial politics. Social factors comprise horizontal and gender inequalities, processes of individual fragmentation and social exclusion, deficient social cohesion (including lack of social capital) and weak civil society. International factors take account of the legacy of colonialism, international strategies of political economy, climate change and global economic crises (Mcloughlin 2010, 16).

Accumulated experience and recent data refute any positive correlation between HIV prevalence and state fragility. On the contrary, a rise in HIV prevalence is (insignificantly) associated with diminished fragility. The AIDS, Security and Conflict Initiative makes this finding clear, both methodologically and substantively, with three main explanations. The first is that current measures of state fragility tend to concentrate on macroeconomic indicators of state capacity to administer development funds, while the most severe impacts of HIV will be felt at household and community levels. The second motivation concerns the yet unmeasured costs and the effects of unpaid services that women and girls disproportionately offer in caring for persons living with HIV. The third explanation underlines how current indicators of state fragility tend to measure state capacity to respond to human calamities, including epidemic diseases, over the short or medium-term, whereas HIV is most visible over the long-term (de Waal, Klot, and Manjari 2009, 35–36).

The fragile state concept is widely used in peacebuilding and state-building. Until now, the notion, as well as its use, has been the subject of animated debate. An internationally agreed definition of what is meant by "fragile state" does not exist (Faria 2011, 1). Most development agencies define it as a crucial collapse of the state in performing its key functions: assuring basic security, maintaining the rule of law and justice, and providing basic services and economic opportunities for citizens (Department for International Development 2005, 9). In essence, they have largely adopted a functional approach which associates state fragility to bad governance and weak state will or capacity (Mcloughlin 2010, 16). Frances Stewart and Graham Brown (2010) advance a three-pronged definition of fragility which aims to include all other definitions approximately. Fragility is then defined as depicting a state that is failing or at high risk of failing in three dimensions: authority failures, service failures and legitimacy failures. The first happens when the state does not have the authority to protect its citizens from different forms of violence. The second occurs when the state is not able to ensure that all citizens have access to basic services. The last takes place when the state is deficient in legitimacy, enjoys limited popular support, and is usually not democratic.

HIV and law enforcement

HIV among law enforcement institutions, and especially the police, remains an underexplored issue, despite the fact that they face significant risks of exposure to HIV (Crofts and Patterson 2016). The first global workshop on HIV and the police was organised in 2007. It emphasised specific vulnerabilities in these forces and the potential role of police and law enforcement agencies in overall state responses and recommended that tailored strategies be identified and put into practice, and United Nations Office on Drugs and Crime (UNODC) together reviewed police practices with most vulnerable populations affected by HIV programming interventions for their personnel. In Latin America, UNODC has implemented, with the support of the UNAIDS Cosponsors Regional Group, a regional observatory on HIV and prisons. In 2009, the Asian representatives of police and law enforcement members of the Pacific area established the Asia and Pacific Regional Network on Police and AIDS. This network organised a regional strategy about how police can intervene to build an enabling environment for HIV programmes among key populations at higher risk of HIV exposure (UNAIDS and DPKO 2011a, 45). In addition, during the same year, Professor Nick Crofts, director of the Centre for Law Enforcement and Public Health in Melbourne, and internationally recognised expert in the field, founded the Law Enforcement and HIV Network (LEAHN). Specifically, LEAHN is a global network of police and health professionals with a focus on HIV prevention (Crofts and Jardine 2016, 9-11).

Issues regarding the police and human immunodeficiency virus fall into two principal areas. The first analyses how police institutions react to HIV within their ranks and the second describes how policing methods influence national HIV epidemics and responses (de Waal, Klot, and Manjari 2009, 77). With reference to the first area, the technical nature of police work creates certain weaknesses. A great deal of experience, skills and personal information could be lost because of staff with HIV retiring from service or dying, and these skills would take years to replace. The police depend on staff with specialist skills, such as detectives, personnel involved in judicial processes and liaison, handwriting experts, and other technical staff, who require specialised (often foreign) training and are hard to replace. A number of organisational factors could be negatively impacted by the epidemic. These include a tendency towards hierarchy that prevents sharing of information and teamwork, the provision of generous funeral benefits, and lenient sick and compassionate leave policies that are financially costly and make it difficult to replace staff (Institute for Security Studies and Malawi Institute for Management 2003, 11).

With regard to the second area, the focus is on the expression "policing the epidemic", namely the way law enforcement practices shape the risk environment and, in turn, influence the course of the epidemic (de Waal, Klot, and Manjari 2009, 77). Civilian police forces that play a part in international peacekeeping operations face the same problems and constraints as their military counterparts in such missions; indeed they may even be less prepared and more exposed to the risk of contracting HIV because of their direct and sometimes violent engagement with the local population. Law enforcement officers have direct and incessant forefront contact with a range of key populations at higher risk of HIV exposure, including people who inject drugs, sex workers, street children, trafficked women, illegal migrants, survivors of sexual abuse and rape, and others, such as detainees and prisoners. Where HIV prevalence is higher among such populations, policing practices can have a decisive function in either preventing or accelerating HIV. In addition, in conflict-affected situations, the police may provide protection from conflict-related sexual violence and develop appropriate norms of conduct. Their responses can either raise or minimise the risk of exposure to HIV (UNAIDS and DPKO 2011b, 17).

Although research shows a higher incidence of infection among African police members than among African citizens in some African countries (Kershaw 2008, 21), this finding cannot be generalised due to a lack of reliable data. In South Africa, for example, police officers may run a higher risk of exposure to HIV than their international colleagues due to two main causes: the first, the presence of one of the most elevated levels of violence on the planet (Abrahams 2010) and, the second, the biggest and most high-profile HIV epidemic in the world, with an estimated 7.7 million people living with HIV in 2018 (UNAIDS 2020).

In South Africa, as in many countries with generalised epidemics, the high HIV prevalence rates are caused in part by people, including police, having unprotected sex with multiple partners (Kirby et al. 2012). Specifically, in the South African police there is a culture of acceptance and practice of having multiple sexual partners, which is believed to be indicative of virility and masculinity. Since many police members are deployed in areas distant from their homes, they often reside in communal hostels. These often lack recreational facilities, and other stress-relieving structures, resulting in police members opting to engage in sexual relationships outside of their marriages or steady relationships (Masuku 2007, 2).

The South African Police Service (SAPS) celebrated 20 years of policing under democratic rule in 2015. In 1995, the SAPS was given a constitutional mandate to protect the citizens of South Africa, uphold and enforce the law and maintain public order (SAPS Strategy, Research, Monitoring and Evaluation 2015, VI). SAPS, however, risks becoming an ineffective institution which is not able to perform its duties fully. Policing and investigation work demand practice and experience, which are necessary to collect different forms of evidence so that a convincing case may be prosecuted before a court. HIV places additional strains on the shrinking number of experienced officers and detectives. A rapid loss of skills means fewer teachers for new recruits and a concomitant increase in the burden placed on experienced police officers (Schönteich 2003, 4).

The HIV epidemic has caused a significant reduction in the number of police officials engaged to carry out clear-cut patrolling tasks on the street. This problematic situation along with a complex process of reorganisation of the police sector can produce a negative effect on investigation strategies, crime prevention approaches and public order policies, which are all based on an efficient community policing model. As a consequence, there could be a growth of street crimes and gang activities across the country over the next years, which could endanger the safety of every South African citizen (Leggett 2002, 23).

Conclusion

This chapter has identified a number of themes of particular relevance, including police officers' fear and risk of occupational HIV transmission (Flavin 1998). Moreover, one should not forget the key role that each police department plays in implementing educational strategies targeting law enforcement officers, specifically at how to prevent casual transmission of HIV during policing activities (National AIDS Trust 2014). To demonstrate this, it is instructive to illustrate the various interventions that the South African Police Service (SAPS) has decided to promote in support of all its employees, including the categories of employees identified as being at high risk of contracting HIV and related diseases (e.g. detectives, functional police members, forensic scientists, and fingerprint experts) (SAPS Strategic Management 2018, 286). These interventions are guided by the following key strategic objectives: first, social and structural approaches to HIV, STI and TB prevention, care and impact (e.g. empowering police officers who operate in various informal settlements, rural and hard-to-reach areas such as farms and ports of entry with knowledge on HIV). Second, preventing new HIV, STI and TB infections (e.g. establishing HIV and TB supporting groups, peer education programmes and HIV, STI and TB awareness-raising activities). Third, providing health and wellness screening, including HIV counselling and testing (e.g. worksite health and wellness screening/assessment sessions in partnership with recognised medical aid plans and accredited healthcare professionals and registration on the various disease risk management programmes). Fourth, protection of human rights and promotion of access to justice (e.g. programmes to reduce HIV-related stigma and discrimination among SAPS employees). Fifth, providing care and support services (health and wellness assessments) (e.g. encouraging rigorous HIV counselling, screening and testing sessions in collaboration with approved external experts, facilitation of HIV, TB and other related support groups, and promotion of safe and consistent condom use as well as male and female condom distribution at all police stations to prevent new infections and re-infection). Sixth, peer education programmes (e.g. recruiting and training new peer educators to produce a change in knowledge, attitudes, beliefs and behaviours associated with HIV, peer support, sharing information and referral, and sustaining the use of coaching, mentoring and peer-network mechanism support). Seventh, information, education and communication (e.g. organising HIV workshops and awareness sessions at police stations, celebrating World AIDS Day and AIDS Memorial Day to discuss HIV prevention, education and treatment in the police community, and marketing and exhibition by using internal communication mediums such as the satellite-based television network of the SAPS, known as POL TV, the Police magazine, the Intranet and salary advice, posters, pamphlets, flyers). Lastly, governance (e.g., organising strategies and related policies, developing effective guidelines and standard operating procedures, and creating constructive partnerships and stakeholder relations such as the South African Police Service Medical Scheme, Government Employees Medical Scheme, Department of Public Service and Administration, Safety and Security Sector Education and Training Authority) (SAPS Strategic Management 2016, 286). The rationale of all these measures is to make sure that the workplace is safe, and that police officers are not at risk of getting infected with HIV at work (Beletsky et al. 2011).

Final considerations

The growing efficiency of pharmaceutical treatments employed over the past few years has produced encouraging results on the anti-HIV front (Iacob, Iacob, and Jugulete 2017), although there is a growing concern for the situation in many countries of Africa, Latin America and the ex-Soviet Union (Kharsany and Karim 2016; Ortblad et al. 2019; Luz, Veloso, and Grinsztejn 2019; Blue 2018). The unprecedented challenge posed by the epidemic for the international community calls for global cooperation aimed at evaluating the diverse aspects of the issues that many actors in this tragic drama must deal with (Hein, Bartsch, and Kohlmorgen 2007). The WHO and UNAIDS and other international organisations are working towards achieving the right objectives, as their work underpins an internationally-accepted policy which concerns the ways in which the designated authorities of the various governments should develop a public health intervention strategy (Jönsson 2010). It is, however, evident that this strategy will be effective only if it is applied with respect for human rights, of which the right to health is an integral part (Enoch and Piot 2017).

In general, when an observer takes a sick person into consideration, he or she wonders about the causes of the disease, but the explanations he or she may find will seldom implicate the person suffering from the disease as being responsible (Levy 2018). Judgments on responsibility are linked to the debasement of the other; the more a person is held responsible for a negative event that has occurred to them, the more they are debased. If this responsibility can absolutely not be invoked, then we are in the presence of a blameless victim (Furedi 2004, 191). The complete absence of objective responsibility can lead to a debasement of an HIV-positive individual (Kontomanolis et al. 2017). In other cases, individual responsibility is always partially inherent to various extents. For example, in the case of people with colorectal cancer, responsibility can only be partially invoked on the basis of a risk-taking behaviour such as cigarette smoking (Gram et al. 2009; Parajuli et al. 2014). In the case of HIV, individual responsibility is more implicit than in cancer. However, when the infected person cannot be held responsible, attempts are made to identify a plausible explanation (Seacat and Hirschman 2011).

It sometimes occurs that society needs to have a disease to blame in order to accuse its victims of every kind of vileness. HIV probably plays this role; a role which is not so different from that of other diseases, such as the plague, typhus, cholera, syphilis, or more recently, cancer. HIV reawakens ancient fears, dormant thanks to advances in medicine: fear of infection, the epidemic and body degeneration. The sudden onset of HIV, the oddness of the virus and the designation of key populations at higher risk of HIV exposure are further elements which have disarmed cancer of its terrifying significance and have somehow put it into its right perspective (Sontag 2001). These key populations, identified by UNAIDS as gay men and other men who have sex with men, sex workers, transgender people and people who inject drugs, have the highest risk of contracting and transmitting HIV, and, at the same time, they frequently lack adequate access to prevention, care, and treatment services because their behaviours are often stigmatised, and even criminalised (Beardsley 2013).

The comprehensible HIV-associated infection alert does not suffice to legitimise state intervention on sexual morality aimed at limiting the sexual freedom of some categories of individuals such as persons who exchange sex for money or nonmonetary items. The maker of criminal laws must find a balance between the scope of crime prevention and the safeguard of an individual's civil rights and liberties. However, there should be an uncompromising refusal on behalf of the state to nurture risky behaviours in society through illiberal provisions which could reward irrational and emotional reactions, even if these were shared by most of the population. The state cannot use criminal law as a weapon in ethicising initiatives aimed at promoting specific lifestyles and prosecuting conducts which are discretionally considered immoral or asocial. Choosing a criminal policy would not only not be effective in addressing HIV, but would actually be gravely counterproductive, as it would generate the false impression that criminal laws could resolve HIV-related health issues and also contrast with an effective preventive strategy based on a rational political-and-health-information promotion (Wainberg 2009).

In some countries, criminal law is being applied to those who transmit or expose others to HIV (WHO 2006; Kazatchkine 2010; Chen 2016). Laws criminalising the transmission of HIV risk bringing within the scope of legal sanction HIV-positive people who are behaving in ways that do not deserve a penalty and may as a result of prosecution face adverse human rights consequences (Brown, Hanefeld, and Welsh 2009). The issue of fundamental importance is that of adopting a preventive, non-repressive programme which gives value to the role, albeit limited, of the penal sanction in defending intangible goods such as individual safety and public health (Cameron 2009). UNAIDS urges governments to limit criminalisation of cases of intentional transmission (for example, when a person knows his or her HIV-positive status and deliberately acts to transmit the human immunodeficiency virus (HIV) to another person). The two principal reasons advanced for criminalising HIV transmission are to punish harmful conduct by imposing criminal penalties and prevent HIV transmission by deterring or changing any behaviour that potentially exposes people to a significant risk of harm. However, criminal law enforcement of HIV transmission does not reach these objectives, except in the rare cases of deliberate or intentional HIV transmission. Extending criminal accountability beyond the aforementioned cases should be avoided as it could expose large sectors of the population to possible prosecution without their being able to foresee their liability for such prosecution. The overly broad application of criminal law to HIV transmission is likely to disproportionately impact on members of marginalised groups, such as sex workers, men who have sex with men, and people who inject drugs. These groups are often accused of transmitting HIV, despite inadequate access to HIV prevention, treatment, care and support services, and risk being further victimised by stigma and discrimination processes (UNAIDS 2013).

In conclusion, I argue that the basic idea that inspires this book is the need to develop a socio-criminological analysis of the multiple dimensions of the HIV epidemic in order to contribute significantly to the current international debate on infectious diseases. The concept of social interaction constitutes an original interpretive lens capable of bringing out the multifaceted nature of the virus. First, the role of social interaction in HIV healing and its implications, both bio-medically and socially are addressed respectively in Chapter 1, Chapter 2 and Chapter 3. Secondly, interactional processes are also particularly important to the gender system because of the extremely elevated frequency of interactions between men and women, including offender-victim interactions in sexually abusive and/or coercive relationships and HIV-related infection risks as examined in Chapter 4 and 5 (Qiao et al. 2015; Ridgeway and Smith-Lovin 1996, 173). Finally, Chapter 6 focuses on the interaction between security and public health in the context of the HIV epidemic according to a global perspective (Dijkstra and De Ruijter 2017; McInnes 2006).

Bibliography

Abong'o, Ngore Vitalis. 2014. "The Socio-Cultural Changes in the Kenyan Luo Society since the British Invasion and the Effects on the Levirate Custom: A Critical Survey." *Research on Humanities and Social Sciences* 4 (18): 1–8.

Abrahams, David. 2010. "A Synopsis of Urban Violence in South Africa." *International Review of the Red Cross* 92, no. 878 (June): 495–520.

Abubakar, Amina, and Patricia Kitsao-Wekulo. 2015. "Gender and Health Inequalities in Sub-Saharan Africa: the Case of HIV." In *Psychology of Gender through the Lens of Culture: Theories and Applications*, edited by Saba Safdar and Natasza Kosakowska-Berezecka, 395–408. New York, NY: Springer.

Africa Check. 2017. "Factsheet: South Africa's Crime Statistics for 2016/17." Last modified 24 October, 2017. https://africacheck.org/factsheets/south-africas-crime-statistics-201617/.

African Commission on Human and Peoples' Rights. 2018. *HIV, the Law and Human Rights in the African Human Rights System: Key Challenges and Opportunities for Rights-Based Responses*. Geneva: Joint United Nations Programme on HIV and AIDS. https://www.unaids.org/en/resources/documents/2018/HIV_Law_AfricanHumanRightsSystem.

Aggleton, Peter, Kate Wood, Anne Malcolm, Richard Parker, and Miriam Maluwa. 2005. *HIV-Related Stigma, Discrimination and Human Rights Violations: Case Studies of Successful Programmes*. Geneva: Joint United Nations Programme on HIV and AIDS. https://www.unaids.org/en/resources/documents/2005/20051005_jc999-humrightsviol_en.pdf.

Agot, Kawango E., Ann Vander Stoep, Melissa Tracy, Billy A. Obare, Elizabeth A. Bukusi, Jeckoniah O. Ndinya-Achola, Stephen Moses, and Noel S. Weiss. 2010. "Widow Inheritance and HIV Prevalence in Bondo District, Kenya: Baseline Results from a Prospective Cohort Study." *PLOS One* 5 (11): e14028. https://doi.org/10.1371/journal.pone.0014028.

Ahmadu, Fuambai. 2000. "Rites and Wrongs: An Insider/Outsider Reflects on Power and Excision." In *Female 'Circumcision' in Africa: Culture, Controversy, and Change*, edited by Bettina Shell-Duncan and Ylva Hernlund, 283–312. Boulder, CO: Lynne Rienner Publishers.

Ahonsi, Babatunde, Nahla Tawab, Scott Geibel, Sam Kalibala, Jerry Okal, Babacar Mane, Nathi Sohaba, Julialynne Walker, and Eric Green. 2014. *HIV/AIDS Vulnerabilities, Discrimination, and Service Accessibility among Africa's Youth: Insights from a Multi-Country Study*. Abuja, Nigeria: Population Council.

Akers, Timothy, and Mark M. Lanier. 2009. "'Epidemiological Criminology': Coming Full Circle." *American Journal of Public Health* 99, no. 3 (March): 397–402.

Akins, Chana K. 2004. "The Role of Pavlovian Conditioning in Sexual Behavior: A Comparative Analysis of Human and Nonhuman Animals." *International Journal of Comparative Psychology* 17 (2): 241–262.

Albert, Edward. 1986. "Illness and Deviance: The Response of the Press to AIDS." In *The Social Dimensions of AIDS: Method and Theory*, edited by

Douglas A. Feldman and Thomas M. Johnson, 163–178. New York, NY: Praeger Publishers.

Aldis, William. 2008. "Health Security as a Public Health Concept: A Critical Analysis." *Health Policy and Planning* 23, no. 6 (November): 369–375.

Aliouat-Denis, Cécile-Marie, Magali Chabé, Christine Demanche, El Moukhtar Aliouat, Eric Viscogliosi, Jacques Guillot, Laurence Delhaes, and Eduardo Dei-Cas. 2008. "Pneumocystis Species, Co-evolution and Pathogenic Power." *Infection, Genetics and Evolution* 8, no. 5 (September): 708–726.

Allen, W. David. 2007. "The Reporting and Underreporting of Rape." *Southern Economic Journal* 73, no. 3 (January): 623–641.

Allinder, Sara M., and Janet Fleischman. 2019. "The World's Largest HIV Epidemic in Crisis: HIV in South Africa." Center for Strategic and International Studies. Last modified April 2, 2019. https://www.csis.org/analysis/worlds-largest-hiv-epidemic-crisis-hiv-south-africa.

Altman, Dennis. 1998. "HIV, Homophobia, and Human Rights." *Health Human Rights* 2 (4): 15–22.

Altman, Lawrence K. 1982. "New Homosexual Disorder Worries Health Officials." *The New York Times,* May 11, 1982. http://www.nytimes.com/1982/05/11/science/new-homosexual-disorder-worries-health-officials.html?pagewanted=all.

Amin, Avni. 2013. *16 Ideas for Addressing Violence against Women in the Context of the HIV epidemic: A Programming Tool.* Geneva: World Health Organization. https://www.who.int/reproductivehealth/publications/violence/vaw_hiv_epidemic/en/.

Amuri, Mbaraka, Steve Mitchell, Anne Cockcroft, and Neil Andersson. 2011. "Socio-Economic Status and HIV/AIDS Stigma in Tanzania." *AIDS Care* 23 (3): 378–382.

Amy, Jean-Jacques. 2008. "Certificates of Virginity and Reconstruction of the Hymen." *European Journal of Contraception & Reproductive Health Care* 13 (2): 111–113.

Andersen, Nic. 2018. "Shocking Stats Reveal 41% of Rapes in SA Are against Children." The South African. Last modified May 18, 2018. https://www.thesouthafrican.com/news/rape-statistics-41-children/.

Anderson, Bebe J. 2009. "HIV Stigma and Discrimination Persist, Even in Health Care." *Virtual Mentor* 11 (12): 998–1001. https://doi.org/10.1001/virtualmentor.2009.11.12.oped1-0912.

Anderson, Michelle J. 2000. "Rape in South Africa." *Georgetown Journal of Gender and the Law* 1, no. 3 (Summer): 789–821.

Aranda, Florencia. 2008. "Intersections between HIV and Violence against Adolescent and Young Women." In *The Multiple Faces of the Intersections between HIV and Violence against Women,* edited by Aracely Barahona-Strittmatter and Dynis Luciano, 28–33. Washington, DC: Development Connections. https://genderandaids.unwomen.org/en/resources/2008/11/the-multiple-faces-of-the-intersections-between-hiv-and-violence-against-women.

Arkell, Camille, and Mallory Harrigan. 2018. *Condoms for the Prevention of HIV Transmission.* Toronto, ON: Canadian AIDS Treatment Information Exchange. https://www.catie.ca/en/fact-sheets/prevention/condoms.

Arluke, Arold. 1988. "The Sick-Role Concept." In *Health Behavior: Emerging Research Perspectives*, edited by David S. Gochman, 169–180. New York, NY: Plenum Press.

Armstrong, Sue. 1993. "South Africa's Rape Epidemic Fuels HIV." *WorldAIDS*, no. 27 (May): 1.

Artz, Lilian, Patrick Burton, Catherine L. Ward, Lezanne Leoschut, Joanne Phyfer, Sam Lloyd, Reshma Kassanjee, and Cara Le Mottee. 2016. *Sexual Victimisation of Children in South Africa. Final Report of the Optimus Foundation Study: South Africa*. Cape Town: UBS Optimus Foundation. http://www.ci.uct.ac.za/overview-violence/reports/sexual-victimisation-of-children-in-SA.

Australasian Society for HIV Medicine and National Centre in HIV Social Research. 2012. *Stigma and Discrimination around HIV and HCV in Healthcare Settings: Research Report*. Sydney: Australasian Society for HIV Medicine. http://www.ashm.org.au/resources/Pages/1976963391.aspx.

Ayala, George, Judy Chang, Rebecca Matheson, Laurel Sprague, and Ruth Morgan Thomas. 2017. *Reconsidering Primary Prevention of HIV: New Steps Forward in the Global Response*. Oakland, CA: MPact Global Action for Gay Men's Health and Rights. https://mpactglobal.org/reconsidering-primary-prevention/.

Ayikukwei, Rose, Ngare Duncan, John Sidle, David Ayuku, Joyce Baliddawa, and James Greene. 2008. "HIV/AIDS and Cultural Practices in Western Kenya: The Impact of Sexual Cleansing Rituals on Sexual Behaviours." *Culture, Health & Sexuality* 10 (6): 587–599.

Azim, Tasnim, Irene Bontell, and Steffanie A. Strathdee. 2015. "Women, Drugs and HIV." *International Journal on Drug Policy* 26, no. Suppl. 1 (February): S16–S21.

Baggaley, Rebecca F., Richard G. White, and Marie-Claude Boily. 2010. "HIV Transmission Risk through Anal Intercourse: Systematic Review, Meta-Analysis and Implications for HIV Prevention." *International Journal of Epidemiology* 39, no. 4 (August): 1048–1063.

Bagheri Amiri, Fahimeh, Amin Doosti-Irani, Abbas Sedaghat, Noushin Fahimfar, and Ehsan Mostafavi. 2018. "Knowledge, Attitude, and Practices Regarding HIV and TB among Homeless People in Tehran, Iran." *International Journal of Health Policy and Management* 7, no. 6 (June): 549–555.

Bailey-King, Ettie. 2018. "Three Things You Need to Know: Child Marriage and HIV." Girls Not Brides. Last modified December 1, 2018. https://www.girlsnotbrides.org/child-marriage-and-hiv/.

Bajos, Nathalie, and Jerome Marquet. 2000. "Research on HIV Sexual Risk: Social Relations-Based Approach in a Cross-Cultural Perspective." *Social Science & Medicine* 50, no. 11 (June): 1533–1546.

Banwari, Meel. 2011. "Poverty, Child Sexual Abuse and HIV in the Transkei Region, South Africa." *African Health Sciences* 11 (1): S117–S121.

Barberis, Daniela S. 2003. "In Search of an Object: Organicist Sociology and the Reality of Society in Fin-De-Siècle France." *History of the Human Sciences* 16, no. 3 (August): 51–72.

Barday, Naseema. 2017. "SA Rape Crisis: 'We Still Blame the Victims.'" Last modified August 29, 2017. Health24. https://www.health24.com/News/Public-Health/sa-rape-crisis-we-still-blame-the-victims-20170829.

Barnett, Tony. 2006. "A Long-Wave Event. HIV/AIDS, Politics, Governance and 'Security': Sundering the Intergenerational Bond?" *International Affairs* 82, no. 2 (March): 297–313.

Barrett-Grant, Kitty, Derrick Fine, Mark Heywood, and Ann Strode, eds. 2001. *HIV/AIDS and the Law: A Resource Manual.* 2nd ed. Johannesburg: The AIDS Law Project and the AIDS Legal Network.

Basile, Kathleen C., Sarah DeGue, Kathryn Jones, Kimberley Freire, Jenny Dills, Sharon G. Smith, and Jerris L. Raiford. 2016. *STOP SV: A Technical Package to Prevent Sexual Violence.* Atlanta, GA: Division of Violence Prevention, National Center for Injury Prevention and Control, Centers for Disease Control and Prevention. https://www.cdc.gov/features/sexual-violence-prevention/index.html.

Battin, Margaret P., Leslie P. Francis, Jay A. Jacobson, and Charles B. Smith. 2009. *The Patient as Victim and Vector: Ethics and Infectious Disease.* New York, NY: Oxford University Press.

Beardsley, Kip. 2013. *Policy Analysis and Advocacy Decision Model for HIV-Related Services: Males Who Have Sex with Males, Transgender People, and Sex Workers.* Washington, DC: Futures Group, Health Policy Project. https://www.healthpolicyproject.com/index.cfm?id=publications&get=publID&pubId=79.

Beauclair, Roxanne, Niel Hens, and Wim Delva. 2015. "Concurrent Partnerships in Cape Town, South Africa: Race and Sex Differences in Prevalence and Duration of Overlap." *Journal of the International AIDS Society* 18, no. 1 (January): 19372. https://doi.org/10.7448/IAS.18.1.19372

Beck, Ulrich. 1992. *Risk Society: Towards a New Modernity.* London: Sage.

Bedeski, Robert. 1999. *Defining Human Security.* Victoria: Centre for Global Studies.

Behrendt, Alice, and Steffen Moritz. 2005. "Posttraumatic Stress Disorder and Memory Problems after Female Genital Mutilation." *American Journal of Psychiatry* 162, no. 5 (May): 1000–1002.

Behrens, Kevin G. 2014. "Virginity Testing in South Africa: A Cultural Concession Taken Too Far?" *South African Journal of Philosophy* 33 (2) 177–187.

Beigbeder, Yves. 2004. *International Public Health: Patients' Rights vs. the Protection of Patents.* Aldershot, UK: Ashgate

Bejide, Folake. 2014. "The Legal Protection of Children Orphaned by HIV/AIDS in Nigeria: An Appraisal." *World Journal of AIDS* 4 (3): 321–331. http://dx.doi.org/10.4236/wja.2014.43038.

Beletsky, Leo, Alpna Agrawal, Bruce Moreau, Pratima Kumar, Nomi Weiss-Laxer, and Robert Heimer. 2011. "Police Training to Align Law Enforcement and HIV Prevention: Preliminary Evidence from the Field." *American Journal of Public Health* 101, no. 11 (November): 2012–2015.

Bennett, John E., Raphael Dolin, and Martin J. Blaser. 2014. *Mandell, Douglas, and Bennett's Principles and Practice of Infectious Diseases.* 8th ed. Philadelphia, PA: Saunders.

Berg, Rigmor C., and Vigdis Underland. 2014. *Immediate Health Consequences of Female Genital Mutilation/Cutting (FGM/C)*. Oslo: Norwegian Knowledge Centre for the Health Services. https://www.fhi.no/en/publ/2014/immediate-health-consequences-of-female-genital-mutilationcutting-fgmc-/.

Berg, Rigmor C., Vigdis Underland, Jan Odgaard-Jensen, Atle Fretheim, and Gunn Elisabeth Vist. 2014. "Effects of Female Genital Cutting on Physical Health Outcomes: A Systematic Review and Meta-Analysis." *BMJ Open* 4, no. 11 (November): e006316. http://dx.doi.org/ 10.1136/bmjopen-2014-006316.

Berkley, Seth. 1991. "Parenteral Transmission of HIV in Africa." *AIDS* 5 (Suppl. 1): S87–S92.

Bernard, Claude. 1865. *Introduction à l'Étude de la Médecine Expérimentale.* Paris: Baillière.

Berten, Hans, and Ronan Van Rossem. 2009. "Doing Worse but Knowing Better: An Exploration of the Relationship between HIV/AIDS Knowledge and Sexual Behavior among Adolescents in Flemish Secondary Schools." *Journal of Adolescence* 32, no. 5 (October): 1303–1319.

Beswick, Stephanie. 2001. "'We Are Bought Like Clothes': The War over Polygyny and Levirate Marriage in South Sudan." *Northeast African Studies* 8 (2): 35–61.

Bimbi, Franca. 2000. "Tipologie di Violenza e Relazioni Sociali." In *Libertà Femminile e Violenza sulle Donne. Strumenti di Lavoro per Interventi con Orientamenti di Genere*, edited by Cristina Adami, Alberta Basaglia, Franca Bimbi and Vittoria Tola, 43–54. Milano: Franco Angeli.

Birungi, Ruth, Dennis Nabembezi, Julius Kiwanuka, Michele Ybarra, and Sheana Bull. 2011. "Adolescents' Perceptions of Sexual Coercion in Uganda." *African Journal of AIDS Research* 10 (4): 487–494.

Blank, Hanne. 2007. *Virgin: The Untouched History.* New York, NY: Bloomsbury USA.

Bloom, Jack. 2013. "Combating South Africa's Rape Culture." Politicsweb. Last modified February 18, 2013. https://www.politicsweb.co.za/news-and-analysis/combating-south-africas-rape-culture.

Blue, Anna. 2018. "The Return of a Grievous Epidemic: Rising HIV/AIDS Infections in the Post-Soviet States." Lossi 36. Last modified 19 December, 2018. https://lossi36.com/2018/12/19/return-epidemic-aids-infections-post-soviet-states/.

Boily, Marie-Claude, Rebecca F. Baggaley, Lei Wang, Benoit Masse, Richard G. White, Richard J. Hayes, and Michel Alary. 2009. "Heterosexual Risk of HIV-1 Infection per Sexual Act: Systematic Review and Meta-Analysis of Observational Studies." *The Lancet Infectious Diseases* 9, no. 2 (February): 118–129.

Bonita, Ruth, Robert Beaglehole, and Tord Kjellström. 2006. *Basic Epidemiology*. 2nd ed. Geneva: World Health Organization.

Bougard, Nigel Bradley, Karen Booyens, and Rene Ehlers. 2015. "Adult Female Rape Survivors' Views about the Constitutional, Human Rights and Compulsory HIV Testing of Alleged Sex Offenders." *Acta Criminologica: African Journal of Criminology and Victimology* 2015, no. Special Edition 4 (January): 50–72.

Boulton, Kate, Pepis Rodriguez, Mayo Schreiber, and Catherine Hanssens. 2017. *HIV Criminalization in the United States: A Sourcebook on State and Federal HIV Criminal Law and Practice.* 3rd ed. New York, NY: The Center for HIV Law and Policy.

Brewer, Devon D., John J. Potterat, John M. Roberts, and Stuart Brody. 2007. "Male and Female Circumcision Associated with Prevalent HIV Infection in Virgins and Adolescents in Kenya, Lesotho, and Tanzania." *Annals of Epidemiology* 17, no. 3 (March): 217–226.

Brown, Brian, Paul Crawford, and Ronald Carter. 2006. *Evidence-Based Health Communication.* Maidenhead, UK: Open University Press.

Brown, Darigg C., Rhonda BeLue, and Collins O. Airhihenbuwa. 2010. "HIV and AIDS-Related Stigma in the Context of Family Support and Race in South Africa." *Ethnicity & Health* 15 (5): 441–458.

Brown, Jennifer L., and Ralph J. DiClemente. 2011. "Secondary HIV Prevention: Novel Intervention Approaches to Impact Populations Most at Risk." *Current HIV/AIDS Reports* 8, no. 4 (December): 269–276.

Brown, Tim. 2000. "AIDS, Risk and Social Governance." *Social Science & Medicine* 50, no. 9 (May): 1273–1284.

Brown, Wideney, Johanna Hanefeld, and James Welsh. 2009. "Criminalising HIV Transmission: Punishment without Protection." *Reproductive Health Matters* 17, no. 34 (November): 119–126.

Browne, Ken. 2006. *Introducing Sociology for AS-Level.* 2nd ed. Cambridge, UK: Polity Press.

Buckley, Stephen. 1997. "Wife Inheritance Spurs AIDS Rise in Kenya." *The Washington Post*, November 8, 1997. http://www.washingtonpost.com/wp-srv/inatl/longterm/africanlives/kenya/kenya_aids.htm.

Burchardt, Marian. 2007. "Managing Risks through Solidarity? HIV/AIDS and the Organisation of Support in South Africa." Working Paper 19, School of Social Policy, Sociology and Social Research, University of Kent, Canterbury, UK. https://www.kent.ac.uk/scarr/publications/Burchardt.pdf.

Burgueño, Eduardo, Silvia Carlos, Cristina Lopez-Del Burgo, Alfonso Osorio, Maria Stozek, Adolphe Ndarabu, Philémon Muamba, Philomene Tshisuaka, and Jokin De Irala. 2017. "Forced Sexual Intercourse and Its Association with HIV Status among People Attending HIV Voluntary Counseling and Testing in a Healthcare Center in Kinshasa (DRC)." *PLOS One* 12 (12): e0189632. https://doi.org/10.1371/journal.pone.0189632.

Burke, Jacquelyn. 2015. "Discretion to Warn: Balancing Privacy Rights with the Need to Warn Unaware Partners of Likely HIV/AIDS Exposure." *Boston College Journal of Law and Social Justice* 35 (1): 89–116. http://lawdigitalcommons.bc.edu/jlsj/vol35/iss1/5.

Burki, Talha Khan. 2011. "Discrimination against People with HIV Persists in China." *The Lancet* 377, no. 9762 (January): 286–287.

Bury, Mike, and Lee F. Monaghan. 2013. "The Sick Role." In *Key Concepts in Medical Sociology*, 2nd ed., edited by Jonathan Gabe and Lee F. Monaghan, 91–95. London: Sage.

Byrne, Deirdre. 2018. "Analysing the Nightmare: Reflections on Rape Culture in South Africa." August 3, 2018. In *Cultures of Sexual Assault: A Symposium*, produced by the Australian National University's Gender Institute, Podcast. MP4 audio, 37:16. http://genderinstitute.anu.edu.au/analysing-nightmare-reflections-rape-culture-south-africa.

Cabal, Luisa, and Patrick Eba. 2017. "Learning from the Past: Confronting Legal, Social, and Structural Barriers to the HIV Response." *Health and Human Rights Journal* 19, no. 2 (December): 113–115. http://www.jstor.org/stable/90016118.

Cabassi, Julia. 2004. *Renewing Our Voice: Code of Good Practice for NGOs Responding to HIV/AIDS.* Geneva: The NGO HIV/AIDS Code of Practice Project. https://www.who.int/3by5/partners/NGOcode/en.

Cairns, James, ed. 2008. *Combating HIV and AIDS Related Stigma, Denial and Discrimination: A Training Guide for Religious Leaders.* New York, NY: Religions for Peace. http://rfp.org/node/61.

Cameron, Edwin. 2009. "Criminalization of HIV Transmission: Poor Public Health Policy." *HIV/AIDS Policy & Law Review* 14, no. 2 (December): 1, 63–75.

Canguilhem, Georges. 1966. *Le Normal et le Pathologique.* Paris: Presses Universitaires de France.

Caraël, M., L. Curran, E. Gacad, E. Gnaore, R. Harding, B. M. Mandofia, A. Schauss, M. Stahlhofer, S. Timberlake, and M. Ummel. 2000. *Protocol for the Identification of Discrimination against People Living with HIV.* Geneva: Joint United Nations Programme on HIV and AIDS.

Carnaghi, Andrea, Rosanna Trentin, Mara Cadinu, and Valentina Piccoli. 2011. "Recasting the HIV-Risk Perception in a Social Context: The Interplay between Group-Based Information and Mood." *International Review of Social Psychology*, 24 (4): 59–71.

Carr, Dara, Traci Eckhaus, Laura Brady, Charlotte Watts, Cathy Zimmerman, and Laura Nyblade. 2010. *Scaling Up the Response to HIV Stigma and Discrimination.* London: International Center for Research on Women and London School of Hygiene and Tropical Medicine. https://www.icrw.org/publications/scaling-up-the-response-to-hiv-stigma-and-discrimination/.

CDC (Centers for Disease Control and Prevention). 1982a. "A Cluster of Kaposi's Sarcoma and Pneumocystis Carinii Pneumonia among Homosexual Male Residents of Los Angeles and Orange Counties, California." *Morbidity and Mortality Weekly Report* 31, no. 23 (June): 305–307. https://www.cdc.gov/mmwr/preview/mmwrhtml/00001114.htm.

CDC (Centers for Disease Control and Prevention). 1982b. "Epidemiologic Notes and Reports Possible Transfusion-Associated Acquired Immune Deficiency Syndrome (AIDS) – California." *Morbidity and Mortality Weekly Report* 31, no. 48 (December): 652–654. https://www.cdc.gov/mmwr/preview/mmwrhtml/00001203.htm.

CDC (Centers for Disease Control and Prevention). 1982c. "Opportunistic Infections and Kaposi's Sarcoma among Haitians in the United States." *Morbidity and Mortality Weekly Report* 31, no. 26 (July): 353–354, 360–361. https://www.cdc.gov/mmwr/preview/mmwrhtml/00001123.htm.

CDC (Centers for Disease Control and Prevention). 2019. "Effectiveness of Prevention Strategies to Reduce the Risk of Acquiring or Transmitting HIV." Division of HIV/AIDS Prevention, National Center for HIV/AIDS, Viral Hepatitis, STD, and TB Prevention. Last modified November 12, 2019. https://www.cdc.gov/hiv/risk/estimates/preventionstrategies.html.

Chapman, Jenifer, Nena do Nascimento, and Mahua Mandal. 2019. "Role of Male Sex Partners in HIV Risk of Adolescent Girls and Young Women in Mozambique." *Global Health: Science and Practice* 7, no. 3 (September): 435–446. https://doi.org/10.9745/GHSP-D-19-00117.

Cheek, Randy B. 2000. *A Generation at Risk: Security Implications of the HIV/AIDS Crisis in Southern Africa.* Washington, DC: Institute for National Strategic Studies, National Defence University.

Cheek, Randy B. 2001. "Playing God with HIV: Rationing HIV Treatment in Southern Africa." *African Security Review* 10 (4): 19–27.

Chemaitelly, Hiam, Helen A. Weiss, Clara Calvert, Manale Harfouche, and Laith J. Abu-Raddad. 2019. "HIV Epidemiology among Female Sex Workers and Their Clients in the Middle East and North Africa: Systematic Review, Meta-Analyses, and Meta-Regressions." *BMC Medicine* 17: 119. https://doi.org/10.1186/s12916-019-1349-y.

Chemical and Biological Arms Control Institute and Center for Strategic and International Studies. 2000. *Contagion and Conflict: Health as a Global Security Challenge.* Washington, DC: Chemical and Biological Arms Control Institute and Center for Strategic and International Studies.

Chen, Amy Jong. 2016. "HIV-Specific Criminal Law: A Global Review." *Intersect: The Stanford Journal of Science, Technology, and Society* 9, no. 3 (Spring). http://ojs.stanford.edu/ojs/index.php/intersect/article/view/829.

Chen, Yea-Hung, H. Fisher Raymond, Willi McFarland, and Hong-Ha M. Truong. 2010. "HIV Risk Behaviors in Heterosexual Partnerships: Female Knowledge and Male Behavior." *AIDS Behavior* 14, no. 1 (February): 87–91.

Chendi, Bih Hycenta, Marie Claire Okomo Assoumou, Graeme Brendon Jacobs, Elsie Laban Yekwa, Emilia Lyonga, Martha Mesembe, Agnes Eyoh, and George Mondinde Ikomey. 2019. "Rate of Viral Load Change and Adherence of HIV Adult Patients Treated with Efavirenz or Nevirapine Antiretroviral Regimens at 24 and 48 Weeks in Yaoundé, Cameroon: A Longitudinal Cohort Study." *BMC Infectious Diseases* 19: 194. https://doi.org/10.1186/s12879-019-3824-7.

Chi, Peilian, and Xiaoming Li. 2013. "Impact of Parental HIV/AIDS on Children's Psychological Well-Being: A Systematic Review of Global Literature." *AIDS and Behavior* 17, no. 7 (September): 2554–2574.

Chikovani, Ivdity, Ketevan Goguadze, Ivana Bozicevic, Natia Rukhadze, and George Gotsadze. 2013. "Determinants of Risky Sexual Behavior among Injecting Drug Users (IDUs) in Georgia." *AIDS and Behavior* 17, no. 5 (June): 1906–1913.

Chingwaru, Walter, and Jerneja Vidmar. 2018. "Culture, Myths and Panic: Three Decades and Beyond with an HIV/AIDS Epidemic in Zimbabwe." *Global Public Health* 13, no. 2 (February): 249–264. https://doi.org/10.1080/17441692.2016.1215485.

Chirambo, Kondwani. 2004. *AIDS and Electoral Democracy: Applying a New Lens to Election Coverage.* Pretoria: Institute for Democracy in Southern Africa.

Choi, Susanne Y. P., and Eleanor Holroyd. 2007. "The Influence of Power, Poverty and Agency in the Negotiation of Condom Use for Female Sex Workers in Mainland China." *Culture, Health & Sexuality* 9 (5): 489–503.

Chowdhury, Ishita, and Mark M. Lanier. 2012. "Rape and HIV as Methods of Waging War: Epidemiological Criminology's Response." *Advances in Applied Sociology* 2, no. 1 (March): 47–52.

Churcher, Sian. 2013. "Stigma Related to HIV and AIDS as a Barrier to Accessing Health Care in Thailand: A Review of Recent Literature." *WHO South-East Asia Journal of Public Health* 2, no. 1 (January-March): 12–22.

Cilliers, Jakkie. 2004. *Human Security in Africa: A Conceptual Framework for Review*. Pretoria: African Human Security Initiative.

Cipolla, Costantino. 2002a. "Introduzione. Per un Approccio Correzionale alla Qualità Sociale della Salute." In *Valutare la Qualità in Sanità. Approcci, Metodologie e Strumenti*, edited by Costantino Cipolla, Guido Giarelli and Leonardo Altieri, 12–13. Milano: Franco Angeli.

Cipolla, Costantino. 2002b. "Introduzione." In *Trasformazione dei Sistemi Sanitari e Sapere Sociologico*, edited by Costantino Cipolla, 22. Milano: Franco Angeli.

Clair, Matthew, Caitlin Daniel, and Michèle Lamont. 2016. "Destigmatisation and Health: Cultural Constructions and the Long-Term Reduction of Stigma". *Social Science & Medicine* 165 (September): 223–232.

Cluver, Lucie, and Don Operario. 2008. "Inter-generational Linkages of AIDS: Vulnerability of Orphaned Children for HIV Infection." *Institute of Development Studies Bulletin* 39, no. 5 (November): 27–35.

Coalition to Stop the Use of Child Soldiers. 1999. *The Use of Children as Soldiers, a Growing Phenomenon*. London: Coalition to Stop the Use of Child Soldiers.

Cohen, Mary Ann, Michael J. Mugavero, and Elise Hall. 2017. "HIV Psychiatry – A Paradigm for Integrated Care." In *Comprehensive Textbook of AIDS Psychiatry: A Paradigm for Integrated Care*, 2nd ed., edited by Mary Ann Cohen, Jack M. Gorman, Jeffrey M. Jacobson, Paul Volberding and Scott L. Letendre, 3–18. New York, NY: Oxford University Press.

Cohn, Susan E., and Rebecca A. Clark. 2014. "Human Immunodeficiency Virus Infection in Women." In *Mandell, Douglas, and Bennett's Principles and Practice of Infectious Diseases*, 8th ed., edited by John E. Bennett, Raphael Dolin and Martin J. Blaser, 1590–1615. Philadelphia, PA: Elsevier Saunders.

Conroy, Sarah J. 2011. "Women's Inheritance and Conditionality in the Fight against AIDS." *Wisconsin International Law Journal* 28 (4): 705–741.

Coombs, Alexandra, and Elizabeth Gold. 2019. *Generating Demand for PrEP: A Desk Review*. Arlington, VA: Strengthening High Impact Interventions for an AIDS-free Generation (AIDSFree) Project. https://www.jsi.com/resource/generating-demand-for-prep-a-desk-review/.

Cree, Viviene E., Helen Kay, Kay Tisdall, and Jennifer Wallace. 2004. "Stigma and Parental HIV." *Qualitative Social Work* 3, no. 1 (March): 7–25.

Crofts, Nick, and David Patterson. 2016. "Police Must Join the Fast Track to End AIDS by 2030." *Journal of the International AIDS Society* 19, no. 4 Suppl. 3 (July): 21153. https://doi.org/10.7448/IAS.19.4.21153.

Crofts, Nick, and Melissa Jardine. 2016. "The Role of the Police in the HIV Response: The Law Enforcement and HIV Network (LEAHN)." *HIV Australia* 14, no. 1 (March): 9-11. https://www.afao.org.au/article/role-police-hiv-response-law-enforcement-hiv-network-leahn/.

Crowell, Nancy A., and Ann W. Burgess, eds. 1996. *Understanding Violence against Women.* Washington, DC: National Academic Press.

Curran, James W., and Harold W. Jaffe. 2011. "AIDS: The Early Years and CDC's Response." *Morbidity and Mortality Weekly Report Supplements* 60, no. 4 (October): 64–69. https://www.cdc.gov/mmwr/preview/mmwrhtml/su6004a11.htm.

Dana, Liyuwork Mitiku,Yohannes Mehretie Adinew, and Mitike Molla Sisay. 2019. "Transactional Sex and HIV Risk among Adolescent School Girls in Ethiopia: Mixed Method Study." *BioMed Research International* 2019: 4523475. https://doi.org/10.1155/2019/4523475

Dannreuther, Charlie, and Rohit Lekhi. 2000. "Globalization and the Political Economy of Risk." *Review of International Political Economy* 7, no. 4 (Winter): 574–594.

David, Antonio C., and Carmen A. Li. 2010. "Exploring the Links between HIV/AIDS, Social Capital and Development." *Journal of International Development* 22, no. 7 (October): 941–961.

Davis, Joseph E. 2010. "Medicalization, Social Control, and the Relief of Suffering." In *The New Blackwell Companion to Medical Sociology*, edited by William C. Cockerham, 211–241. Oxford: Wiley-Blackwell.

De Cock, Kevin M., Mary Glenn Fowler, Eric Mercier, Isabelle de Vincenzi, Joseph Saba, Elizabeth Hoff, David J. Alnwick, Martha Rogers, and Nathan Shaffer. 2000. "Prevention of Mother-to-Child HIV Transmission in Resource-Poor Countries: Translating Research into Policy and Practice." *JAMA* 283, no. 9 (March): 1175–1182. https://doi.org/10.1001/jama.283.9.1175.

de Waal, Alex, Jennifer Klot, and Mahajan Manjari. 2009. *HIV/AIDS, Security and Conflict: New Realities, New Responses.* New York, NY: Social Science Research Council.

Deacon, Harriet, Inez Stephney, and Sandra Prosalendis. 2005. *Understanding HIV/AIDS Stigma: A Theoretical and Methodological Analysis.* Cape Town: Human Sciences Research Council Press.

Decker, Michele R., Amanda D. Latimore, SuzumiYasutake, Miriam Haviland, Saifuddin Ahmed, Robert W. Blum, Freya Sonenstein, and Nan Marie Astone. 2015. "Gender-Based Violence against Adolescent and Young Adult Women in Low-and Middle-Income Countries." *Journal of Adolescent Health* 56, no. 2 (February): 188–196.

Decosas, Josef. 2002. "The Social Ecology of AIDS in Africa." Draft Paper Prepared for the UNRISD Project on HIV/AIDS and Development, United Nations Research Institute for Social Development (UNRISD), Geneva. http://www.unrisd.org/unrisd/website/document.nsf/(httpPublications)/E60AAD2EFA4882F4C1256BB8004F2F3F?OpenDocument.

Delva, Wim. 2010. "How Supportive Is the Social Network of AIDS Orphans and Other Orphaned Children in Conakry and N'Zérékoré, Guinea?" *SACEMA Quarterly*, November. http://www.sacemaquarterly.com/aids/how-supportive-is-the-social-network-of-aids-orphans-and-other-orphaned-children-in-conakry-and-n'zerekore-guinea.html.

Department for International Development. 2005. *Why We Need to Work Effectively in Fragile States*. London: Department for International Development.

Department of Foreign Affairs and International Trade. 1999. *Human Security: Safety for People in a Changing World*. Ottawa, ON: Department of Foreign Affairs and International Trade

Derlega, Valerian J., and Anita P. Barbee, eds. 1998. *HIV and Social Interaction*. London: Sage.

Dijkstra, Hylke, and Anniek De Ruijter. 2017. "The Health-Security Nexus and the European Union: Toward a Research Agenda." *European Journal of Risk Regulation* 8, no. 4 (December): 613–625.

Dingake, Oagile Bethuel Key. 2018. "The State of Human Rights in Relation to Key Populations, HIV and Sexual and Reproductive Health." *Reproductive Health Matters* 26 (52): 46–50.

Dingwall, Robert, Lily M. Hoffman, and Karen Staniland. 2013. "Introduction: Why a Sociology of Pandemics?" *Sociology of Health & Illness* 35, no. 2 (February): 167–173.

Diouf, Khady, and Nawal Nour. 2013. "Female Genital Cutting and HIV Transmission: Is There an Association?" *American Journal of Reproductive Immunology* 69, no. Suppl. 1 (February): S45–S50.

Dlamini, Bathabile. 2016. "Forced Virginity-Testing Is Unlawful and Offensive, and Will Not Prevent HIV-AIDS." *Daily Maverick*, February 2, 2016. https://www.dailymaverick.co.za/opinionista/2016-02-02-forced-virginity-testing-is-unlawful-and-offensive-and-will-not-prevent-hiv-aids/.

Do, Mai, and Dominique Meekers. 2009. "Multiple Sex Partners and Perceived Risk of HIV Infection in Zambia: Attitudinal Determinants and Gender Differences." *AIDS Care* 21 (10): 1211–1221.

Doerner, William G., and Steven P. Lab. 2015. *Victimology*. 7th ed. New York, NY: Routledge.

Douek, Daniel C., Mario Roederer, and Richard A. Koup. 2009. "Emerging Concepts in the Immunopathogenesis of AIDS." *Annual Review of Medicine* 60: 471–484.

Doyle, Priscilla, Jane Sixsmith, Margaret Mary Barry, Samir Akram Mahmood, Laura MacDonald, Maeve O'Sullivan, C. Oroviogoichoechea, Georgina Anne Cairns, Francisco Guillén-Grima, and Jorge Maria Núñez-Córdoba. 2012. *Public Health Stakeholders' Perceived Status of Health Communication Activities for the Prevention and Control of Communicable Diseases across the EU and EEA/EFTA Countries*. Stockholm: European Centre for Disease Prevention and Control. https://aran.library.nuigalway.ie/handle/10379/4585.

Drakes, Nicole, Clarissa Perks, Alok Kumar, Kim Quimby, Colin Clarke, Rajul Patel, Ian Hambleton, and Robert Clive Landis. 2013. "Prevalence and Risk Factors for Inter-Generational Sex: A Cross-Sectional Cluster Survey of Barbadian Females Aged 15–19." *BMC Women's Health* 13: 53. https://doi.org/10.1186/1472-6874-13-53.

Duger, Angela, Sarah Dougherty, Till Baeringhausen, and Ralf Jurgens. 2013. "HIV, AIDS, and Human Rights." In *Health and Human Rights Resource Guide*, 5th ed., edited by Angela Duger, 94-178. Boston, MA: François-Xavier Bagnoud Center for Health and Human Rights, Harvard University. https://www.hhrguide.org.

Duke, Thomas Scott. 2007. "Hidden, Invisible, Marginalized, Ignored: A Critical Review of the Professional and Empirical Literature (or Lack Thereof) on Gay and Lesbian Teachers in the United States." *Journal of Gay and Lesbian Issues in Education* 4 (4): 19–38.

Dunkle, Kristin L., Rachel K. Jewkes, Heather C. Brown, Glenda E. Gray, James A. McIntryre, and Siobán D. Harlow. 2004. "Gender-Based Violence, Relationship Power, and Risk of HIV Infection in Women Attending Antenatal Clinics in South Africa." *The Lancet* 363, no. 9419 (May): 1415–1421.

Durkheim, David Émile. 1895. *Les Règles de la Méthode Sociologique*. Paris: Alcan.

Earnshaw, Valerie A., and R. Stephenie Chaudoir. 2009. "From Conceptualizing to Measuring HIV Stigma: A Review of HIV Stigma Mechanism Measures." *AIDS and Behavior* 13, no. 6 (December): 1160–1177.

Eaton, Jeffrey W., Felicia R. Takavarasha, Christina Schumacher, Owen Mugurungi, Geoffrey P. Garnett, Constance Nyamukapa, and Simon Gregson. 2014. "Trends in Concurrency, Polygyny, and Multiple Sex Partnerships During a Decade of Declining HIV Prevalence in Eastern Zimbabwe." *The Journal of Infectious Diseases* 210, Suppl. 2 (December): S562–S568.

Eba, Patrick M. 2015. "HIV-Specific Legislation in Sub-Saharan Africa: A Comprehensive Human Rights Analysis." *African Human Rights Law Journal* 15 (2): 224–262.

Elbe, Stefan. 2006. "Should HIV/AIDS Be Securitized? The Ethical Dilemmas of Linking HIV/AIDS and Security." *International Studies Quarterly* 50, no. 1 (March): 119–144.

Elbe, Stefan. 2008. "Risking Lives: AIDS, Security and Three Concepts of Risk." *Security Dialogue* 39, no. 2-3 (April/June): 177–198.

Elder, Kay, Doris Baker, and Julie A. Ribes. 2004. *Infections, Infertility, and Assisted Reproduction*. Cambridge: Cambridge University Press.

Elias, Robert. 1986. *The Politics of Victimization: Victims, Victimology and Human Rights*. New York, NY: Oxford University Press.

Ellard-Gray, Amy, Nicole K. Jeffrey, Melisa Choubak, and Sara E. Crann. 2015. "Finding the Hidden Participant: Solutions for Recruiting Hidden, Hard-to-Reach, and Vulnerable Populations." *International Journal of Qualitative Methods* 14, no. 5 (December): 1–10.

Ellsberg, Mary, and Lori Heise. 2005. *Researching Violence against Women: A Practical Guide for Researchers and Activists*. Washington, DC: World Health Organization and Program for Appropriate Technology in Health.

EngenderHealth. 2004. *Reducing Stigma and Discrimination Related to HIV and AIDS: Training for Health Care Workers*. New York, NY: EngenderHealth.

Enoch, Jamie, and Peter Piot. 2017. "Human Rights in the Fourth Decade of the HIV/AIDS Response: An Inspiring Legacy and Urgent Imperative." *Health and Human Rights Journal* 19, no. 2 (December): 117–122. https://www.jstor.org/stable/90016119.

Epstein, Helen, and Rackel Jewkes. 2009. "The Myth of the Virgin Rape Myth." *The Lancet* 374, no. 9699 (October): 1419.

Erb-Leoncavallo, Ann, Gill Holmes, Gloria Jacobs, Stephanie Urdang, Joann Vanek, and Micol Zarb. 2004. *Women and HIV/AIDS: Confronting the Crisis*. Geneva and New York, NY: Joint United Nations Programme on HIV and

AIDS, United Nations Development Programme and United Nations Development Fund for Women. https://gcwa.unaids.org/external-resource/unaids-unfpa-unifem-women-and-hivaids-confronting-crisis.

Evatt, Bruce L. 2006. "The Tragic History of AIDS in the Hemophilia Population 1982-1984." *Journal of Thrombosis and Haemostasi*s 4, no. 11 (November): 2295–2301.

Fairchild, Amy L., and Eileen A. Tynan. 1994. "Policies of Containment: Immigration in the Era of AIDS." *American Journal of Public Health* 84, no. 12 (December): 2011–2022.

Fallon, Amy. 2018. "South Africa Pushes to Combat HIV among Girls #Blessed by Sugar Daddies." Reuters. Last modified March 26, 2018. https://www.reuters.com/article/us-safrica-women-aids/south-africa-pushes-to-combat-hiv-among-girls-blessed-by-sugar-daddies-idUSKBN1H2031.

Family Health International. 2001. *Care for Orphans, Children Affected by HIV/AIDS and Other Vulnerable Children: A Strategic Framework.* Arlington, VA: Family Health International. http://hivhealthclearinghouse.unesco.org/library/documents/care-orphans-children-affected-hivaids-and-other-vulnerable-children-strategic.

Faria, Fernanda. 2011. "Fragile States: A Fluid Concept for Peacebuilding and Statebuilding." NOREF Policy Brief 3 (July), Norwegian Peacebuilding Resource Centre (NOREF), Oslo. https://noref.no/Publications/Themes/Peacebuilding-and-mediation/Fragile-states-a-fluid-concept-for-peacebuilding-and-statebuilding.

Farmer, Paul. 1992. *AIDS and Accusation: Haiti and the Geography of Blame.* Berkeley, CA: University of California Press.

Farrington, David P. 1986. "Age and crime." In *Crime and Justice: An Annual Review of Research*, vol. 7, edited by Michael Tonry and Norval Morris, 189–250. Chicago, IL: University of Chicago Press.

Farrington, John. 2003. "HIV/AIDS and Development." Background Paper 21, Overseas Development Institute, London. https://www.odi.org/publications/2323-hiv-aids-development?reduced=true.

Fattah, Ezzat A. 1991. *Understanding Criminal Victimization: An Introduction to Theoretical Victimology.* Scarborough, ON: Prentice-Hall Canada.

Fauk, Nelsensius Klauk, Anastasia Suci Sukmawati, Pius Almindu Leki Berek, Ernawati, Elisabeth Kristanti, Sri Sunaringsih Ika Wardojo, Isaias Budi Cahaya, and Lillian Mwanri. 2018. "Barriers to HIV Testing among Male Clients of Female Sex Workers in Indonesia." *International Journal for Equity in Health* 17: 68. https://doi.org/10.1186/s12939-018-0782-4.

Ferris, Margaret G., Michael B. Mizwa, and Gordon E. Schutze. 2010. "Prevention of Sexual Transmission of HIV/AIDS." In *HIV Curriculum for the Health Professional*, 4th ed., edited by Gabe Waggoner, 120-127. Houston, TX: Baylor College of Medicine International Pediatric AIDS Initiative, Texas Children's Hospital. https://bipai.org/hiv-curricula.

Finerman, Ruth, and Linda A. Bennett. 1995. "Overview: Guilt, Blame and Shame in Sickness." *Social Science & Medicine* 40, no. 1 (January): 1–3.

Fisher, Jeffrey D., and Laramie Smith. 2009. "Secondary Prevention of HIV Infection: The Current State of Prevention for Positives." *Current Opinion in HIV and AIDS* 4, no. 4 (July): 279–287.

Fishman, Hannah R. 2013. "HIV Confidentiality and Stigma: A Way Forward." *University of Pennsylvania Journal of Constitutional Law* 16 (1): 199–231. https://scholarship.law.upenn.edu/jcl/vol16/iss1/5.

Flanagan, Jane. 2001. "South African Men Rape Babies as 'Cure' for AIDS." *The Telegraph*, November 11, 2001. https://www.telegraph.co.uk/news/ worldnews/africaandindianocean/southafrica/1362134/South-African-men-rape-babies-as-cure-for-Aids.html.

Flavin, Jeanne. 1998. "Police and HIV/AIDS: The Risk, the Reality, the Response." *American Journal of Criminal Justice* 23, no. 1 (September): 33–58.

Fleming, Kathryn E. 2015. "Improving Access to Education for Orphans or Vulnerable Children Affected by HIV/AIDS." Background Paper Prepared for the Education for All Global Monitoring Report 2015, Education for All 2000–2015: Achievements and Challenges, United Nations Educational, Scientific and Cultural Organization, Paris. https://unesdoc.unesco.org/ark:/48223/pf0000232423.

Flint, Adrian. 2011. *HIV/AIDS in Sub-Saharan Africa: Politics, Aid and Globalization.* Basingstoke, UK: Palgrave Macmillan.

Florom-Smith, Aubrey L., and Joseph P. De Santis. 2012. "Exploring the Concept of HIV-Related Stigma." *Nursing Forum* 47, no. 3 (July-September): 153–165.

Foucault, Michel. 1999. *Les Anormaux.* Paris: Éditions du Seuil.

Fourie, Pieter, and Martin Schönteich. 2001. "Africa's New Security Threat: HIV/AIDS and Human Security in Southern Africa." *African Security Review* 10 (4): 29–41.

Fox, Ashley M. 2014. "Marital Concurrency and HIV Risk in 16 African Countries." *AIDS and Behavior* 18, 4 (April): 791–800.

Fox, Vivian C. 2002. "Historical Perspectives on Violence against Women." *Journal of International Women's Studies* 4 (1): 15-34. http://vc.bridgew.edu/jiws/vol4/iss1/2.

Fraser, Sandy. 2015. "Explainer: Behind the Scourge of Child Rape in South Africa." The Conversation. Last modified June 29, 2015. https://theconversation.com/ explainer-behind-the-scourge-of-child-rape-in-south-africa-43436.

Fredriksen-Goldsen, Karen I., Jane M. Simoni, Hyun-Jun Kim, Keren Lehavot, Karina L. Walters, Joice Yang, Charles P. Hoy-Ellis, and Anna Muraco. 2014. "The Health Equity Promotion Model: Reconceptualization of Lesbian, Gay, Bisexual, and Transgender (LGBT) Health Disparities." *American Journal of Orthopsychiatry* 84, no. 6 (November): 653–663.

Freidson, Eliot. 1970. *Profession of Medicine: A Study of the Sociology of Applied Knowledge.* New York, NY: Harper and Row.

Fulu, Emma, Xian Warner, Stephanie Miedema, Rachel Jewkes, Tim Roselli, and James Lang. 2013. *Why Do Some Men Use Violence against Women and How Can We Prevent It? Quantitative Findings from the United Nations Multi-Country Study on Men and Violence in Asia and the Pacific.* Bangkok: United Nations Development Programme, United Nations Population Fund, United Nations Entity for Gender Equality and the Empowerment of Women and United Nations Volunteers. http://www.partners4prevention.org/node/515.

Furedi, Frank. 2004. *Therapy Culture: Cultivating Vulnerability in an Uncertain Age.* London: Routledge.

Fustos, Kata. 2011. "Gender-Based Violence Increases Risk of HIV/AIDS for Women in Sub-Saharan Africa." Population Reference Bureau. Last modified April 12, 2011. https://www.prb.org/gender-based-violence-hiv/.

Gable, Lance, Katharina Gamharter, Lawrence O. Gostin, James G. Hodge Jr., and Rudolf V. Van Puymbroeck. 2007. *Legal Aspects of HIV/AIDS: A Guide for Policy and Law Reform.* Washington, DC: World Bank. https://openknowledge.worldbank.org/handle/10986/6754.

Garcia, Patricia M., Leslie A. Kalish, Jane Pitt, Howard Minkoff, Thomas C. Quinn, Sandra K. Burchett, Janet Kornegay, Brooks Jackson, John Moye, Celine Hanson, Carmen Zorrilla, and Judy F. Lew. 1999. "Maternal Levels of Plasma Human Immunodeficiency Virus Type 1 RNA and the Risk of Perinatal Transmission." *New England Journal of Medicine* 341, no. 6 (August): 394–402.

Garcia-Moreno, Claudia, Christina Pallitto, Karen Devries, Heidi Stöckl, Charlotte Watts, and Naeema Abrahams. 2013. *Global and Regional Estimates of Violence against Women: Prevalence and Health Effects of Intimate Partner Violence and Non-Partner Sexual Violence.* Geneva: World Health Organization. https://www.who.int/reproductivehealth/publications/violence/9789241564625/en/.

Garkawe, Sam. 2004. "Revising the Scope of Victimology: How Broad a Discipline Should It Be?" *International Review of Victimology* 11, no. 2/3 (November): 275–294.

Garsd, Jasmine, and Andrea Crossan. 2017. "What It Means in South Africa When You Are #Blessed." Public Radio International. Last modified August 10, 2017. https://www.pri.org/stories/2017-08-10/what-it-means-south-africa-when-you-are-blessed.

Gbadamosi, Olaide. 2008. "Female Genital Mutilation: A Life-Threatening Health and Human Rights Issue." *Exchange on HIV/AIDS, Sexuality and Gender*, no. 1: 1–3.

Geary, David C. 2000. "Evolution and Proximate Expression of Human Paternal Investment." *Psychological Bulletin* 126, no. 1 (January): 55–77.

George, Erika R. 2008. "Virginity Testing and South Africa's HIV/AIDS Crisis: Beyond Rights Universalism and Cultural Relativism toward Health Capabilities." *California Law Review* 96, no. 6 (December): 1447–1517. https://scholarship.law.berkeley.edu/californialawreview/vol96/iss6/2/.

Ghanotakis, Elena, Susannah Mayhew, and Charlotte Watts. 2009. "Tackling HIV and Gender-Based Violence in South Africa: How Has PEPFAR Responded and What Are the Implications for Implementing Organizations?" *Health Policy and Planning* 24, no. 5 (September): 357–366.

Ghys, Peter D., Brian G. Williams, Mead Over, Timothy B. Hallett, and Peter Godfrey-Faussett. 2018. "Epidemiological Metrics and Benchmarks for a Transition in the HIV Epidemic." *PLOS Medicine* 15, no. 10 (October): e1002678. https://doi.org/10.1371/journal.pmed.1002678.

Giddens, Anthony, Mitchell Duneier, Richard P. Appelbaum, and Debora Carr. 2009. *Introduction to Sociology.* 7th ed. New York, NY: W. W. Norton & Company.

Giddens, Anthony. 1992. *The Transformation of Intimacy: Sexuality, Love and Eroticism in Modern Societies.* Stanford, CA: Stanford University Press.

Gill, Aisha K. 2008. "'Crimes of Honour' and Violence against Women in the UK." *International Journal of Comparative and Applied Criminal Justice* 32 (2): 243–263.

Gillespie, Stuart. 2006. *Children Vulnerability and AIDS: Case Studies from Southern Africa.* Washington, DC: International Food Policy Research Institute. https://www.ifpri.org/publication/child-vulnerability-and-aids.

Gillespie, Susan L., Mary E. Paul, Javier Chinen, and William T. Shearer. 2013. "HIV Infection and Acquired Immunodeficiency Syndrome." In *Clinical Immunology: Principles and Practice*, 4th ed., edited by Robert R. Rich, Thomas A. Fleisher, William T. Shearer, Harry W. Schroeder Jr., Anthony J. Frew and Cornelia M. Weyand, 465–479. Philadelphia, PA: Elsevier Saunders.

Goffman, Erving. 1959. *The Presentation of Self in Everyday Life.* New York, NY: Anchor Books.

Goffman, Erving. 1963. *Stigma: Notes on the Management of Spoiled Identity.* Englewood Cliffs, NJ: Prentice-Hall.

Goh, Debbie. 2008. "It's the Gays' Fault: News and HIV as Weapons against Homosexuality in Singapore." *Journal of Communication Inquiry* 32, no. 4 (October): 383–399.

Goldstein, Richard. 1991. "The Implicated and the Immune: Responses to AIDS in the Arts and Popular Culture." In *A Disease of Society: Cultural and Institutional Responses to AIDS*, edited by Dorothy Nelkin, David P. Willis and Scott V. Parris, 17-42. New York, NY: Cambridge University Press.

Gomes do Espirito Santo, Maria Eugenia, and Gina D. Etheredge. 2005. "Male Clients of Brothel Prostitutes as a Bridge for HIV Infection between High Risk and Low Risk Groups of Women in Senegal." *Sexually Transmitted Infections* 81, no. 4 (August): 342–344.

Gordon, David F. 2000. *The Global Infectious Disease Threat and Its Implications for the United States.* NIE 99-17D. Washington, DC: National Intelligence Council. https://www.dni.gov/files/documents/infectiousdiseases_2000.pdf.

Gordon, David F. 2002. *The Next Wave of HIV/AIDS: Nigeria, Ethiopia, Russia, India, and China.* ICA 2002-04 D. Washington, DC: National Intelligence Council. https://apps.dtic.mil/dtic/tr/fulltext/u2/a511661.pdf.

Gori, Luca, Piero Manfredi, and Mauro Sodini. 2019. "HIV/AIDS, Demography and Development: Individual Choices Versus Public Policies in SSA." In *Human Capital and Economic Growth: The Impact of Health, Education and Demographic Change*, edited by Alberto Bucci, Klaus Prettner and Alexia Prskawetz, 323–356. Cham, CH: Palgrave Macmillan.

Govender, Prega. 1999. "Child Rape: A Taboo within the AIDS Taboo." *Sunday Times,* April 4, 1999. http://www.aegis.com/news/suntimes/1999/ST990401.html.

Gqola, Pumla Dineo. 2015. *Rape: A South African Nightmare.* Johannesburg: MFBooks Joburg.

Gram, Inger T., Tonje Braaten, Eiliv Lund, Loic Le Marchand, and Elisabete Weiderpass. 2009. "Cigarette Smoking and Risk of Colorectal Cancer among Norwegian Women." *Cancer Causes & Control* 20, no. 6 (August): 895–903.

Grassivaro Gallo, Pia, Marica Livio, and Franco Viviani. 2004. "Changes in Infibulation Practice in East Africa: Comments on a Ritual Alternative to Infibulation in Merka, Somalia." In *Flesh and Blood: Perspectives on the Problem of Circumcision in Contemporary Society*, edited by George C. Denniston, Frederick M. Hodges and Marilyn Fayre Milos, 133–142. New York, NY: Kluwer Academic/Plenum Publishers.

Green, Edward C., and Allison Herling Ruark. 2011. *AIDS, Behavior, and Culture: Understanding Evidence-Based Prevention.* Walnut Creek, CA: Left Coast Press.

Green, Geoff, Jan M. Gilbertson, and Michael F.J. Grimsley. 2002. "Fear of Crime and Health in Residential Tower Blocks: A Case Study in Liverpool, UK." *European Journal of Public Health* 12, no. 1 (March): 10–15.

Greenblott, Kara, and Kate Greenaway. 2007. *Food Security and Nutrition: Meeting the Needs of Orphans and Other Children Affected by HIV and AIDS in Africa.* Rome: World Food Programme. http://www.wfp.org/food_aid/doc/Food_Security_and_Nutrition_Meeting.pdf.

Grigsby, Byron L. 2004. *Pestilence in Medieval and Early Modern English Literature.* New York, NY: Routledge.

Groce, Nora E., and Reshma Trasi. 2004. "Rape of Individuals with Disability: AIDS and the Folk Belief of Virgin Cleansing." *The Lancet* 363, no. 9422 (May): 1663–1664.

Gruskin, Sofia, and Daniel Tarantola. 2008. "Universal Access to HIV Prevention, Treatment and Care: Assessing the Inclusion of Human Rights in International and National Strategic Plans." *AIDS* 22, no. Suppl. 2 (August): S123–S132.

Gündüz, Zuhal Yeşilyurt. 2006. "The HIV/AIDS Epidemic - What's Security Got to Do with It?" *Perceptions* 11, no. 2 (Summer): 49–84. http://sam.gov.tr/the-hivaids-epidemic-whats-security-got-to-do-with-it/.

Gunga, Samson O. 2009. "The Politics of Widowhood and Re-Marriage among the Luo of Kenya." *Thought and Practice* 1 (1): 161–174.

Haber, Lawrence D., and Richard T. Smith. 1971. "Disability and Deviance: Normative Adaptations of Role Behavior." *American Sociological Review* 36, no.1 (February): 87–97.

Hadingham, Jenny. 2000. "Human Security and Africa: Polemic Opposites." *South African Journal of International Affairs* 7 (2): 113–121.

Halasz, Jacek. 2018. "About the Right to Be Ill." *Medicine, Health Care, and Philosophy* 21, no. 1 (March): 113–123.

Hall, Katherine, and Winnie Sambu. 2018. "Income Poverty, Unemployment and Social Grants." In *South African Child Gauge 2018. Children, Families and the State: Collaboration and Contestation*, edited by Katherine Hall, Linda Richter, Zitha Mokomane and Lori Lake, 137–143. Cape Town: Children's Institute, University of Cape Town. http://www.ci.uct.ac.za/ci/child-gauge/2018.

Halperin, Daniel T., Stephen Shiboski, Joel Palefsky, and Nancy Padian. 2002. "High Level of HIV-1 Infection from Anal Intercourse: A Neglected Risk

Factor in Heterosexual AIDS Prevention." Poster Presented at the XIV International AIDS Conference, Barcelona.

Harper, Cynthia C., and Sara S. McLanahan. 2004. "Father Absence and Youth Incarceration." *Journal of Research on Adolescence* 14, no. 3 (September): 369–397.

Harrisberg, Kim. 2019. "Rape Map and Murdered Women - Welcome to South Africa's Republic of Sexual Abuse." Reuters. Last modified December 10, 2019. https://www.reuters.com/article/us-safrica-rape-exhibition-trfn/ rape-map-and-murdered-women-welcome-to-south-africas-republic-of-sexual-abuse-idUSKBN1YE2FT.

Harsono, Dini, Carol L. Galletly, Elaine O'Keefe, and Zita Lazzarini. 2017. "Criminalization of HIV Exposure: A Review of Empirical Studies in the United States." *AIDS and Behavior* 21, no. 1 (January): 27–50.

Hassen, Fatuma, and Ngussie Deyassa. 2013. "The Relationship between Sexual Violence and Human Immunodeficiency Virus (HIV) Infection among Women Using Voluntary Counseling and Testing Services in South Wollo Zone, Ethiopia." *BMC Research Notes* 6: 271. https://doi.org/10.1186/1756-0500-6-271.

Hatzenbuehler, Mark L., Jo C. Phelan, and Bruce G. Link. 2013. "Stigma as a Fundamental Cause of Population Health Inequalities." *American Journal of Public Health* 103, no. 5 (May): 813–821.

Heiberg, Turid, ed. 2005. *10 Essential Learning Points: Listen and Speak Out against Child Sexual Abuse of Girls and Boys.* Oslo: Save The Children Norway. https://resourcecentre.savethechildren.net/library/listen-and-speak-out-against-sexual-abuse-boys-and-girls-10-essential-learning-points-global.

Heidarnia, Mohmmad Ali, and Ali Heidarnia. 2016. "Sick Role and a Critical Evaluation of Its Application to Our Understanding of the Relationship between Physician and Patients." *Novelty in Biomedicine* 4, no. 3 (Summer): 126–134.

Hein, Wolfgang, Sonja Bartsch, and Lars Kohlmorgen, eds. 2007. *Global Health Governance and the Fight against HIV/AIDS.* Basingstoke, UK: Palgrave Macmillan.

Heinecken, Lindy. 2001. "Living in Terror: The Looming Security Threat to Southern Africa." *African Security Review* 10 (4): 7–17.

Helman, Cecil G. 2007. *Culture, Health and Illness: An Introduction for Health Professionals.* 5th ed. London: Hodder Arnold.

Hendrick, Clyde, and Susan S. Hendrick, eds. 2000. *Close Relationships: A Sourcebook.* Thousand Oaks, CA: Sage.

Herek, Gregory M. 1986. "The Instrumentality of Attitudes: Towards a Neo-Functional Theory." *Journal of Social Issues* 42, no. 2 (Summer): 99–114.

Herek, Gregory M. 1999. "AIDS and Stigma." *American Behavioral Scientist* 42, no. 7 (April): 1106–1116.

Herek, Gregory M. 2002. "Thinking about AIDS and Stigma: A Psychologist's Perspective." *The Journal of Law, Medicine & Ethics* 30, no. 4 (December): 594–607.

Herek, Gregory M. 2009. "Sexual Stigma and Sexual Prejudice in the United States: A Conceptual Framework." *In Contemporary Perspectives on Lesbian, Gay, and Bisexual Identities: The 54th Nebraska Symposium on Motivation,* edited by Debra A. Hope, 65–111. New York, NY: Springer.

Herek, Gregory M., and Erik K. Glunt. 1988. "An Epidemic of Stigma: Public Reactions to AIDS." *American Psychologist* 43, no. 11 (November): 886–891.

Herek, Gregory M., and John P. Capitanio. 1998. "Symbolic Prejudice or Fear of Infection? A Functional Analysis of AIDS-Related Stigma among Heterosexual Adults." *Basic and Applied Social Psychology* 20 (3): 230–241.

Heuveline, Patrick. 2004. "Impact of the Epidemic on Population and Household Structure: The Dynamics and Evidence to Date." *AIDS* 18, no. Suppl. 2 (June): S45–S53.

Heyman, Bob, Mette Henriksen, and Karen Maughan. 1998. "Probabilities and Health Risks: A Qualitative Approach." *Social Science & Medicine* 47, no. 9 (November): 1295–1306.

Hicks, Esther K. 1996. *Infibulation: Female Mutilation in Islamic Northeastern Africa.* New Brunswick, NJ: Transaction Publishers.

Highleyman, Liz. 2011. "HIV Eradication: Time to Talk about a Cure." *Bulletin of Experimental Treatment for AIDS* 23, no. 2 (Winter-Spring): 13–27.

Hlatshaneni, Simnikiwe. 2019. "Rape 'Pushes up Number of HIV Infections, Also among Children'." *The Citizen,* November 27, 2019. https://citizen.co.za/news/south-africa/health/2211070/rape-pushes-up-number-of-hiv-infections-also-among-children/.

Holloway, Linda. 2014. "HIV/AIDS." In *Encyclopedia of Social Deviance,* vol. 1, edited by Craig J. Forsyth and Heith Copes, 327–-329. Thousand Oaks, CA: Sage.

Hood, Johanna. 2013. "AIDS Phobia (aizibingkongjuzheng) and the People Who Panic about AIDS (kong'aiZu): The Consequences of HIV Representations in China." In *HIV in World Cultures: Three Decades of Representations,* edited by Gustavo Subero, 203–234. Farnham, UK: Ashgate.

Hope, Ruth. 2007. *Addressing Cross-Generational Sex: A Desk Review of Research and Programs.* Washington, DC: Population Reference Bureau. https://www.igwg.org/resources/addressing-cross-generational-sex-a-desk-review-of-research-and-programs/.

Hubert, Don. 1999. "Human Security: Safety for People in a Changing World." Paper Presented at the Regional Conference on the Management of African Security in the Twenty-First Century, Nigerian Institute of International Affairs, Lagos, Nigeria, 23–24 June 1999.

Hugo, Nicola. 2012. "Virginity Testing and HIV/AIDS: Solution or Human Rights Violation." Polity.org.za. Last modified July 19, 2012. http://www.polity.org.za/article/virginity-testing-and-hivaids-solution-or-human-rights-violation-2012-07-19.

Husbands, Winston, Jessica Cattaneo, Lydia Makoroka, Rui Pires, Jocelyn Watchorn, and Jessica Whitbread. 2012. *HIV-Related Stigma: Synthesis Paper.* Toronto, ON: AIDS Committee of Toronto. http://www.actoronto.org/research.nsf/pages/act.research.0390.

Iacob, Simona, Iacob Diana G., and Gheorghita Jugulete. 2017. "Improving the Adherence to Antiretroviral Therapy, a Difficult but Essential Task for a Successful HIV Treatment-Clinical Points of View and Practical Considerations." *Frontiers in Pharmacology* 8, no. 831 (November). https://doi.org/10.3389/fphar.2017.00831.

Icard, Larry D. 2008. "Reaching African-American Men on the 'Down Low': Sampling Hidden Populations: Implications for HIV Prevention." *Journal of Homosexuality* 55 (3): 437–449.

ICF Macro. 2010. *AIDS Indicator Survey: Interviewer's Manual.* Calverton, MD: ICF Macro. https://dhsprogram.com/pubs/pdf/AISM1/AIS_Interviewer's_Manual_28Dec2010.pdf.

Institute for Security Studies and Malawi Institute for Management. 2003. *HIV/AIDS and Attrition: Assessing the Impact on the Safety, Security and Access to Justice in Malawi.* Pretoria: Institute for Security Studies.

Institute of Medicine, Board on Children, Youth, and Families, Board on Global Health, Committee for the Evaluation of the President's Emergency Plan for AIDS Relief (PEPFAR) Implementation, Jamie Sepúlveda, Charles Carpenter, James Curran, William Holzemer, Helen Smits, Kimberly Scott, and Michele Orza, eds. 2007. *PEPFAR Implementation: Progress and Promise.* Washington, DC: National Academies Press.

Interagency Coalition on AIDS and Development. 2006. *Best Practices for Care of Children Orphaned by AIDS.* Ottawa, ON: Interagency Coalition on AIDS and Development. http://www.icad-cisd.com/pdf/Orphans_FS_EN.pdf.

International HIV/AIDS Alliance and Vasavya Mahila Mandali. 2004. *Moving Forward: A Report on Pioneering Responses to Children Affected by HIV/AIDS in Andhra Pradesh, India.* Hove, UK: International HIV/AIDS Alliance. https://www.streetchildren.org/resources/moving-forward-a-report-on-pioneering-responses-to-children-affected-by-hivaids-in-andhra-pradesh-india/.

Israel, Ellen, Carlos Laudari, and Cecilia Simonetti. 2008. *HIV Prevention, among Vulnerable Populations: The Pathfinder International Approach.* Pathfinder International Technical Guidance Series Number 6. Watertown, MA: Pathfinder International. https://www.pathfinder.org/publications/hiv-prevention-among-vulnerable-populations-pathfinder-approach/.

Jadhav, Apoorva, Parinita Bhattacharjee, Thalinja Raghavendra, James Blanchard, Stephen Moses, Shajy Isac, and Shiva S. Halli. 2013. "Risky Behaviors among HIV-Positive Female Sex Workers in Northern Karnataka, India." *AIDS Research and Treatment* 2013: 878151.
http://dx.doi.org/10.1155/2013/878151.

Jamieson, Lucy, Lizette Berry, and Lori Lake. 2017. "Transforming South Africa: A Call to Action." In *South African Child Gauge 2017,* edited by Lucy Jamieson, Lizette Berry and Lori Lake, 91–95. Cape Town: Children's Institute, University of Cape Town. http://www.ci.uct.ac.za/ci/child-gauge/2017.

Jenness, Samuel M., Elizabeth M. Begier, Alan Neaigus, Christopher S. Murrill, Travis Wendel, and Holly Hagan. 2011. "Unprotected Anal Intercourse and Sexually Transmitted Diseases in High-Risk Heterosexual Women." *American Journal of Public Health* 101, no. 4 (April): 745–750.

Jewkes, Rachel K., Kristin Dunkle, Mzikazi Nduna, and Nwabisa Shai. 2010a. "Intimate Partner Violence, Relationship Power Inequity, and Incidence of HIV Infection in Young Women in South Africa: A Cohort Study." *The Lancet* 376, no. 9734 (July): 41–48.

Jewkes, Rachel K., Kristin Dunkle, Mzikazi Nduna, P. Nwabisa Jama, and Adrian Puren. 2010b. "Associations between Childhood Adversity and Depression, Substance Abuse and HIV & HSV2 Incident Infections in Rural South African Youth." *Child Abuse & Neglect* 34, no. 11 (November): 833–841.

Jewkes, Rachel, and Naeemah Abrahams. 2000. *Violence against Women in South Africa: Rape and Sexual Coercion.* Pretoria: Crime Prevention Research Resources Centre, Council for Scientific and Industrial Research.

Jewkes, Rachel, Naeemah Abrahams, Shanaaz Mathews, Mohammed Seedat, Ashley Van Niekerk, Shanaaz Suffla, and Kopano Ratele. 2009. "Preventing Rape and Violence in South Africa: Call for Leadership in a New Agenda for Action." MRC Policy Brief 2, South African Medical Research Council, Pretoria.

Jewkes, Rachel. 2004. "Child Sex Abuse and HIV Infection." In *Sexual Abuse of Young Children in Southern Africa,* edited by Linda M. Richter, Andrew Dawes and Craig Higson-Smith, 130–142. Cape Town: Human Sciences Research Council Press.

Johnson, Shannon. 2019. "How Long Can a Person Live with HIV?" Medical News Today. Last modified January 30, 2019. https://www.medicalnewstoday.com/articles/324321.

Jones, Nancy Lee. 2003. "The Americans with Disabilities Act (ADA): Statutory Languages and Recent Issues." In *The Americans with Disabilities Act (ADA): Overview, Regulations and Interpretations,* edited by Nancy Lee Jones, 85-126. Hauppauge, NY: Nova Science Publishers.

Jönsson, Christer. 2010. "Coordinating Actors in the Fight against HIV/AIDS: From 'Lead Agency' to Public-Private Partnerships." In *Democracy and Public-Private Partnerships in Global Governance,* edited by Magdalena Bexell and Ulrika Mörth, 167–189. Basingstoke, UK: Palgrave Macmillan.

Jörgens, Viktor, and Monika Grüsser. 2013. "Happy Birthday, Claude Bernard." *Diabetes* 62, no. 7 (July): 2181–2182.

Jürgens, Ralf, and Jonathan Cohen. 2009. *Human Rights and HIV/AIDS: Now More Than Ever - 10 Reasons Why Human Rights Should Occupy the Center of the Global AIDS Struggle.* 4th ed. New York, NY: Open Society Law and Health Initiative. https://www.opensocietyfoundations.org/publications/human-rights-and-hivaids-now-more-ever.

Jürgens, Ralf, Manfred Nowak, and Marcus Day. 2011. "HIV and Incarceration: Prisons and Detention." *Journal of the International AIDS Society* 14, no 1 (January): 26. https://doi.org/10.1186/1758-2652-14-26.

Kabeer, Naila. 2014. "Violence against Women as 'Relational' Vulnerability Engendering the Sustainable Human Development Agenda." Occasional Paper, Human Development Report Office. http://hdr.undp.org/en/content/violence-against-women-%E2%80%98relational%E2%80%99-vulnerability-engendering-sustainable-human-development.

Kalichman, Seth C., Dolly Ntseane, Keitseope Nthomang, Mosarwa Segwabe, Odireleng Phorano, and Leickness C. Simbayi. 2007. "Recent Multiple Sexual Partners and HIV Transmission Risks among People Living with HIV/AIDS in Botswana." *Sexually Transmitted Infections* 83, no. 5 (August): 371–375.

Kalichman, Seth C., Steven D. Pinkerton, Michael P. Carey, Demetria Cain, Vuyelwa Mehlomakulu, Kate B. Carey, Leickness Chisamu Simbayi, Kelvin

Mwaba, and Ofer Harel. 2011. "Heterosexual Anal Intercourse and HIV Infection Risks in the Context of Alcohol Serving Venues, Cape Town, South Africa." *BMC Public Health* 11: 807. https://doi.org/10.1186/1471-2458-11-807.

Kalra, Gurvinder, and Dinesh Bhugra. 2013. "Sexual Violence against Women: Understanding Cross-Cultural Intersections." *Indian Journal of Psychiatry* 55, no. 3 (July-September): 244–249.

Kane, Stephanie. 1994. "Sacred Deviance and AIDS in a North American Buddhist Community." *Law and Policy* 16, no. 3 (July): 323–339.

Kaplan, Adriana, Mary Forbes, Isabelle Bonhoure, Mireia Utzet, Miguel Martín, Malick Manneh, and Haruna Ceesay. 2013. "Female Genital Mutilation/Cutting in the Gambia: Long-Term Consequences and Complications during Delivery and for the Newborn." *International Journal of Women's Health* 5: 323–331. https://doi.org/10.2147/IJWH.S42064.

Karanja, Daniel Njoroge. 2003. *Female Genital Mutilation in Africa*. Maitland, FL: Xulon Press.

Kazatchkine, Cécile. 2010. "Criminalizing HIV Transmission or Exposure: The Context of Francophone West and Central Africa." *HIV/AIDS Policy & Law Review* 14, no. 3 (June): 1, 5–12.

Keetile, Mpho. 2014. "High-Risk Behaviors among Adult Men and Women in Botswana: Implications for HIV/AIDS Prevention Efforts." *SAHARA-J: Journal of Social Aspects of HIV/AIDS* 11 (1): 158–166.

Kelly, Jeffrey A., and Seth C. Kalichman 2002. "Behavioral Research in HIV/AIDS Primary and Secondary Prevention: Recent Advances and Future Directions." *Journal of Consulting and Clinical Psychology* 70, no. 3 (June): 626–639.

Keown, Mary Katherine. 2007. "Health Activists Link Spread of HIV-AIDS to FGM." Women's eNews. Last modified August 10, 2007. http://womensenews.org/2007/08/health-activists-link-spread-hiv-aids-fgm/.

Kershaw, Robert J. 2008. *The impact of HIV/AIDS on the Operational Effectiveness of Military Forces*. ASCI Research Report 4. New York, NY: AIDS, Security and Conflict Initiative. http://asci.researchhub.ssrc.org/working-papers/Kershaw.pdf.

Kharsany, Ayesha B. M., and Quarraisha A. Karim. 2016. "HIV Infection and AIDS in Sub-Saharan Africa: Current Status, Challenges and Opportunities." *The Open AIDS Journal* 10: 34–48. https://doi.org/10.2174/1874613601610010034.

Kidd, Ross, and Sue Clay. 2003. *Understanding and Challenging HIV Stigma: Toolkit for Action*. Washington, DC: International Center for Research on Women. https://www.icrw.org/publications/understanding-and-challenging-hiv-stigma-toolkit-for-action/.

Killianova, Tereza. 2013. "Risky Behavior." In *Encyclopedia of Behavioral Medicine*, edited by Marc D. Gellman and J. Rick Turner. New York, NY: Springer. Accessed May 4, 2010. https://doi.org/10.1007/978-1-4419-1005-9_1551.

Kim, Young Soo. 2015. "World Health Organization and Early Global Response to HIV/AIDS: Emergence and Development of International Norms." *Journal of International and Area Studies* 22, no. 1 (June): 19–40. http://www.jstor.org/stable/43490278.

Kirby, Douglas, Robyn Dayton, Kelly L'Engle, and Allison Pricke. 2012. *Promoting Partner Reduction: Helping Young People Understand and Avoid HIV Risks from*

Multiple Partnerships. Durham, NC: FHI 360. https://www.fhi360.org/resource/ promoting-partner-reduction-helping-young-people-understand-and-avoid-hiv-risks-multiple.

Klouman, Elise, Rachel Manongi, and Knut-Inge Klepp. 2005. "Self-Reported and Observed Female Genital Cutting in Rural Tanzania: Associated Demographic Factors, HIV and Sexually Transmitted Infections." *Tropical Medicine & International Health* 10, no. 1 (January): 105–115.

Knipscheer, Jeroen, Erick Vloeberghs, Anke van der Kwaak, and Maria van den Muijsenbergh. 2015. "Mental Health Problems Associated with Female Genital Mutilation." *BJPsych Bulletin* 39, no. 6 (December): 273–277.

Knox, Michael D., and Tiffany Chenneville. 2006. "Prevention and Education Strategies." In *Psychiatric Aspects of HIV/AIDS*, edited by Francisco Fernandez and Pedro Ruiz, 395–403. Philadelphia, PA: Lippincott Williams & Wilkins.

Kontomanolis, Emmanuel N., Spyridon Michalopoulos, Grigorios Gkasdaris, and Zacharias Fasoulakis. 2017. "The Social Stigma of HIV-AIDS: Society's Role." *HIV/AIDS - Research and Palliative Care* 9: 111-118. https://doi.org/10.2147/ HIV.S129992.

Koon-Magnin, Sarah. 2014. "National Crime Victimization Survey." In *Encyclopedia of Social Deviance*, vol. 2, edited by Craig J. Forsyth and Heith Copes, 457–458. Thousand Oaks, CA: Sage.

Krishnan, Suneeta, Megan S. Dunbar, Alexandra M. Minnis, Carol A. Medlin, Caitlin E. Gerdts, and Nancy S. Padian. 2008. "Poverty, Gender Inequities, and Women's Risk of Human Immunodeficiency Virus/AIDS." *Annals of the New York Academy of Sciences* 1136, no. 1 (June) 101–110.

Larsen, Pamela D., Patricia Ryan Lewis, and Ilene Morof Lubkin. 2006. "Illness Behavior and Roles." In *Chronic Illness: Impact and Intervention*, 6th ed., edited by Ilene Morof Lubkin and Pamela D. Larsen, 23-44. Sudbury, MA: Jones and Bartlett Publishers.

Lasco, Chanté. 2002. "Virginity Testing in Turkey: A Violation of Women's Human Rights." *Human Rights Brief* 9 (3): 10–13. http://digitalcommons.wcl. american.edu/hrbrief/vol9/iss3/3.

Lata, Swaran, and Shikha Verma. 2013. "Mental Health of HIV/AIDS Orphans: A Review." *Journal of AIDS and HIV Research* 5, no. 12 (December): 455–467. https://doi.org/10.5897/JAHR2013.0271.

Laurie, Roberta. 2015. *Weaving a Malawi Sunrise: A Woman, a School, a People.* Edmonton, AB: University of Alberta Press.

Lawson, Erica, Fauzia Gardezi, Liviana Calzavara, Winston Husbands, Ted Myers, and Wangari Esther Tharao. 2006. *HIV/AIDS Stigma, Denial, Fear and Discrimination: Experiences and Responses of People from African and Caribbean Communities in Toronto.* Toronto, ON: African and Caribbean Council on HIV/AIDS in Ontario and HIV Social, Behavioural and Epidemiological Studies Unit, University of Toronto.
https://tspace.library.utoronto.ca/handle/1807/10304.

Leclerc-Madlala, Suzanne. 2001. "Virginity Testing: Managing Sexuality in a Maturing HIV/AIDS Epidemic." *Medical Anthropology Quarterly* 15, no. 4 (December): 533–552.

Leclerc-Madlala, Suzanne. 2003. "Protecting Girlhood? Virginity Revivals in the Era of AIDS." *Agenda* 17 (56): 16–25.

Leclerc-Madlala, Suzanne. 2008. "Sugar Daddies and HIV: Is It Really about Money, Money, Money?" *HSRC Review* 6, no. 3 (September): 11–12.

Leclerc-Madlala, Suzanne. 2010. "Virginity Testing: Managing Sexuality in a Maturing HIV/AIDS epidemic." In *Perspectives on Africa: A Reader in Culture, History and Representation*, 2nd ed., edited by Roy Richard Grinker, Stephen C. Lubkemann and Christopher B. Steiner, 411–422. Oxford: Wiley-Blackwell.

Lee, Rachel S., Arlene Kochman, and Kathleen J. Sikkema. 2002. "Internalized Stigma among People Living with HIV/AIDS." *AIDS and Behavior* 6, no. 4 (December): 309–319.

Leggett, Ted. 2002. "Everyone's an Inspector: The Crisis of Rank Inflation and the Decline of Visible Policing." *South African Crime Quarterly*, no. 1 (July): 23–26.

Lehman, J. Stan, Meredith H. Carr, Allison J. Nichol, Alberto Ruisanchez, David W. Knight, Anne E. Langford, Simone C. Gray, and Jonathan H. Mermin. 2014. "Prevalence and Public Health Implications of State Laws That Criminalize Potential HIV Exposure in the United States." *AIDS and Behavior* 18, no. 6 (June): 997–1006.

Lemelle Jr., Anthony J., Charlene Harrington, and Allen J. LeBlanc. 1999. *Readings in the Sociology of AIDS*. Upper Saddle River, NJ: Prentice-Hall.

Lemert, Edwin H. 1951. *Social Pathology: A Systematic Approach to the Theory of Sociopathic Behavior*. New York, NY: McGraw-Hill.

Levi, Jacob, Alice Raymond, Anton Pozniak, Pietro Vernazza, Philipp Kohler, and Andrew Hill. 2016. "Can the UNAIDS 90-90-90 Target Be Achieved? A Systematic Analysis of National HIV Treatment Cascades." *BMJ Global Health* 1, no. 2 (August): e000010. http://dx.doi.org/10.1136/bmjgh-2015-000010.

Levy, Neil. 2018. "Responsibility as an Obstacle to Good Policy: The Case of Lifestyle Related Disease." *Journal of Bioethical Inquiry* 15, no. 3 (September): 459–468.

Lewis, Nathalie M., Greta R. Bauer, Todd A. Coleman, Soraya Blot, Daniel Pugh, Meredith Fraser, and Leanne Powell. 2015. "Community Cleavages: Gay and Bisexual Men's Perceptions of Gay and Mainstream Community Acceptance in the Post-AIDS, Post-Rights Era." *Journal of Homosexuality* 62 (9): 1201–1227.

Li, Li, Zunyou Wu, Sheng Wu, Manhong Jia, Eli Lieber, and Yao Lu. 2008. "Impacts of HIV/AIDS Stigma on Family Identity and Interactions in China." *Families, Systems and Health* 26, no. 4 (December): 431–442.

Li, Ying, Caitlin M. Marshall, Hilary C. Rees, Annabelle Nunez, Echezona E. Ezeanolue, and John E. Ehiri. 2014. "Intimate Partner Violence and HIV Infection among Women: A Systematic Review and Meta-Analysis." *Journal of the International AIDS Society* 17, no. 1 (January): 18845. https://doi.org/10.7448/IAS.17.1.18845.

Lichtenstein, Bronwen. 2005. "Domestic Violence, Sexual Ownership, and HIV Risk in Women in the American Deep South." *Social Science & Medicine* 60, no. 4 (February): 701–714.

Lin, Xiuyun, Guoxiang Zhao, Xiaoming Li, Bonita Stanton, Liying Zhang, Yan Hong, Junfeng Zhao, and Xiaoyi Fang. 2010. "Perceived HIV Stigma among

Children in a High HIV-Prevalence Area in Central China: Beyond the Parental HIV-Related Illness and Death." *AIDS Care* 22 (5): 545–555.

Lloyd, Mary Elizabeth. 2008. *AIDS Orphans Rising: What You Should Know and What You Can Do to Help Them Succeed.* Ann Arbor, MI: Loving Healing Press.

Loeber, Rolf, and Magda Stouthamer-Loeber. 1986. "Family Factors as Correlates and Predictors of Juvenile Conduct Problems and Delinquency". In *Crime and Justice: An Annual Review of Research,* vol. 7, edited by Michael Tonry and Norval Morris, 29–149. Chicago, IL: University of Chicago Press.

Loewenson, Rene, and Alan Whiteside. 2001. "HIV/AIDS: Implications for Poverty Reduction." Background Paper Prepared for the United Nations Development Programme for the United Nations General Assembly Special Session on HIV/AIDS, 25-27 June 2001, New York.

Loftspring, Rachel C. 2007. "Inheritance Rights in Uganda: How Equal Inheritance Rights Would Reduce Poverty and Decrease the Spread of HIV/AIDS in Uganda." *University of Pennsylvania Journal of International Law* 29 (1): 243–281. https://scholarship.law.upenn.edu/jil/vol29/iss1/5.

Longman, Chia, and Gily Coene. 2015. "Harmful Cultural Practices and Minority Women in Europe: From Headscarf Bans to Forced Marriages and Honour Related Violence." In *Interrogating Harmful Cultural Practices: Gender, Culture and Coercion,* edited by Chia Longman and Tamsin Bradley, 51–66. Farnham, UK: Ashgate.

Loosli, B. Clarence. 2004. *Traditional Practices and HIV Prevention in Sub-Saharan Africa.* Geneva: Geneva Foundation for Medical Education and Research. https://www.gfmer.ch/GFMER_members/pdf/Traditional_HIV_Loosli.pdf.

Loutfy, Mona R., Carmen H. Logie, Yimeng Zhang, Sandra L. Blitz, Shari L. Margolese, Wangari E. Tharao, Sean B. Rourke, Sergio Rueda, and Janet M. Raboud. 2012. "Gender and Ethnicity Differences in HIV-Related Stigma Experienced by People Living with HIV in Ontario, Canada." *PLOS One* 7 (12): e48168. https://doi.org/10.1371/journal.pone.0048168.

Luke, Nancy. 2005. "Confronting the 'Sugar Daddy' Stereotype: Age and Economic Asymmetries and Risky Sexual Behavior in Urban Kenya." *International Family Planning Perspectives* 31, no. 1 (March): 6–14.

Luthy-Kaplan, Katrina. 2015. "An Epidemic of Child Rape in Khayelitsha." Global Health NOW. Last modified July 1, 2015. https://www.globalhealthnow.org/2015-07/epidemic-child-rape-khayelitsha.

Luz, Paula M, Benjamin Osher, Beatriz Grinsztejn, Rachel L. Maclean, Elena Losina, Madeline E. Stern, Claudio J. Struchiner, Robert A. Parker, Kenneth A. Freedberg, Fabio Mesquita, Rochelle P. Walensky, Valdilea G. Veloso, and A. David Paltiel. 2018. "The Cost-Effectiveness of HIV Pre-Exposure Prophylaxis in Men Who Have Sex with Men and Transgender Women at High HIV Infection in Brazil." *Journal of the International AIDS Society* 21, no. 3 (March): e25096. https://doi.org/10.1002/jia2.25096.

Luz, Paula M., Valdilea G Veloso, and Beatriz Grinsztejn. 2019. "The HIV Epidemic in Latin America: Accomplishments and Challenges on Treatment and Prevention." *Current Opinion in HIV and AIDS* 14, no. 5 (September): 366–373.

Machisa, Mercilene, Rachel Jewkes, Colleen Lowe Morna, and Kubi Rama. 2011. *The War at Home: Gender Based Violence Indicators Project. Gauteng Research Report, South Africa.* Johannesburg: Gender Links and South African Medical Research Council. http://genderlinks.org.za/programme-web-menu/publications/the-war-at-home-gbv-indicators-project-2011-08-16/.

Machisa, Mercilene, Ruxana Jina, Gerard Labuschagne, Lisa Vetten, Lizle Loots, Sheena Swemmer, Bonita Meyersfeld, and Rachel Jewkes. 2017. *Rape Justice in South Africa: A Retrospective Study of the Investigation, Prosecution and Adjudication of Reported Rape Cases from 2012.* Pretoria: Gender and Health Research Unit, South African Medical Research Council. http://www.mrc.ac.za/reports/rape-justice-south-africa-retrospective-study-investigation-prosecution-and-adjudication.

Macia, Manuel, Pranitha Maharaj, and Ashley Gresh. 2011. "Masculinity and Male Sexual Behaviour in Mozambique." *Culture, Health & Sexuality* 13 (10): 1181–1192.

Madiba, Sphiwe, and Nomsa Ngwenya. 2017. "Cultural Practices, Gender Inequality and Inconsistent Condom Use Increase Vulnerability to HIV Infection: Narratives from Married and Cohabiting Women in Rural Communities in Mpumalanga Province, South Africa." *Global Health Action* 10 (Suppl. 2): 55–62.

Maleche, Allan, and Emma Day. 2011. "Traditional Cultural Practices and HIV: Reconciling Culture and Human Rights." Working Paper Prepared for the Third Meeting of the Technical Advisory Group of the Global Commission on HIV and the Law, 7-9 July 2011. http://www.hivlawcommission.org/index.php/workingpapers?task=document.viewdoc&id=102.

Maman, Suzanne, Jacquelyn Campbell, Michael D. Sweat, and Andrea C. Gielen. 2000. "The Intersections of HIV and Violence: Directions for Future Research and Interventions." *Social Science & Medicine* 50, no. 4 (February): 459–478.

Mampane, Johannes N. 2018. "Exploring the 'Blesser and Blessee' Phenomenon: Young Women, Transactional Sex, and HIV in Rural South Africa." *Sage Open* 8, no. 4 (October-December): 1–9. https://doi.org/10.1177/2158244018806343.

Manning, Ryann. 2002. "HIV/AIDS and Democracy: What Do We Know?" In *HIV/AIDS, Economics and Governance in South Africa: Key Issues in Understanding Response,* edited by Kevin Kelly, Warren Parker and Stephen Gelb, 21–36. Johannesburg: Centre for AIDS Development, Research and Evaluation.

Manning, Wendy D., Peggy C. Giordano, Monica A. Longmore, and Christine M. Flanagan. 2012. "Young Adult Dating Relationships and the Management of Sexual Risk." *Population Research and Policy Review* 31, no. 2 (April): 165–185.

Maphagela, Amy. 2016. "Bitter Themes and Sugar Daddies: Inter-Generational Sex and the Spread of HIV in South Africa." In *Sizonqoba! Outliving AIDS in Southern Africa,* edited by Busani Ngcaweni, 197–220. Pretoria: Africa Institute of South Africa.

Mash, Rachel, and Robert Mash. 2013. "Faith-Based Organisations and HIV Prevention in Africa: A Review." *African Journal of Primary Health Care & Family Medicine* 5 (1): a464. https://doi.org/10.4102/phcfm.v5i1.464.

Maslovskaya, Olga, James Brown, and Sabu S. Padmadas. 2009. "Disentangling the Complex Association between Female Genital Cutting and HIV among Kenyan Women." *Journal of Biosocial Science* 41, no. 6 (November): 815–830.

Masuku, Sibusiso. 2002. "Prevention Is Better Than Cure: Addressing Violent Crime in South Africa." *South African Crime Quarterly*, no. 2 (November): 5–12.

Masuku, Themba. 2007. *An Overview of the Implementation of the SAPS Policy and Five Year (2000–2005) Strategic Plan on HIV and AIDS: The Case of Johannesburg Policing Area*. Johannesburg: Centre for the Study of Violence and Reconciliation. https://www.csvr.org.za/publications/1501-an-overview-of-the-implementation-of-the-saps-policy-a-five-year-2000-2005-strategic-plan-on-hiv-a-aids-the-case-of-the-johannesburg-policing-area.

Mattes, Robert. 2003. "Health Democracies? The Potential Impact of AIDS on Democracy in Southern Africa." ISS Paper 71, Institute for Security Studies, Pretoria.

Mawar, Nita, Seema Saha, Apoorvaa Pandit, and Uma Patil Mahajan. 2005. "The Third Phase of HIV Pandemic: Social Consequences of HIV/AIDS Stigma and Discrimination and Future Needs." *Indian Journal of Medical Research* 122, no. 6 (December): 471–484.

Mbatha, Blessing. 2013. "AIDS-Related Stigma as a Barrier to HIV and AIDS Prevention, Care and Treatment in South African Public Universities." *Mediterranean Journal of Social Sciences* 4, no. 14 (November): 517–524.

Mburu, Gitau, Mark Limmer, and Paula Holland. 2019. "HIV Risk Behaviours among Women Who Inject Drugs in Coastal Kenya: Findings from Secondary Analysis of Qualitative Data." *Harm Reduction Journal* 16: 10. https://doi.org/10.1186/s12954-019-0281-y.

McGhee, Sarah Theresa. 2012. "Masculinity Sexuality and Soccer: An Exploration of Three Grass Sport-for-Social-Change Organizations in South Africa." PhD diss., University of South Florida. https://scholarcommons.usf.edu/etd/4368/.

McInnes, Colin. 2006. "HIV/AIDS and Security." *International Affairs (Royal Institute of International Affairs 1944-)* 82, no. 2 (March): 315–326.

Mcloughlin, Claire. 2010. *Topic Guide on Fragile States*. Birmingham, UK: Governance and Social Development Resource Centre, University of Birmingham.

McNeill, Fraser G. 2011. *AIDS, Politics, and Music in South Africa*. New York, NY: Cambridge University Press.

Médecins Sans Frontières. 2016. *Untreated Violence: The Need for Patient-Centred Care for Survivors of Sexual Violence in the Platinum Mining Belt*. Cape Town: Médecins Sans Frontières. https://www.msf.org.za/about-us/publications/reports/untreated-violence.

Medie, Peace A. 2019. "Women and Violence in Africa." In *Oxford Research Encyclopedia of African History*. Oxford: Oxford University Press. Accessed Apr 21, 2020. https://doi.org/ 10.1093/acrefore/9780190277734.013.56.

Meel, Banwari Lal. 2003. "The Myth of Child Rape as a Cure for HIV/AIDS in Transkei: A Case Report." *Medicine, Science and the Law* 43, no. 1 (January): 85–88.

Meinck, Franziska, Lucie D. Cluver, Mark E. Boyes, and Elsinah L. Mhlongo. 2015. "Risk and Protective Factors for Physical and Sexual Abuse of Children and Adolescents in Africa: A Review and Implications for Practice." *Trauma, Violence, & Abuse* 16, no. 1 (January): 81–107.

Meini, Bruno, and Mara Tognetti Bordogna. 2018. "The Impact of HIV-Related Stigma on Children Orphaned by AIDS or Living with Seropositive Caregivers." *International Review of Sociology* 28 (3): 541–555.

Meini, Bruno, and Mara Tognetti Bordogna. 2019. "The Contribution of Harmful Traditional Practices to HIV Transmission among Adolescent and Adult Females in Sub-Saharan Africa: A Victimological Approach." *International Journal of Gender Studies in Developing Societies* 3 (1): 37–59.

Meini, Bruno. 2008a. "HIV/AIDS, Crime and Security in Southern Africa." *African Journal of Criminology and Justice Studies* 3, no. 2 (Spring): 35–84. https://www.umes.edu/uploadedFiles/_WEBSITES/AJCJS/Content/vol3.2%20meini%20final1.pdf.

Meini, Bruno. 2008b. "La Relazione tra la Questione Sociale degli Orfani da AIDS e il Crimine." *Nuove Esperienze di Giustizia Minorile/ New Experiences of Juvenile Justice*, no. 3: 23–33.

Meini, Bruno. 2013. "The HIV/AIDS Pandemic: Social Risks and Moral Panic in a Global Context." In *Global Society, Cosmopolitanism and Human Rights*, edited by Vittorio Cotesta, Vincenzo Cicchelli and Mariella Nocenzi, 185–196. Newcastle upon Tyne: Cambridge Scholars Publishing.

Mendelsohn, Benjamin. 1976. "Victimology and Contemporary Society's Trends." *Victimology* 1, no. 1 (Spring): 8–28.

Mishra, Vinod, and Simona Bignami-Van Assche. 2008. *Orphans and Vulnerable Children in High HIV Prevalence Countries in Sub-Saharan Africa.* DHS Analytical Studies 15. Calverton, MD: Macro International Inc. https://dhsprogram.com/publications/publication-AS15-Analytical-Studies.cfm.

Mkhwanazi, Nolwazi, Tawanda Makusha, Deidre Blackie, Lenore Manderson, Katharine Hall, and Mayke Huijbregts. 2018. "Negotiating the Care of Children and Support for Caregivers." In *South African Child Gauge 2018. Children, Families and the State: Collaboration and Contestation*, edited by Katharine Hall, Linda Richter, Zitha Mokomane and Lori Lake, 70–80. Cape Town: Children's Institute, University of Cape Town.

Mojapelo, Lebohang. 2016. "Virginity Testing 'Sacred' but Not a Science." Africa Check. Last modified February 10, 2016. https://africacheck.org reports/virginity-testing-sacred-but-not-a-science.

Mokwena, Steve. 1991. "The Era of the Jackrollers: Contextualising the Rise of the Youth Gangs in Soweto." Paper Presented at the Centre for the Study of Violence and Reconciliation, Johannesburg, South Africa, Seminar 7, October 30. https://www.csvr.org.za/publications/1805-the-era-of-the-jackrollers-contextualising-the-rise-of-the-youth-gangs-in-soweto.

Moletsane, Mokgadi. 2013. "Educational and Psychosocial Effects of AIDS on Orphans from a Previously Disadvantaged South African Township." *Journal of Human Ecology* 44 (3): 297–303.

Monjok, Emmanuel, Ekere J. Essien, and Laurens Holmes. 2007. "Female Genital Mutilation: Potential for HIV Transmission in Sub-Saharan Africa and Prospects for Epidemiologic Investigation and Intervention." *African Journal of Reproductive Health* 11 (1): 33–42.

Moodley, Prevan, and Sumayya Ebrahim. 2019. "#Blesser: A Critical Evaluation of Conceptual Antecedents and the Allure of a Transactional Relationship." *Acta Academica* 51 (2): 21–40.

Mookodi, Godisang. 2004. "Male Violence against Women in Botswana: A Discussion of Gendered Uncertainties in a Rapidly Changing Environment." *African Sociological Review/ Revue Africaine de Sociologie* 8 (1): 118–138.

Morgan, Myfanwy. 2003. "The Doctor-Patient Relationship." In *Sociology as Applied to Medicine*, 5th ed., edited by Graham Scambler, 55–70. London: Saunders.

Morison, Linda, Caroline Scherf, Gloria Ekpo, Katie Paine, Beryl West, Rosalind Coleman, and Gijs Walraven. 2001. "The Long-Term Reproductive Health Consequences of Female Genital Cutting in Rural Gambia: A Community-Based Survey." *Tropical Medicine & International Health* 6, no. 8 (August): 643–653.

Morse, Stephen S. 2001. "Factors in the Emergence of Infectious Diseases." In *Plagues and Politics: Infectious Disease and International Policy*, edited by Andrew T. Price-Smith, 8–26. Basingstoke, UK: Palgrave Macmillan.

Mtenga, Sally M., Constanze Pfeiffer, Sonja Merten, Masuma Mamdani, Amon Exavery, Joke Haafkens, Marcel Tanner, and Eveline Geubbels. 2015. "Prevalence and Social Drivers of HIV among Married and Cohabitating Heterosexual Adults in South-Eastern Tanzania: Analysis of Adult Health Community Cohort Data." *Global Health Action* 8 (1): 28941. https://doi.org/10.3402/gha.v8.28941.

Mujuzi, Jamil. 2012. "Widow Inheritance in Uganda." In *The International Survey of Family Law: 2012 Edition*, edited by Bill Atkin, 393–403. Bristol: Jordan Publishing.

Mulieri, Ilaria, Flavia Santi, Anna Colucci, Emanuele Fanales Belasio, Pietro Gallo, and Anna Maria Luzi. 2014. "Sex Workers Clients in Italy: Results of a Phone Survey on HIV Risk Behaviour and Perception." *Annali dell'Istituto Superiore di Sanità* 50 (4): 363–368.

Murphy, William D., Emily M. Coleman, and Mary R. Haynes. 1986. "Factors Related to Coercive Sexual Behavior in a Nonclinical Sample of Males." *Violence and Victims* 1 (4): 255–278.

Musariri-Chipatiso, Linda, Violet Nyambo, Mercilene Machisa, and Kevin Chiramba. 2014. *The Western Cape Gender Based Violence Indicators Study.* Johannesburg: Gender Links.

Musheno, Michael. 1994. "Social-Legal Dynamics of AIDS: Constructing Identities, Protecting Boundaries amidst Crisis." *Law & Policy* 16, no. 3 (July): 235–247.

Muthumbi, Jane, Joar Svanemyr, Elisa Scolaro, Marleen Temmerman, and Lale Say. 2015. "Female Genital Mutilation: A Literature Review of the Current Status of Legislation and Policies in 27 African Countries and Yemen." *African Journal of Reproductive Health* 19 (3): 32–40.

Mutinta, Given. 2014. "Multiple Sexual Partnerships and Their Underlying Risk Influences at the University of KwaZulu-Natal." *Journal of Human Ecology* 46 (2): 147–155.

Muula, Adamson S., and Joseph M. Mfusto-Bengo. 2004. "Important but Neglected Ethical and Cultural Considerations in the Fight against HIV/AIDS in Malawi." *Nursing Ethics* 11, no. 5 (September): 479–488.

Mwoma, Teresa, and Jace Pillay. 2016. "Educational Support for Orphans and Vulnerable Children in Primary Schools: Challenges and Interventions." *Issues in Educational Research* 26 (1): 82–97. http://www.iier.org.au/iier26/mwoma.pdf.

Nachman, Steven R., and Ginette Dreyfuss. 1986. "Haitians and AIDS in South Florida." *Medical Anthropology Quarterly* 17, no. 2 (February): 32–33.

Nagtegaal, Jackie. 2018. "The Cost of Rape: Seeking Justice in South Africa." *Daily Maverick*, September 7, 2018. https://www.dailymaverick.co.za/opinionista/2018-09-07-the-cost-of-rape-seeking-justice-in-south-africa/.

Naidoo, Ruben K., and Karthy Govender. 2011. "Compulsory HIV Testing of Alleged Sexual Offenders: A Human Rights Violation." *South African Journal of Bioethics and Law* 4, no. 2 (December): 95–101. http://www.sajbl.org.za/index.php/sajbl/article/view/126.

Nambiar, Puja, and William R. Short. 2019. "Mechanisms of HIV Transmission." In *Fundamental of HIV Medicine 2019*, edited by W. David Hardy, 21–24. New York, NY: Oxford University Press.

Namey, Emily, Brian Perry, Jennifer Headley, Albert Kouakou Yao, Mariame Louise Ouattara, Coulibaly Shighata, and Michael Ferguson. 2018. "Understanding the Financial Lives of Female Sex Workers in Abidjan, Côte d'Ivoire: Implications for Economic Strengthening Interventions for HIV Prevention." *AIDS Care* 30 (Suppl. 3): 6–17.

Namy, Sophie, Catherine C. Carlson, Kathleen O'Hara, Janet Nakuti, Paul Bukuluki, Julius Lwanyaaga, Sylvia Namakula, Barbrah Nanyunja, Milton L Wainberg, Dipak Naker, and Lori Michau. 2017. "Towards a Feminist Understanding of Intersecting Violence against Women and Children in the Family." *Social Science & Medicine* 184 (July): 40–48.

Nare, Prince. 2013. "Implementing the Right to Post-Exposure Prophylaxis for HIV Prevention in a Broken System: Lessons from a Community-Based Organisation in South Africa." *Diversity and Equality in Health and Care* 10 (4): 231–235. http://diversityhealthcare.imedpub.com/implementing-the-right-to-postexposure-prophylaxis-for-hiv-prevention-in-a-broken-system-lessons-from-a-communitybased-organisation-in-south-africa.pdf.

National AIDS Trust. 2003. "Fact Sheet 3: Examples of HIV-Related Discrimination." The Learning Exchange. Accessed March 6, 2020. https://lx.iriss.org.uk/content/examples-hiv-related-discrimination.

National AIDS Trust. 2014. *HIV: A Guide for Police Forces. How to Address in Police Occupational Health Policies and Blood-Borne Virus (BBV) Training*. London: National AIDS Trust. https://www.nat.org.uk/publication/hiv-guide-police-forces.

Ndahinda, Felix Mukwiza. 2007. "Victimization of African Indigenous Peoples: Appraisal of Violations of Collective Rights under Victimological and International Law Lenses." *International Journal on Minority and Group Rights* 14 (1): 1–23.

Newburn, Tim. 2017. *Criminology*. 3rd ed. New York, NY: Routledge.

Ngige, Lucy W., Alice. N. Ondigi, and Stephan M. Wilson. 2008. "Family Diversity in Kenya." In *Families in a Global Context*, edited by Charles B. Hennon and Stephan M. Wilson, 207–231. New York, NY: Routledge.

Nicholson, Tamaryn Jane. 2016. "A Call to Action." *Psychology in Society*, no. 52: 121–124.

Nicolosi, Alfredo, Maria Léa Corrêa Leite, Massimo Musicco, Claudio Arici, Giovanna Gavazzeni, and Adriano Lazzarin. 1994. "The Efficiency of Male-to-Female and Female-to-Male Sexual Transmission of the Human Immunodeficiency Virus: A Study of 730 Stable Couples." *Epidemiology* 5, no. 6 (November): 570–575.

Nieweglowski, Katherine, and Patrik W. Corrigan. 2017. "Stigma and Health." In *Oxford Research Encyclopedia of Psychology*, edited by Ada Brunstein and Oliver Braddick. New York, NY: Oxford University Press. https://doi.org/10.1093/acrefore/9780190236557.013.8.

Noroozinejad, Gholamhossein, Mosaieb Yarmohmmadi Vasel, Fatemeh Bazrafkan, Mahmoud Sehat, Majid Rezazadeh, and Khodabakhsh Ahmadi. 2013. "Perceived Risk Modifies the Effect of HIV Knowledge on Sexual Risk Behaviors." *Frontiers in Public Health*, no. 1 (September): 33. https://doi.org/10.3389/fpubh.2013.00033.

Nöstlinger, Christiana, Daniela Rojas Castro, Tom Platteau, Sonia Dias, and Jean Le Gall. 2014. "HIV-Related Discrimination in European Health Care Settings." *AIDS Patient Care and STDs* 28, no. 3 (March): 155–161.

Ntozi, James P. M., Innocent Najjumba Mulindwa, Fred Ahimbisibwe, Natal Ayiga, and Jonathan Odwee. 2003. "Has the HIV/AIDS Epidemic Changed Sexual Behaviour of High Risk Groups in Uganda?" *African Health Sciences* 3 (3): 107–116.

Nwaneri, Onyi. 2019. "Children Are Our Future: Why Do We Rape, Abuse and Kill Them?" *Daily Maverick*, May 29, 2019. https://www.dailymaverick.co.za/article/2019-05-29-children-are-our-future-why-do-we-rape-abuse-and-kill-them/.

Nyblade, Laura, and Kerry MacQuarrie. 2006. *Can We Measure HIV/AIDS-Stigma and Discrimination? Current Knowledge about Quantifying Stigma in Developing Countries*. Washington, DC: United States Agency for International Development. http://www.policyproject.com/pubs/generalreport/Measure%20HIV%20Stigma.pdf.

Ochillo, Marylyn A., Edwin van Teijlingen, and Martin Hind. 2017. "Influence of Faith-Based Organisations on HIV Prevention Strategies in Africa: A Systematic Review." *African Health Sciences* 17 (3): 753–761.

Odu, Bimbola Kemi, and Florence Foluso Akanle. 2008. "Knowledge of HIV/AIDS and Sexual Behaviour among the Youths in South West Nigeria." *International Journal of Tropical Medicine*: 3 (4): 79–84.

Office of the US Global AIDS Coordinator. 2012. *Guidance for Orphans and Vulnerable Children Programming*. Washington, DC: Office of the US Global AIDS Coordinator.

Ogbebo, Winifred. 2010. "Africa: Female Genital Mutilation Helps Spread of HIV/AIDS - Obasanjo-Bello." AllAfrica Global Media. Last modified August 29, 2010. http://allafrica.com/stories/201008300148.html.

Ogden, Jane. 1995. "Psychosocial Theory and the Creation of the Risky Self." *Social Science & Medicine* 40, no. 3 (February): 409–415.

Ogolla, Maurice. 2014. "Levirate Unions in both the Bible and African Cultures: Convergence and Divergence." *International Journal of Humanities and Social Science* 4, no. 10 (1) (August): 287–292.

Ogunbodede, Eyitope O. 2004. "HIV/AIDS Situation in Africa." *International Dental Journal* 54, no. Suppl. 6 (December): 352–360.

OHCHR (Office of the High Commissioner for Human Rights) and UNAIDS (Joint United Nations Programme on HIV/AIDS). 2006. *International Guidelines on HIV/AIDS and Human Rights: 2006 Consolidated Version.* Geneva: Office of the High Commissioner for Human Rights and Joint United Nations Programme on HIV/AIDS. https://www.ohchr.org/Documents/Issues/HIV/Consolidated GuidelinesHIV.pdf.

OHCHR (Office of the High Commissioner for Human Rights) and WHO (World Health Organization). 2008. *Fact Sheet No. 31: The Right to Health.* Geneva: Office of the High Commissioner for Human Rights. https://www.refworld.org/docid/48625a742.html.

OHCHR (Office of the High Commissioner for Human Rights). 1995. *Fact Sheet No. 23: Harmful Traditional Practices Affecting the Health of Women and Children.* Geneva: Office of the High Commissioner for Human Rights. http://www.refworld.org/docid/479477410.html.

Okello, Elialilia S., Glenn J. Wagner, Bonnie Ghosh-Dastidar, Jeffrey Garnett, Dickens Akena, Noeline Nakasujja, and Seggane Musisi. 2015. "Depression, Internalized HIV Stigma and HIV Disclosure." *World Journal of AIDS* 5, no. 1 (March): 30–40. https://doi.org/10.4236/wja.2015.51004.

O'Mathúna, Dónal, and Walt Larimore. 2006. *Alternative Medicine: The Christian Handbook, Updated and Expanded.* Grand Rapids, MI: Zondervan.

Onyeneho, Nkechi G. 2009. "HIV/AIDS Risk Factors and Economic Empowerment Needs of Female Sex Workers in Enugu Urban, Nigeria." *Tanzania Journal of Health Research* 11, no. 3 (July): 126–135.

Oppenheimer, Gerald M. 1992. "Causes, Cases, and Cohorts: The Role of Epidemiology in the Historical Construction of AIDS." In *AIDS: The Making of a Chronic Disease*, edited by Elizabeth Fee and Daniel M. Fox, 49–83. Berkeley, CA: University of California Press.

Oriji, Christian Chigozi, and Rosemary Ekechukwu. 2015. "Relationship between Cultural Practices and HIV/AIDS Transmission in Rivers State, Nigeria." *European Journal of Research in Social Sciences* 3 (3): 52–60.

Ortblad, Katrina F., Jared M. Baeten, Peter Cherutich, Joyce Njeri Wamicwe, and Judith N. Wasserheit. 2019. "The Arc of HIV Epidemics in Sub-Saharan Africa: New Challenges with Concentrating Epidemics in the Era of 90–90–90." *Current Opinion in HIV and AIDS* 14, no. 5 (September): 354–365.

Ostergard Jr., Robert L. 2002. "Politics in the Hot Zone: AIDS and National Security in Africa." *Third World Quarterly* 23 (2): 333–350.

Outwater, Anne, Naeema Abrahams, and Jacquelyn C. Campbell. 2005. "Women in South Africa: Intentional Violence and HIV/AIDS: Intersections and Prevention." *Journal of Black Studies* 35, no. 4 (March): 135–154.

Overseas Security Advisory Council. 2018. *South Africa 2018 Crime & Safety Report.* Washington, DC: United States Department of State. https://www.osac.gov/Pages/ContentReportDetails.aspx?cid=23940.

Padian, Nancy. S., Stephen C. Shiboski, Sarah O. Glass, and Eric Vittinghoff. 1997. "Heterosexual Transmission of Human Immunodeficiency Virus (HIV) in Northern California: Results from a Ten-Year Study." *American Journal of Epidemiology* 146, no. 4 (August): 350–357.

Paltiel, A. David, Kenneth A. Freedberg, Callie A. Scott, Bruce R. Schackman, Elena Losina, Bingxia Wang, George R. Seage, III, Caroline E. Sloan, Paul E. Sax, and Rochelle P. Walensky 2009. "HIV Pre-Exposure Prophylaxis in the United States: Impact on Lifetime Infection Risk, Clinical Outcomes, and Cost-effectiveness." *Clinical Infectious Diseases* 48, no. 6 (March): 806–815.

Parajuli, Ranjan, Eivind Bjerkaas, Aage Tverdal, Loïc Le Marchand, Elisabete Weiderpass, and Inger T Gram. 2014. "Cigarette Smoking and Colorectal Cancer Mortality among 602,242 Norwegian Males and Females." *Clinical Epidemiology* 6: 137–145. https://doi.org/10.2147/CLEP.S5872.

Parker, Richard, and Peter Aggleton. 2003. "HIV and AIDS-Related Stigma and Discrimination: A Conceptual Framework and Implications for Action." *Social Science & Medicine* 57, no. 1 (July): 13–24.

Parker, Richard, Peter Aggleton, Kathy Attawell, Julie Pulerwitz, and Lisanne Brown. 2002. *HIV/AIDS Related Stigma and Discrimination: A Conceptual Framework and an Agenda for Action.* Washington, DC: Population Council.

Parker, Richard. 2012. "Stigma, Prejudice and Discrimination in Global Public Health." *Cadernos de Saúde Pública* 28, no. 1 (January): 164–169.

Parsons, Talcott. 1951. *The Social System.* Glencoe, IL: Free Press.

Parsons, Talcott. 1964. *Social Structure and Personality.* New York, NY: Free Press.

Parsons, Talcott. 1975. "The Sick Role and the Role of the Physician Reconsidered." *The Milbank Memorial Fund Quarterly: Health ad Society* 53, no. 3 (Summer): 257–278.

Parsons, Talcott. 1978. *Action Theory and the Human Condition.* New York, NY: Free Press.

Patterson, David, and Leslie London. 2002. "International Law, Human Rights and HIV/AIDS." *Bulletin of the World Health Organization* 80 (12): 964–969. https://apps.who.int/iris/handle/10665/71665.

Patterson, David. 2004. *Programming HIV/AIDS: A Human Rights Approach – A Tool for International Development and Community-Based Organizations Responding to HIV/AIDS (Canadian Version).* Toronto, ON: Canadian HIV/AIDS Legal Network. https://npin.cdc.gov/publication/programming-hivaids-human-rights-approach-tool-international-development-and-community.

Pépin, Jacques, Mireille Plamondon, Alfredo Claudino Alves, Mélissa Beaudet, and Annie-Claude Labbé. 2006. "Parenteral Transmission during Excision and Treatment of Tuberculosis and Trypanosomiasis May Be Responsible for the HIV-2 Epidemic in Guinea-Bissau." *AIDS* 20, no. 9 (June): 1303–1311.

Perron, Liette, Vyta Senikas, Margaret Burnett, Victoria Davis, Social Sexual Issues Committee, and Ethics Committee. 2013. "Female Genital Cutting." *Journal of Obstetrics and Gynaecology Canada* 35, no. 11 (November): 1028–1045.

Perrow, Charles, and Mauro F. Guillén. 1990. *The AIDS Disaster: The Failure of Organizations in New York and the Nation.* New Haven, CT: Yale University Press.

Peterson, Zoë D., and Charlene L. Muehlenhard. 2007. "Conceptualizing the 'Wantedness' of Women's Consensual and Nonconsensual Sexual Experiences: Implications for How Women Label Their Experiences with Rape." *The Journal of Sex Research* 44 (1): 72–88.

Pharoah, Robyn, and Taya Weiss. 2005. "AIDS, Orphans, Crime, and Instability: Exploring the Linkages." ISS Paper 107, Institute for Security Studies, Pretoria.

Pharoah, Robyn, and Martin Schönteich. 2003. "AIDS, Security and Governance in Southern Africa: Exploring the Impact." ISS Paper 65, Institute for Security Studies, Pretoria.

Pharoah, Robyn. 2004a. "Introduction". In *A Generation at Risk? HIV/AIDS, Vulnerable Children and Security in Southern Africa*, edited by Robyn Pharoah, 1–8. Institute for Security Studies Monograph Series, no. 109. Pretoria: Institute for Security Studies.

Pharoah, Robyn. 2004b. "Conclusion". In *A Generation at Risk? HIV/AIDS, Vulnerable Children and Security in Southern Africa*, edited by Robyn Pharoah, 115–122. Institute for Security Studies Monograph Series, no. 109. Pretoria: Institute for Security Studies.

Phillips, J. Craig, and Elizabeth M. Saewyc. 2010. "HIV Disease and Gay, Lesbian, Bisexual, and Transgender Persons." In *The Person with HIV/AIDS: Nursing Perspectives*, 4th ed., edited by Jerry D. Durham and Felissa R. Lashley, 365–404. New York City, NY: Springer.

Pinto, Carla M. A., Ana R. M. Carvalho, Dumitru Baleanu, and Hari M. Srivastava. 2019. "Efficacy of the Post-Exposure Prophylaxis and of the HIV Latent Reservoir in HIV Infection." *Mathematics* 7, no. 6 (June): 515. https://doi.org/10.3390/math7060515.

Pitchenik, Arthur E., Margaret A. Fischl, Gordon M. Dickinson, Daniel M. Becker, Arthur M. Fournier, Mark T. O'Connell, Robert M. Colton, and Thomas J. Spira. 1983. "Opportunistic Infections and Kaposi's Sarcoma among Haitians: Evidence of a New Acquired Immunodeficiency State." *Annals of Internal Medicine* 98, no. 3 (March): 277–284.

Pitpitan, Eileen V., Seth C. Kalichman, Lisa A. Eaton, Steffanie A. Strathdee, and Thomas L. Patterson. 2013. "HIV/STI Risk among Venue-Based Female Sex Workers across the Globe: A Look Back and the Way Forward." *Current HIV/AIDS Reports* 10, no. 1 (March): 65–78.

Poorolajal, Jalal, Elham Hooshmand, Hossein Mahjub, Nader Esmailnasab, and Ensiyeh Jenabi. 2016. "Survival Rate of AIDS Disease and Mortality in HIV-Infected Patients: A Meta-Analysis." *Public Health* 139 (October): 3–12.

Population Services International. 2005. *The Sugar Daddy Syndrome: African Campaign Battle Ingrained Phenomenon.* Washington, DC: Population Services International.

Powers, Kimberly A., Charles Poole, Audrey E. Pettifor, and Myron S. Cohen. 2008. "Rethinking the Heterosexual Infectivity of HIV-1: A Systematic Review and Meta-Analysis." *The Lancet Infectious Diseases* 8, no. 9 (September): 553–563.

Pulerwitz, Julie, Annie Michaelis, Ellen Weiss, Lisanne Brown, and Vaishali Mahendra. 2010. "Reducing HIV-Related Stigma: Lessons Learned from Horizons Research and Programs." *Public Health Reports* 125, no. 2 (March-April): 272–281.

Qiao, Shan, Jing-Bao Nie, Joseph Tucker, Stuart Rennie, and Xiao-Ming Li. 2015. "The Role of Social Relationship in HIV Healing and Its Implications in HIV Cure in China." *Health Psychology and Behavioral Medicine* 3 (1): 115–127.

Quam, Michael D. 1990. "The Sick Role, Stigma and Pollution: The Case of AIDS." In *Culture and AIDS*, edited by Douglas A. Feldman, 29–44. New York, NY: Praeger.

Quinn, Sandra C., and Supriya Kumar. 2014. "Health Inequalities and Infectious Disease Epidemics: A Challenge for Global Health Security." *Biosecurity and Bioterrorism: Biodefense Strategy, Practice, and Science* 12, no. 5 (September): 263–273.

Qukula, Qama. 2019. "Why Life Sentences Aren't the Solution to SA's Rape Crisis." CapeTalk. Last modified 27 November, 2019. http://www.capetalk.co.za/articles/368215/why-life-sentences-aren-t-the-solution-to-sa-s-rape-crisis.

Reed, Elizabeth, Jhumka Gupta, Monica Biradavolu, Vasavi Devireddy, and Kim M. Blankenship. 2010. "The Context of Economic Insecurity and Its Relation to Violence and Risk Factors for HIV among Female Sex Workers in Andhra Pradesh, India." *Public Health Reports* 125, no. Suppl. 4 (July-August): 81–89.

Reidpath, Daniel D., and Kit Y. Chan. 2005. "A Method for the Quantitative Analysis of the Layering of HIV-Related Stigma." *AIDS Care* 17 (4): 425–432.

Reisel, Dan, and Sarah M. Creighton. 2015. "Long Term Consequences of Female Genital Mutilation (FMG)." *Maturitas* 80, no. 1 (January): 48–51.

Reniers, Georges, and Rania Tfaily. 2012. "Polygyny, Partnership Concurrency, and HIV Transmission in Sub-Saharan Africa." *Demography* 49, no. 3 (August): 1075–1101.

Reniers, Georges, and Susan Watkins. 2010. "Polygyny and the Spread of HIV in Sub-Saharan Africa: A Case of Benign Concurrency." *AIDS* 24, no. 2 (January): 299–307.

Research Directorate of the Immigration and Refugee Board of Canada. 2006a. *Nigeria: Levirate Marriage Practices among the Yoruba, Igbo and Hausa-Fulani; Consequences for a Man or Woman Who Refuses to Participate in the Marriage; Availability of State Protection (February 2006)*. Ottawa, ON: Immigration and Refugee Board of Canada. https://www.refworld.org/docid/45f1478811.html.

Research Directorate of the Immigration and Refugee Board of Canada. 2006b. *Zimbabwe: The Custom of Wife 'Inheritance'; the Government's Attitude towards This Custom; Protection Available to Women Who Refuse to Observe This Custom (2004–January 2006)*. Ottawa, ON: Immigration and Refugee Board of Canada. https://www.refworld.org/docid/45f147cb23.html.

Ridgeway, Cecilia L., and Lynn Smith-Lovin. 1996. "Gender and Social Interaction [Introduction]." *Social Psychology Quarterly* 59, no. 3 (September): 173-175.

Robatjazi, Mehri, Masoumeh Simbar, Fatemeh Nahidi, Jaber Gharehdaghi, Mohammadali Emamhadi, Abou-Ali Vedadhir, and Hamid Alavimajd. 2016. "Virginity Testing Beyond a Medical Examination." *Global Journal of Health Sciences* 8 (7): 152–164.

Rodriguez, Sarah B. 2014. *Female Circumcision and Clitoridectomy in the United States: A History of a Medical Treatment.* Rochester, NY: University of Rochester Press.

Roseman, Mindy Jane, Sofia Gruskin, and Sumita Banerjee. 2004. *HIV/AIDS and Human Rights in a Nutshell: A Quick and Useful Guide for Action, as Well as a Framework to Carry HIV/AIDS and Human Rights Actions Forward.* Boston, MA: Program on International Health and Human Rights, François-Xavier Bagnoud Center for Health and Human Rights, Harvard School of Public Health and Toronto, ON: International Council of AIDS Service Organizations. https://www.hivlawandpolicy.org/resources/hivaids-and-human-rights-nutshell-program-international-health-and-human-rights-harvard.

Rueda, Sergio, Katherine Gibson, Sean B. Rourke, Tsegaye Bekele, Sandra Gardner, John Cairney, and the OHTN Cohort Study Team. 2012. "Mastery Moderates the Negative Effect of Stigma on Depressive Symptoms in People Living with HIV." *AIDS and Behavior* 16, no. 3 (April): 690–699.

Saag, Michael S., Constance A. Benson, Rajesh T. Gandhi, Jennifer F. Hoy, Raphael J. Landovitz, Michael J. Mugavero, Paul E. Sax, Davey M. Smith, Melanie A. Thompson, Susan P. Buchbinder, Carlos del Rio, Joseph J. Eron Jr, Gerd Fätkenheuer, Huldrych F. Günthard, Jean-Michel Molina, Donna M. Jacobsen, and Paul A. Volberding. 2018. "Antiretroviral Drugs for Treatment and Prevention of HIV Infection in Adults: 2018 Recommendations of the International Antiviral Society–USA Panel." *JAMA* 320, no. 4 (July): 379-396. https://doi.org/10.1001/jama.2018.8431.

Sabatier, Renée. 1988. *Blaming Others: Prejudice, Race and Worldwide AIDS.* Washington, DC: Panos Institute; Philadelphia, PA: New Society Publishers.

Sahasrabuddhe, Vikrant V., and Sten H. Vermund. 2007. "The Future of HIV Prevention: Control of Sexually Transmitted Infections and Circumcision Interventions." *Infectious Disease Clinics of North America* 21, no. 1 (March): 241–257.

Saki, Mandana, Sima Mohammad Khan Kermanshahi, Eesa Mohammadi, and Minoo Mohraz. 2015. "Perception of Patients with HIV/AIDS from Stigma and Discrimination." *Iranian Red Crescent Medical Journal* 17, no. 6 (June): e23638. https://doi.org10.5812/ircmj.23638v2.

Salbu, Steven R. 1996. "AIDS and the Blood Supply: An Analysis of Law, Regulation, and Public Policy." *Washington University Law Quarterly* 74 (4): 913–980.

Samson, Anda. 2008. "Lack of Empowerment: A Driving Force behind the HIV and VAW epidemics." In *The Multiple Faces of the Intersections between HIV and Violence against Women*, edited by Aracely Barahona-Strittmatter and Dynis Luciano, 17–21. Washington, DC: Development Connections. https://genderandaids.unwomen.org/en/resources/2008/11/the-multiple-faces-of-the-intersections-between-hiv-and-violence-against-women.

Samudzi, Zoé, and Jenevieve Mannell. 2016. "Cisgender Male and Transgender Female Sex Workers in South Africa: Gender Variant Identities and Narratives of Exclusion." *Culture, Health & Sexuality* 18 (1): 1–14.

Samuelsen, Helle, Ole Norgaard, and Lise Rosendal Ostergaard. 2012. "Social and Cultural Aspects of HIV and AIDS in West Africa: A Narrative Review of Qualitative Research." *SAHARA-J: Journal of Social Aspects of HIV/AIDS* 9, no. 2 (June): 64–73.

Sander, Dirk, Matthias Wentzlaff-Eggebert, Martin Kruspe, Alexandra Gurinova, and Matthias Kuske. 2016. *Communication Strategies for the Prevention of HIV, STI, and Hepatitis among MSM in Europe*. Stockholm: European Centre for Disease Prevention and Control. https://ecdc.europa.eu/en/publications-data/communication-strategies-prevention-hiv-sti-and-hepatitis-among-msm-europe.

Sands, Peter, Carmen Mundaca-Shah, and Victor J. Dzau. 2016. "The Neglected Dimension of Global Security: A Framework for Countering Infectious-Disease Crises." *The New England Journal of Medicine* 374, no. 13 (March): 1281-1287.

Sanjel, Seshananda. 2013. "Gender-Based Violence: A Crucial Challenge for Public Health." *Kathmandu University Medical Journal* 11, no. 1 (April-June): 179–184.

SAPS (South African Police Service) Strategic Management. 2016. *Annual Report 2015/2016*. Pretoria: South African Police Service. https://www.saps.gov.za/about/stratframework/annual_report/2015_2016/saps_annual_report_2015_2016.pdf.

SAPS (South African Police Service) Strategic Management. 2018. *Annual Report 2017/2018*. Pretoria: South African Police Service. https://www.saps.gov.za/about/stratframework/annual_report/2017_2018/saps_annual_report_2017_2018.pdf.

SAPS (South African Police Service) Strategy, Research, Monitoring and Evaluation. 2015. *Strategic Plan 2014–2019*. Pretoria: South African Police Service. https://www.saps.gov.za/about/stratframework/strategic_plan/2015_2019/strategic_plan_%202015.pdf.

SAPS (South African Police Service). 2018. *Crime Situation in RSA: Twelve Months 01 April 2017 to 31 March 2018*. Pretoria: South African Police Service. https://pmg.org.za/page/SAPSCrimeStats.

Sarbin, Theodore R. 1967. "The Dangerous Individual: An Outcome of Social Identity Transformation." *British Journal of Criminology* 7, no. 3 (July): 285–295.

Sartorius, Norman. 2007. "Stigmatized Illnesses and Health Care." *Croatian Medical Journal* 48, no. 3 (June): 396–397.

Sawers, Larry, Alan G. Isaac, and Eileen Stillwaggon. 2011. "HIV and Concurrent Sexual Partnerships: Modelling the Role of Coital Dilution." *Journal of the International AIDS Society* 14, no.1 (January): 44. https://doi.org/10.1186/1758-2652-14-44.

Scambler, Graham, and Frederique Paoli. 2008. "Health Work, Female Sex Workers and HIV/AIDS: Global and Local Dimensions of Stigma and Deviance as Barriers to Effective Interventions." *Social Science & Medicine* 66, no. 8 (April): 1848–1862.

Scheper-Hughes, Nancy, and Margaret Lock. 1991. "The Message in the Bottle: Illness and the Micropolitics of Resistance." *Journal of Psychohistory* 18 (4): 409–432.

Schiltz, Marie-Angie, and Theodorus G. M. Sandfort. 2000. "HIV-Positive People, Risk and Sexual Behaviour." *Social Science & Medicine* 50, no. 11 (June): 1571–1588.

Schleifer, Rebecca. 2004. *Deadly Delay: South Africa's Efforts to Prevent HIV in Survivors of Sexual Violence*. New York, NY: Human Right Watch. https://www.hrw.org/report/2004/03/03/deadly-delay/south-africas-efforts-prevent-hiv-survivors-sexual-violence.

Schlein, Lisa. 2013. "UN: Epidemic of Violence against Women is Global." Voice of America. Last modified June 20, 2013. https://www.voanews.com/science-health/un-epidemic-violence-against-women-global.

Schneider, Michael. F., Stephen Gange, Carolyn M. Williams, Kathryn Anastos, Ruth M. Greenblatt, Lawrence A. Kingsley, Roger Detels and Alvaro Muñoz. 2005. "Patterns of the Hazard of Death after AIDS through the Evolution of Antiretroviral Therapy: 1984–2004." *AIDS* 19, no. 17 (November): 2009–2018.

Schneider, Michelle, Matthew Chersich, Marleen Temmerman, Olivier Degomme, and Charles D. Parry. 2014. "The Impact of Alcohol on HIV Prevention and Treatment for South Africans in Primary Healthcare." *Curationis* 37 (1): a1137. https://doi.org/10.4102/curationis.v37i1.1137.

Schönteich, Martin. 1999. "Age and AIDS: South Africa's Crime Time Bomb?" *African Security Review* 8 (4): 34–43.

Schönteich, Martin. 2002. "The Coming Crime Wave? AIDS, Orphans and Crime in South Africa." *Southern African Journal of HIV Medicine* 3 (1): 30–34.

Schönteich, Martin. 2003. "A Bleak Outlook: HIV/AIDS and the South African Police Service." *South African Crime Quarterly*, no. 5 (September): 1–6.

Schwerhoff, Gerd. 2013. "Early Modern Violence and the Honour Code: From Social Integration to Social Distinction?" *Crime, Histoire & Sociétés /Crime, History & Societies* 17 (2): 27–46.

Sciolla, L. ed. 1983. *Identità. Percorsi di Analisi in Sociologia.* Torino: Rosenberg and Sellier.

Scott, John, and Gordon Marshall. 2009. "Sick Role." In *A Dictionary of Sociology*, 3rd rev. ed., 687. Oxford: Oxford University Press.

Seacat, Jason D., and Richard Hirschman. 2011. "Attributions and Expectancies about People Living with HIV/AIDS: Implications for Stereotyping." *Current Research in Social Psychology* 17, Article 5. https://uiowa.edu/crisp/sites/uiowa.edu.crisp/files/17.5.pdf.

Shannon, Kate, Shira M. Goldenberg, Kathleen N. Deering, and Steffanie A. Strathdee. 2014. "HIV Infection among Female Sex Workers in Concentrated and High Prevalence Epidemics: Why a Structural Determinants Framework Is Needed." *Current Opinion in HIV and AIDS* 9, no. 2 (March): 174–182.

Shannon, Kate, Steffanie A. Strathdee, Jean Shoveller, Melanie Rusch, Thomas Kerr, and Mark W. Tyndall. 2009. "Structural and Environmental Barriers to Condom Use Negotiation with Clients among Female Sex Workers: Implications for HIV-Prevention Strategies and Policy." *American Journal of Public Health* 99, no. 4 (April): 659–665.

Sharif, Pamela D. 1990. "Haitians Fight Blood War against AIDS Discrimination." *Black Enterprise*, July 1990, 13.

Shaw, George M., and Eric Hunter. 2012. "HIV Transmission." *Cold Spring Harbor Perspectives in Medicine* 2, no. 11 (November): a006965. https://doi:10.1101/cshperspect.a006965

Shayo, Festo K., and Mariam H. Kalomo. 2019. "Prevalence and Correlates of Sexual Intercourse among Sexually Active In-School Adolescents: An Analysis of Five Sub-Sahara African Countries for the Adolescent's Sexual Health Policy Implications." *BMC Public Health* 19, no. 1 (December): 1285. https://doi.org/10.1186/s12889-019-7632-1.

Shields, Rachel. 2010. "South Africa's Shame: The Rise of Child Rape." *The Independent*, May 16, 2010. http://www.independent.co.uk/news/world/africa/south-africas-shame-the-rise-of-child-rape-1974578.html.

Shrestha, Roman, Pramila Karki, and Michael M. Copenhaver. 2016. "Early Sexual Debut: A Risk Factor for STIs/HIV Acquisition among a Nationally Representative Sample of Adults in Nepal." *Journal of Community Health* 41, no. 1 (February): 70–77.

Sibanda-Moyo, Nonhlanhla, Eleanor Khonje, and Maame Kyerewaa Brobbey. 2017. *Violence against Women in South Africa: A Country in Crisis*. Johannesburg: Centre for the Study of Violence and Reconciliation. https://www.csvr.org.za/publications/2735-violence-against-women-in-sa.

Siegal, Frederick, and Marta Siegal. 1983. *AIDS: The Medical Mystery*. New York, NY: Grove Press.

Simbayi, Leickness C., Seth Kalichman, Anna Strebel, Allanise Cloete, Nomvo Henda, and Ayanda Mqeketo. 2007. "Internalized Stigma, Discrimination, and Depression among Men and Women Living with HIV/AIDS in Cape Town, South Africa." *Social Science & Medicine* 64, no. 9 (May): 1823–1831.

Smart, Rose. 2003. *Policies for Orphans and Vulnerable Children: A Framework for Moving Ahead*. Washington, DC: POLICY Project. https://eldis.org/document/A14519.

Smit, Peter J., Michael Brady, Michael Carter, Ricardo Fernandes, Lance Lamore, Michael Meulbroek, Michel Ohayon, Tom Platteau, Peter Rehberg, Jürgen K. Rockstroh, and Marc Thompson. 2012. "HIV-Related Stigma within Communities of Gay Men: A Literature Review." *AIDS Care* 24 (4): 405–412.

Smith, Candace. 2019. "How Communities Are Addressing Violence against Women in South Africa." ABC. Last modified July 18, 2019. https://abcnews.go.com/International/communities-addressing-violence-women-south-africa/story?id=64389896.

Smith, Charlene. 2001. *Proud of Me. Speaking Out against Sexual Violence and HIV*. Johannesburg: Penguin Books.

Smith, David J. 1995. "Youth Crime and Conduct Disorders: Trends, Patterns and Causal Explanations." In *Psychosocial Disorders in Young People: Time Trends and Their Causes*, edited by Michael Rutter and David J. Smith, 389–489. Chichester, UK: John Wiley and Sons Ltd.

Smythe, Dee. 2015. *Rape Unresolved: Policing Sexual Offences in South Africa*. Cape Town: University of Cape Town Press.

Solnes Miltenburg, Andrea. 2010. "Female Genital Mutilation: The Three Feminine Pains in Somaliland." *Global Medicine*, no. 9 (February): 6–10. https://ifmsa.nl/projecten/global-medicine-issue9.pdf.

Somerville, Jamice. 1990. "FDA Reverses Policy, Drops Ban on Haitian Blood Donors." *American Medical News*, December 28, 1990. Westlaw.

Sontag, Susan. 2001. *Illness as Metaphor and AIDS and Its Metaphors*. New York, NY: Picador.

Special Representative of the Secretary-General on Violence against Children and Plan International. 2012. *Protecting Children from Harmful Practices in Plural Legal Systems with a Special Emphasis on Africa*. New York, NY: Office of the Special Representative of the Secretary-General on Violence against Children.

https://resourcecentre.savethechildren.net/library/protecting-children--practices-plural-legal-systems-special-emphasis-africa.

Stangl, Anne L., Laura Brady, and Katherine Fritz. 2012. *Technical Brief: Measuring HIV Stigma and Discrimination.* Washington, DC: International Center for Research on Women. http://strive.lshtm.ac.uk/system/files/attachments/STRIVE%20stigma%20measurement.pdf.

Statistics South Africa. 2018. *Victims of Crime Survey 2017/18.* Pretoria: Statistics South Africa. http://www.statssa.gov.za/?page_id=1854&PPN=P0341&SCH=7373.

Steen, Richard, Jan A. C., Hontelez, Owen Mugurungi, Amon Mpofu, Suzette M Matthijsse, Sake J. de Vlas, Gina A. Dallabetta, and Frances M. Cowan. 2019. "Economy, Migrant Labour and Sex Work: Interplay of HIV Epidemic Drivers in Zimbabwe over Three Decades." *AIDS* 33, no. 1 (January): 123–131.

Steffenson, Annie E., Audrey E. Pettifor, George R. 3rd Seage, Helen V. Rees, and Paul D. Cleary. 2011. "Concurrent Sexual Partnerships and Human Immunodeficiency Virus Risk among South African Youth." *Sexually Transmitted Diseases* 38, no. 6 (June): 459–466.

Stewart, Frances, and Graham Brown. 2010. "Fragile States: CRISE Overview 3." Oxford: Centre for Research on Inequality, Human Security and Ethnicity (CRISE), University of Oxford. https://gsdrc.org/document-library/fragile-states-crise-overview-3/.

Stöckl, Heidi, Naira Kalra, Jantine Jacobi, and Charlotte Watts. 2013. "Is Early Sexual Debut a Risk Factor for HIV Infection among Women in Sub-Saharan Africa? A Systematic Review." *American Journal of Reproductive Immunology* 69, no. Suppl. 1 (February): 27–40.

Stockman, Jamila K., Jacquelyn C. Campbell, and David D. Celentano. 2010. "Sexual Violence and HIV Risk Behaviors among a Nationally Representative Sample of Heterosexual American Women: The Importance of Sexual Coercion." *Journal of Acquired Immune Deficiency Syndromes* 53, no. 1 (January): 136–143.

Stoner, Marie, Nadia Nguyen, Kelly Kilburn, F. Xavier Gomez-Olive, Jessie K. Edwards, Amanda Selin, James P. Hughes, Yaw Agyei, Catherine Macphail, Kathleen Kahn, and Audrey Pettifor. 2019. "Age-Disparate Partnerships and Incident HIV Infection in Adolescent Girls and Young Women in Rural South Africa." *AIDS* 33, 1 (January): 83–91.

Stuber, Jennifer, Ilan Meyer, and Bruce Link. 2008. "Stigma, Prejudice, Discrimination and Health." *Social Science & Medicine* 67, no. 3 (August): 351–357.

Stuijt, Adriana. 2009. "Half of South Africa's Young Have AIDS from Rape." Digital Journal. Last modified January 8, 2009. http://www.digitaljournal.com/article/264771.

Sutherland, Edwin Hardin, and Donald R. Cressey. 1974. *Criminology.* Philadelphia, PA: Lippincott.

Sydor, Anna. 2013. "Conducting Research into Hidden or Hard-to-Reach Populations." *Nurse Researcher* 20, no. 3 (January): 33–37.

Tadjbakhsh, Shahrbanou, and Anuradha M. Chenoy. 2007. *Human Security: Concepts and Implications.* New York, NY: Routledge.

Tamarit, Josep, Carolina Villacampa, and Gemma Filella. 2010. "Secondary Victimization and Victim Assistance." *European Journal of Crime, Criminal Law and Criminal Justice* 18 (3): 281–298.

The Antiretroviral Therapy Cohort Collaboration. 2017. "Survival of HIV-Positive Patients Starting Antiretroviral Therapy between 1996 and 2013: A Collaborative Analysis of Cohort Studies." *The Lancet HIV* 4, no. 8 (August): e349-e356. https://doi.org/10.1016/S2352-3018(17)30066-8.

Thi, Mai Doan Ahn, Deborah Bain Brickley, Dang Thi Nhat Vinh, Don J. Colby, Annette H. Sohn, Nguyen Quang Trung, Le Truong Giang, and Jeffrey S. Mandel. 2008. "A Qualitative Study of Stigma and Discrimination against People Living with HIV in Ho Chi Minh City, Vietnam." *AIDS and Behavior* 12, no. Suppl. 1 (July): S63–S70.

Thisyakorn, Usa. 2017. "Elimination of Mother-to-Child Transmission of HIV: Lessons Learned from Success in Thailand." *Paediatrics and International Child Health* 37 (2): 99–108.

Thobejane, Tsoaledi Daniel, and Tsetselelani Decide Mdhluli. 2015. "Probing the Efficacy of Virginity Testing on the Fight against HIV/AIDS: The Case of the KwaZulu-Natal, South Africa." *OIDA International Journal of Sustainable Development* 8 (7): 11–20.

Thobejane, Tsoaledi Daniel, Tshilidzi Patrecia Mulaudzi, and Rally Zitha. 2017. "Factors Leading to 'Blesser-Blessee' Relationships amongst Female Students: The Case of a Rural University in Thulamela Municipality, Limpopo Province, South Africa." *Gender and Behaviour* 15 (2): 8716–8731.

Thomas, Caroline. 2001. "Global Governance, Development and Human Security: Exploring the Links." *Third World Quarterly* 22 (2): 159–175.

Thomas, Lynn. 2000. "'Ngaitana (I Will Circumcise Myself)': Lessons from Colonial Campaigns to Ban Excision in Meru, Kenya." In *Female, 'Circumcision' in Africa: Culture, Controversy and Change*, edited by Bettina Shell-Duncan and Ylva Hernlund, 129–150. Boulder, CO: Lynne Rienner Publishers.

Thomas, Richard K. 2003. *Society and Health: Sociology for Health Professionals*. New York, NY: Plenum Publishers

Todres, Jonathan. 2007. "Rights Relationships and the Experience of Children Orphaned by AIDS." *UC Davis Law Review* 41, no. 2 (December): 417–476.

Tomasevski, Katarina. 2006. "Why a Human Rights Approach to HIV/AIDS Makes All the Difference." In *Human Rights and Poverty Reduction: Realities, Controversies and Strategies - An ODI Meeting Series*, edited by Tammie O'Neal, 71–76. London: Overseas Development Institute.

Tomaszewski, Evelyn P. 2012. "Human Rights Update: Understanding HIV/AIDS Stigma and Discrimination." Human Rights and International Affairs Division, National Association of Social Workers. Accessed November 18, 2019. https://www.socialworkers.org/LinkClick.aspx?fileticket=Ehw3d_90z30%3D&portalid=0.

Tortu, Stephanie, Lloyd A. Goldsamt, and Rahul Hamid. 2001. *A Practical Guide to Research and Services with Hidden Populations*. Boston, MA: Allyn & Bacon.

Treichler, Paula A. 1987. "AIDS, Homophobia and Biomedical Discourse: An Epidemic of Signification." *Cultural Studies* 1 (3): 263–305.

Udehn, Lars. 2001. *Methodological Individualism: Background, History and Meaning*. London: Routledge.

UN Women (United Nations Entity for Gender Equality and the Empowerment of Women). 2012. *Handbook for Legislation on Violence against Women*. New York, NY: United Nations Entity for Gender Equality and the Empowerment of Women. https://www.unwomen.org/en/digital-library/publications/2012/12/handbook-for-legislation-on-violence-against-women.

UNAIDS (Joint United Nations Programme on HIV and AIDS) and DPKO (Department of Peacekeeping Operations). 2011a. *On The Front Line: A Review of Programmes That Address HIV among International Peacekeepers and Uniformed Services 2005–2010*. New York, NY: United Nations.

UNAIDS (Joint United Nations Programme on HIV and AIDS) and DPKO (Department of Peacekeeping Operations). 2011b. *The Responsibility of the Security Council in the Maintenance of International Peace and Security: HIV/AIDS and International Peacekeeping Operations*. Geneva: Joint United Nations Programme on HIV and AIDS. https://www.unaids.org/en/resources/documents/2011/20110512_UNSC_UNAIDS_DPKO_NonPaper.

UNAIDS (Joint United Nations Programme on HIV and AIDS) and the European Commission. 2013. "Right to Health, Right to Life: Why We Need to Act Now on HIV and Human Rights – High Level Meeting on HIV and Human Rights in the European Union and Neighbouring Countries." Discussion Paper, Joint United Nations Programme on HIV and AIDS, Geneva. https://ec.europa.eu/health/sites/health/files/sti_prevention/docs/ev_20130527_discussion_paper_en.pdf.

UNAIDS (Joint United Nations Programme on HIV and AIDS) and WHO (World Health Organization). 2005. *AIDS Epidemic Update: December 2005*. Geneva: Joint United Nations Programme on HIV and AIDS. https://www.who.int/hiv/pub/epidemiology/epiupdate2005/en/.

UNAIDS (Joint United Nations Programme on HIV and AIDS) Interagency Task Team on Education. 2004. *The Role of Education in the Protection, Care and Support of Orphans and Vulnerable Children Living in a World with HIV and AIDS*. Geneva: Joint United Nations Programme on HIV and AIDS. http://unesdoc.unesco.org/images/0013/001355/135531e.pdf.

UNAIDS (Joint United Nations Programme on HIV and AIDS). 2007. *Reducing HIV Stigma and Discrimination: A Critical Part of National AIDS Programmes*. Geneva: Joint United Nations Programme on HIV and AIDS. https://www.unaids.org/en/resources/documents/2009/20090401_jc1521_stigmatisation_en.pdf.

UNAIDS (Joint United Nations Programme on HIV and AIDS). 2008. *Report on the Global AIDS Epidemic 2008*. Geneva: Joint United Nations Programme on HIV and AIDS. http://www.unaids.org/en/resources/documents/2008/20081107_jc1510_2008globalreport_en.pdf.

UNAIDS (Joint United Nations Programme on HIV and AIDS). 2011. *UNAIDS Terminology Guidelines*. Geneva: Joint United Nations Programme on HIV and AIDS. https://www.unaids.org/en/resources/documents/2011/20111025_JC2118_UNAIDS_Terminology_Guidelines.

UNAIDS (Joint United Nations Programme on HIV and AIDS). 2013. *Ending Overly Broad Criminalisation of HIV Non-Disclosure, Exposure and Transmission: Critical Scientific, Medical and Legal Considerations*. Geneva:

Joint United Nations Programme on HIV and AIDS. https://www.unaids.org/ en/resources/documents/2013/20130530_Guidance_Ending_Criminalisation.

UNAIDS (Joint United Nations Programme on HIV and AIDS). 2014. *Reduction of HIV-Related Stigma and Discrimination.* Geneva: Joint United Nations Programme on HIV and AIDS. https://www.catie.ca/en/resources/reduction-hiv-related-stigma-and-discrimination.

UNAIDS (Joint United Nations Programme on HIV and AIDS). 2015a. *UNAIDS 2016-2021 Strategy: On the Fast-Track to End AIDS.* Geneva: Joint United Nations Programme on HIV and AIDS. https://www.unaids.org/en/resources/ documents/2015/UNAIDS_PCB37_15-18.

UNAIDS (Joint United Nations Programme on HIV and AIDS). 2015b. *UNAIDS Terminology Guidelines.* Geneva: Joint United Nations Programme on HIV and AIDS. http://www.unaids.org/en/resources/documents/2015/2015_ terminology_guidelines.

UNAIDS (Joint United Nations Programme on HIV and AIDS). 2016. *On the Fast-Track to an AIDS-Free Generation: The Incredible Journey of the Global Plan towards the Elimination of New HIV Infections among Children by 2015 and Keeping Their Mothers Alive.* Geneva: Joint United Nations Programme on HIV and AIDS. https://reliefweb.int/report/world/fast-track-aids-free-generation-incredible-journey-global-plan-towards-elimination-new.

UNAIDS (Joint United Nations Programme on HIV and AIDS). 2017. *Disability and HIV.* Geneva: Joint United Nations Programme on HIV and AIDS. https://www.unaids.org/en/resources/documents/2017/jc2905_disability-and-hiv.

UNAIDS (Joint United Nations Programme on HIV and AIDS). 2018a. *UNAIDS Data 2018.* Geneva: Joint United Nations Programme on HIV and AIDS. http://www.unaids.org/en/resources/documents/2018/unaids-data-2018.

UNAIDS (Joint United Nations Programme on HIV and AIDS). 2018b. *Implementation of the HIV Prevention 2020 Road Map.* Geneva: Joint United Nations Programme on HIV and AIDS. https://reliefweb.int/report/world/ implementation-hiv-prevention-2020-road-map-first-progress-report-march-2018.

UNAIDS (Joint United Nations Programme on HIV and AIDS). 2018c. *Women and Girls and HIV.* Geneva: Joint United Nations Programme on HIV and AIDS. https://www.unaids.org/en/resources/documents/2018/women_girls_hiv.

UNAIDS (Joint United Nations Programme on HIV and AIDS). 2019. *UNAIDS Data 2019.* Geneva: Joint United Nations Programme on HIV and AIDS. https://www.unaids.org/en/resources/documents/2019/2019-UNAIDS-data.

UNAIDS (Joint United Nations Programme on HIV and AIDS). 2020. "Country: South Africa." Accessed June 1, 2020. https://www.unaids.org/en/ regionscountries/countries/southafrica.

UNDP (United Nations Development Programme). 1994. *Human Development Report 1994: New Dimensions of Human Security.* New York, NY: Oxford University Press. http://www.hdr.undp.org/en/content/human-development-report-1994.

UNDP (United Nations Development Programme). 2013. *Legal Protection against HIV-Related Human Rights Violations: Experiences and Lessons Learned from National HIV Laws in Asia and the Pacific.* Bangkok: United Nations Development Programme. https://www.undp.org/content/undp/en/home/

librarypage/hiv-aids/legal-protections-against-hiv-related-human-rights-violations.html.

UNDP (United Nations Development Programme). 2016. *Connecting the Dots: Strategy Note on HIV, Health and Development 2016-2021.* New York, NY: United Nations Development Programme. http://www.undp.org/content/undp/en/home/librarypage/hiv-aids/hiv--health-and-development-strategy-2016-2021.html.

UNESCO (United Nations Educational, Scientific and Cultural Organization). 2013. *Addressing the Links between Gender-Based Violence and HIV in the Great Lakes Region: Background Information on GBV and HIV.* Paris: United Nations Educational, Scientific and Cultural Organization. https://genderandaids.unwomen.org/en/resources/2014/09/addressing-the-links-between-gender-based-violence-and-hiv-in-the-great-lakes-region-background-information-on-gbv-and-hiv.

UNFPA (United Nations Population Fund), UNHCR (United Nations High Commissioner for Refugees), UNICEF (United Nations Children's Fund), UNIFEM (United Nations Development Fund for Women), WHO (World Health Organization), FIGO (International Federation of Gynecology and Obstetrics), ICN (International Council of Nurses), MWIA (Medical Women's International Association), WCPT (World Confederation for Physical Therapy), and WMA (World Medical Association). 2010. *Global Strategy to Stop Health-Care Providers from Performing Female Genital Mutilation.* Geneva: World Health Organization. http://www.unfpa.org/publications/global-strategy-stop-health-care providers-performing-fgm.

UNHCHR (United Nations High Commissioner for Human Rights). 2011. *The Protection of Human Rights in the Context of Human Immunodeficiency Virus (HIV) and Acquired Immune Deficiency Syndrome (AIDS).* A/HRC/19/37. Geneva: United Nations Human Rights Council. https://www.right-docs.org/doc/a-hrc-19-37/.

UNICEF (United Nations Children's Fund). 2006. *Africa's Orphaned and Vulnerable Generations: Children Affected by AIDS.* New York, NY: United Nations Children's Fund. https://www.unicef.org/publications/index_35645.html.

UNICEF (United Nations Children's Fund). 2013. *Female Genital Mutilation/Cutting: A Statistical Overview and Exploration of the Dynamics of Change.* New York, NY: United Nations Children's Fund. https://www.unicef.org/publications/index_69875.html.

UNICEF (United Nations Children's Fund). 2016a. *For Every Child, End AIDS: Seventh Stocktaking Report, 2016.* New York, NY: United Nations Children's Fund. https://www.unicef.org/publications/index_93427.html.

UNICEF (United Nations Children's Fund). 2016b. *Protection and Resilience: A Simple Checklist for Why, Where and How, to Coordinate HIV and Child Protection Policy and Programming.* New York, NY: United Nations Children's Fund. https://ovcsupport.org/wp-content/uploads/2015/10/FINAL_HIV_CP_Tool_4C.pdf.

UNICEF (United Nations Children's Fund). 2016c. *Female Genital Mutilation/Cutting: A Global Concern.* New York, NY: United Nations Children's

Fund. https://data.unicef.org/resources/female-genital-mutilationcutting-global-concern/.

UNICEF (United Nations Children's Fund). 2019. *The State of the World's Children 2019. Children, Food and Nutrition: Growing Well in a Changing World.* New York, NY: United Nations Children's Fund. https://www.unicef.org/reports/state-of-worlds-children-2019.

United Nations General Assembly. 2011. *Political Declaration on HIV/AIDS: Intensifying Our Efforts to Eliminate HIV/AIDS.* A/65/L.77. New York, NY: United Nations General Assembly. https://www.unwomen.org/en/docs/2011/6/political-declaration-on-hiv-aids-a-65-l77.

United Nations Security Council. 2000a. "Security Council Holds Debate on Impact of Peace and Security in Africa." Press Release SC/6781, 4086th Meeting. 10 January, 2000. United Nations Website. https://www.un.org/press/en/2000/20000110.sc6781.doc.html.

United Nations Security Council. 2000b. "Security Council, Adopting 'Historic' Resolution 1308 (2000) on HIV/AIDS, Calls For Pre-Deployment Testing, Counselling for Peacekeeping Personnel." Press Release SC/6890, 4172nd Meeting, Resolution 1308. 17 July, 2000. United Nations Website. https://www.un.org/press/en/2000/20000717.sc6890.doc.html.

United Nations Security Council. 2011. "Unanimously Adopting 1983 (2011), Security Council Encourages Inclusion of HIV Prevention, Treatment, Care, Support in Implementing Peacekeeping Mandates." Press Release SC/10272, 6547th Meeting, Resolution 1983. 7 June, 2011. United Nations Website. https://www.un.org/press/en/2011/sc10272.doc.htm.

Utan, Kathryn. 2005. "Collateral Damage: HIV/AIDS Creates a Generation of Orphans and Vulnerable Children." *CommonHealth*, Spring: 59–66. http://www.aiha.com/wp-content/uploads/2015/07/15-Collateral-Damage-HIV-AIDS-Creates-a-Generation-of-Orphans-and-Vulnerable-Children.pdf.

Vahlne, Anders. 2009. "A Historical Reflection on the Discovery of Human Retroviruses." *Retrovirology* 6: 40. https://doi.org/10.1186/1742-4690-6-40.

Valdiserri, Ronald O. 2002. "HIV/AIDS Stigma: An Impediment to Public Health." *American Journal of Public Health* 92, no. 3 (March): 341–342.

Van Dyk, Alta C. 2008. *HIV/AIDS, Care and Counselling: A Multidisciplinary Approach.* 4th ed. Cape Town: Pearson Education.

Vanable, Peter A., Michael P. Carey, Donald C. Blair, and Rae A. Littlewood. 2006. "Impact of HIV-Related Stigma on Health Behaviors and Psychological Adjustment among HIV-Positive Men and Women." *AIDS and Behavior* 10, no. 5 (September): 473–482.

Varas-Díaz, Nelson, Irma Serrano-García, and José Toro-Alfonso. 2005. "AIDS-Related Stigma and Social Interaction: Puerto Ricans Living with HIV/AIDS." *Qualitative Health Research* 15, no. 2 (February): 169–187.

Varul, Matthias Zick. 2010. "Talcott Parsons, the Sick Role and Chronic Illness." *Body & Society* 16, no. 2 (June), 72–94.

Verbrugge, Lois M., and Alan M. Jette. 1994. "The Disablement Process." *Social Science & Medicine* 38, no. 1 (January): 1–14.

Vernal, Fiona. 2011. "Discourse Networks in South African Slave Society." *African Historical Review* 43 (2): 1–36.

Veterans Health Administration. 2008. "Secondary HIV Prevention: Information for VA Health Care Providers." Washington, DC: US Department of Veterans Affairs. https://www.hiv.va.gov/products/secondary-hiv-prevention.asp.

Vetten, Lisa. 2007. "New Crimes and Old Procedures: Can the New Sexual Offences Bill Deliver on Its Promises?" *South African Crime Quarterly*, no. 22 (December): 21–25.

Vetten, Lisa. 2014. "Rape and Other Forms of Sexual Violence in South Africa." *Institute for Security Studies Policy Brief* 72: 1–8.

Vian, Taryn, Katherine Semrau, Davidson H. Hamer, Le Thi Thanh Loan, and Lora Sabin. 2012. "HIV/AIDS-Related Knowledge and Behaviors among Most-at-Risk Populations in Vietnam." *The Open AIDS Journal* 6: 259–265. https://doi.org/10.2174/1874613601206010259.

Vickers, Steve. 2006. "Staging Sex Myths to Save Zimbabwe's Girls." BBC. Last modified October 24, 2006. http://news.bbc.co.uk/2/hi/africa/6076758.stm.

Viljoen, Frans, and Susan Precious. 2007. "Introduction: Human Rights under Threat in Attempts to Address HIV and AIDS." In *Human Rights under Threat: Four Perspectives on HIV, AIDS and the Law in Southern Africa*, edited by Frans Viljoen and Susan Precious, 1–12. Pretoria: Pretoria University Law Press.

Vincent, Louise. 2006. "Virginity Testing in South Africa: Re-Traditioning the Post-Colony." *Culture, Health & Sexuality* 8 (1): 17–30.

Vogelman, Lloyd, and Sharon Lewis. 1993. *Gang Rape and the Culture of Violence in South Africa*. Johannesburg: Centre for the Study of Violence and Reconciliation.

Vriniotis, Mary. 2015. *Victimization Survey 101: Recommendations for Funding and Implementing a Victimization Survey*. Washington, DC: Inter-American Development Bank. https://publications.iadb.org/en/publication/12316/victimization-surveys-101-recommendations-funding-and-implementing-victimization.

Wadesango, Newman, Symphorosa Rembe, and Owence Chabaya. 2011. "Violation of Women's Rights by Harmful Traditional Practices." *The Anthropologist* 13 (2): 121–129.

Wæver, Ole. 1995. "Securitization and Desecurization." In *On Security*, edited by Ronnie D. Lipschutz, 46–86. New York, NY: Columbia University Press.

Wainberg, Mark A. 2009. "Criminalizing HIV Transmission May Be a Mistake." *Canadian Medical Association Journal* 180, no. 6 (March): 688. https://doi.org/10.1503/cmaj.090249.

Watkins-Hayes, Celeste. 2014. "Intersectionality and the Sociology of HIV/AIDS: Past, Present, and Future Research Directions." *Annual Review of Sociology* 40: 431–457.

Weiss, Gregory L., and Lynne Lonnquist. 1997. *The Sociology of Health, Healing, and Illness*. 2nd ed. Upper Saddle River, NJ: Prentice-Hall.

Weiss, Mitchell G., Jayashree Ramakrishna, and Daryl Somma. 2006. "Health-Related Stigma: Rethinking Concepts and Interventions." *Psychology, Health & Medicine* 11 (3): 277–287.

White Hughto, Jaclyn M., Sari L. Reisner, and John. E. Pachankis. 2015. "Transgender Stigma and Health: A Critical Review of Stigma Determinants, Mechanisms, and Interventions." *Social Science & Medicine* 147 (December): 222–231.

Whiteside, Alan. 1998. *Implications of AIDS for Demography and Policy in Southern Africa*. Pietermaritzburg, South Africa: University of Natal Press.

WHO (World Health Organization) Department of Gender, Women and Health and Global Coalition on Women and AIDS. 2004. "Violence against Women and HIV/AIDS: Critical Intersections - Intimate Partner Violence and HIV/AIDS." *WHO Information Bulletin Series*, no. 1 (November): 1–9. https://www.who.int/hac/techguidance/pht/InfoBulletinIntimatePartnerViolenceFinal.pdf.

WHO (World Health Organization) Department of Violence and Injury Prevention and Disability and Centre for Public Health, WHO Collaborating Centre for Violence Prevention, Liverpool John Moores University. 2010. *Violence Prevention: The Evidence*. Geneva: World Health Organization. https://www.who.int/violence_injury_prevention/violence/the-evidence/en/.

WHO (World Health Organization) Regional Office for the Eastern Mediterranean. n.d. "Vulnerable Groups and Key Populations at Increased Risk of HIV – Definitions." World Health Organization. Accessed April 20, 2020. http://www.emro.who.int/asd/health-topics/vulnerable-groups-and-key-populations-at-increased-risk-of-hiv.html.

WHO (World Health Organization). 2006. *Report of the WHO European Region Technical Consultation, in Collaboration with the European AIDS Treatment Group (EATG) and AIDS Action Europe (AAE), on the Criminalization of HIV and Other Sexually Transmitted Infections*. Copenhagen: World Health Organization Regional Office for Europe. https://www.hivlawandpolicy.org/resources/technical-consultation-collaboration-european-aids-treatment-group-and-aids-action-europe.

WHO (World Health Organization). 2007. *The World Health Report 2007 - A Safer Future: Global Public Health Security in the 21st Century*. Geneva: World Health Organization. https://www.who.int/whr/2007/en/.

WHO (World Health Organization). 2008a. *Eliminating Female Genital Mutilation: An Interagency Statement – OHCHR, UNAIDS, UNDP, UNECA, UNESCO, UNFPA, UNHCR, UNICEF, UNIFEM, WHO*. Geneva: World Health Organization. http://www.who.int/reproductivehealth/publications/fgm/9789241596442/en/.

WHO (World Health Organization). 2008b. *The World Health Report 2008 - Primary Health Care: Now More Than Ever*. Geneva: World Health Organization. https://www.who.int/whr/2008/en/.

WHO (World Health Organization). 2011. *An Update on WHO's Work on Female Genital Mutilation (FGM): Progress Report*. Geneva: World Health Organization. http://www.who.int/reproductivehealth/publications/fgm/rhr_11_18/en/.

WHO (World Health Organization). 2013. *Consolidated Guidelines on the Use of Antiretroviral Drugs for Treating and Preventing HIV Infection: Recommendations for a Public Health Approach*. Geneva: World Health Organization. https://www.who.int/hiv/pub/guidelines/arv2013/en/.

WHO (World Health Organization). 2014a. *Global Update on the Health Sector Response to HIV, 2014.* Geneva: World Health Organization. https://www.who.int/hiv/pub/progressreports/update2014/en/.

WHO (World Health Organization). 2014b. *Global Guidance on Criteria and Processes for Validation: Elimination of Mother-to-Child Transmission of HIV and Syphilis.* Geneva: World Health Organization. https://apps.who.int/iris/handle/10665/112858.

WHO (World Health Organization). 2014c. *Guidelines on Post-Exposure Prophylaxis for HIV and the Use of Co-Trimoxazole Prophylaxis for HIV-Related Infections among Adults, Adolescents and Children: Recommendations for a Public Health Approach - December 2014 Supplement to the 2013 Consolidated ARV Guidelines.* Geneva: World Health Organization. https://www.who.int/hiv/pub/guidelines/arv2013/arvs2013upplement_dec2014/en/.

WHO (World Health Organization). 2014d. "Gender, Women and Health: What Do We Mean by 'Sex' and 'Gender'?" May 28, 2014. https://www.legal-tools.org/doc/a33dc3/pdf/.

WHO (World Health Organization). 2014e. "HIV Prevention: Offering Hope to Victims of Sexual Violence." November, 2014. https://www.who.int/features/2014/pep-antiretrovirals/en/.

WHO (World Health Organization). 2015. *HIV and Young People Who Sell Sex.* Geneva: World Health Organization. https://www.who.int/hiv/pub/toolkits/hiv-young-sexworkers/en/.

WHO (World Health Organization). 2016a. *Global Health Sector Strategy on HIV, 2016–2021: Towards Ending AIDS.* Geneva: World Health Organization. https://www.who.int/hiv/strategy2016-2021/ghss-hiv/en/.

WHO (World Health Organization). 2016b. *Consolidated Guidelines on HIV Prevention, Diagnosis, Treatment and Care for Key Populations.* Geneva: World Health Organization. https://www.who.int/hiv/pub/guidelines/keypopulations-2016/en/.

WHO (World Health Organization). 2017. *WHO Guidelines on Ethical Issues in Public Health Surveillance.* Geneva: World Health Organization. https://www.who.int/ethics/publications/public-health-surveillance/en/.

WHO (World Health Organization). 2019. *The Public Health Dimension of the World Drug Problem: How WHO Works to Prevent Drug Misuse, Reduce Harm and Improve Safe Access to Medicine.* Geneva: World Health Organization. https://www.who.int/hiv/pub/idu/world-drug-problem-public-health/en/.

Wickström, Annette. 2010. "Virginity Testing as a Local Public Health Initiative: A 'Preventive Ritual' More Than a 'Diagnostic Measure'." *Journal of the Royal Anthropological Institute* 16, no. 3 (September): 532–550.

Wild, Lauren. 2001. "The Psychosocial Adjustment of Children Orphaned by AIDS." *Southern African Journal of Child and Adolescent Mental Health* 13 (1): 3–22.

Wilkinson, Kate. 2016. "Guide: Rape Statistics in South Africa." Africa Check. Last modified June 22, 2016. https://africacheck.org/factsheets/guide-rape-statistics-in-south-africa/.

Wilkinson, Richard G. 1996. *Unhealthy Societies: The Afflictions of Inequality.* London: Routledge.

Willan, Samantha. 2000. *Considering the Impact of HIV/AIDS on Democratic Governance and Vice Versa.* Durban: Health Economics and HIV/AIDS Research Division, University of Natal.

Williams, Simon J. 2003. *Medicine and the Body.* London: Sage.

Williams, Simon. J. 2005. "Parsons Revisited: From the Sick Role to...?" *Health* 9, no. 2 (April): 123-144.

Win, Everjoice J. 2004. "Virginity Testing as HIV/AIDS Prevention Strategy: Clutching at Straws, The Way I See It." *Sexuality in Africa Magazine* 1, no. 1 (March): 13–14.

Winter, Bronwyn, Denise Thompson, and Sheila Jeffreys. 2002. "The UN Approach to Harmful Traditional Practices." *International Feminist Journal of Politics* 4 (1): 72–94.

Youde, Jeremy. 2007. "HIV/AIDS and Democratic Legitimacy and Stability." In *HIV/AIDS and Threat to National and International Security*, edited by Robert L. Ostergard Jr., 197–222. Basingstoke, UK: Palgrave Macmillan.

Young, J. T. 2004. "Illness Behaviour: A Selective Review and Synthesis." *Sociology of Health & Illness* 26, no. 1 (January): 1–31.

Yount, Kathryn M., and Bisrat K. Abraham. 2007. "Female Genital Cutting and HIV/AIDS among Kenyan Women." *Studies in Family Planning* 38, no. 2 (June): 73–88.

Zaba, Basia, Jimmy Whitworth, Milly Marston, Jessica Nakiyingi, Anthony Ruberantwari, Mark Urassa, Raphaeli Issingo, Gabriel Mwaluko, Sian Floyd, Andrew Nyondo, and Amelia Crampin. 2005. "HIV and Mortality of Mothers and Children: Evidence from Cohort Studies in Uganda, Tanzania, and Malawi." *Epidemiology* 16, no. 3 (May): 275–280.

Zablotska, Iryna B., Ronald H. Gray, Michael A. Koenig, David Serwadda, Fred Nalugoda, Godfrey Kigozi, Nelson Sewankambo, Tom Lutalo, Fred Wabwire Mangen, and Maria J. Wawer. 2009. "Alcohol Use, Intimate Partner Violence, Sexual Coercion and HIV among Women Aged 15-24 in Rakai, Uganda." *AIDS and Behavior* 13, no. 2. (April): 225–233.

Zhang, Meiwen, Sarah Jane Steele, Amir Shroufi, Gilles van Cutsem, Junaid Khan, Garret Barnwell, Julia Hill, and Kristal Duncan. 2017. "The Health Impact of Sexual Violence among Women in a Platinum Mining Belt." Paper Presented at the Annual Conference on Retroviruses and Opportunistic Infections, Seattle, WA. http://www.croiconference.org/sessions/health-impact-sexual-violence-among-women-platinum-mining-belt.

Zhu, Bang-Yong, Jin Bu, Pei-Yong Huang, Zhi-Guang Zhou, Yue-Ping Yin, Xiang-Sheng Chen, Wan-Hui Wei, Ming-ying Zhong, Hong-Chu Wang, Hong Wang, and Quan Gan. 2012. "Epidemiology of Sexually Transmitted Infections, HIV, and Related High-Risk Behaviors among Female Sex Workers in Guangxi Autonomous Region, China." *Japanese Journal of Infectious Diseases* 65 (1): 75–78.

Ziguras, Christopher. 2004. *Self-Care: Embodiment, Personal Autonomy and the Shaping of Health Consciousness.* London: Routledge.

Zululand District Municipality. 2015. *Zululand Integrated Development Plan Review 2015/2016.* Ulundi, South Africa: Zululand District Municipality. http://www.zululand.org.za/planning/integrated-development-plan/2015---2016-(final).aspx.

List of acronyms

AIDS	Acquired Immunodeficiency Syndrome
AIS	AIDS Indicator Survey
ART	Antiretroviral Therapy
CDC	Centers for Disease Control and Prevention
DHS	Demographic and Health Survey
DPKO	Department of Peacekeeping Operations
FDA	Food and Drug Administration
GRID	Gay-Related Immunodeficiency
HAART	Highly Active Antiretroviral Therapy
HIV	Human Immunodeficiency Virus
KDHS	Kenya Demographic and Health Survey
LGBT	Lesbian, Gay, Bisexual, and Transgender
LEAHN	Law Enforcement and HIV Network
OHCHR	Office of the High Commissioner for Human Rights
PCP	Pneumocystis Pneumonia
PEP	Post-Exposure Prophylaxis
PrEP	Pre-Exposure Prophylaxis
SAPS	South African Police Service
STIs	Sexually Transmitted Infections
TB	Tuberculosis
UN	United Nations
UN Women	United Nations Entity for Gender Equality and the Empowerment of Women
UNAIDS	Joint United Nations Programme on HIV and AIDS
UNDP	United Nations Development Programme
UNESCO	United Nations Educational, Scientific and Cultural Organization
UNFPA	United Nations Population Fund
UNHCHR	United Nations High Commissioner for Human Rights

UNICEF	United Nations Children's Fund
UNODC	United Nations Office on Drugs and Crime
VOCS	Victims of Crime Survey
WHO	World Health Organization

Index

V

Vernal, Fiona, 53
victimology, 79
violence against women, 51, 55, 56
violence on minors, 62
virgin cleansing myth, 73
virginity testing, 71, 72, 74
vulnerability, 40

W

Wæver, Ole, 85
Whiteside, Alan, 90
WHO (World Health
    Organization), vii, 47, 73, 74
widow inheritance, 70
Willan, Samantha, 90
Win, Everjoice J., 74

World AIDS Day, 96

X

Xhosa, 53

Y

Yemen, 75
Youde, Jeremy, 90
Yount, Kathryn M., 78

Z

Zambia, 73
Zimbabwe, 69, 70, 73
Zulu, 72
Zululand, 72

www.ingramcontent.com/pod-product-compliance
Lightning Source LLC
Chambersburg PA
CBHW050519280326
41932CB00014B/2379